Chinese Economic Reform

How Far, How Fast?

Chinese Economic Reform

How Far, How Fast?

Edited by

Bruce L. Reynolds

Department of Economics
Union College
Schenectady, New York

ACADEMIC PRESS, INC.
Harcourt Brace Jovanovich, Publishers
Boston   San Diego   New York
Berkeley   London   Sydney
Tokyo   Toronto

ACADEMIC PRESS
1250 Sixth Avenue, San Diego, CA 92101

United Kingdom Edition published by
ACADEMIC PRESS INC. (LONDON) LTD.
24-28 Oval Road, London NW1 7DX

HC
427.92
. C4664
1988

Library of Congress Cataloging-in-Publication Data

Chinese economic reform.

  Bibliography: p.
  Includes index.
  1. China — Economic policy — 1976- . I. Reynolds,
Bruce Lloyd, Date-   .
HC427.92.C4664 1988   338.951   88-6306
ISBN 0-12-587045-0

Printed in the United States of America
88 89 90 91   9 8 7 6 5 4 3 2 1

Contents

v

Contributors

Numbers in parentheses indicate the pages on which the authors' contributions begin.

Irma Adelman (154), *University of California, Berkeley, California 94720*
Bela Balassa (120), *The Johns Hopkins University, Baltimore, Maryland 21218 and World Bank, Washington, DC 20433*
William A. Byrd (5), *The World Bank, Washington, DC 20433*
Chen Yizi (172), *China Economic System Reform Research Institute, Beijing, China*
Gregory C. Chow (29), *Princeton University, Princeton, New Jersey 08544*
John Fei (200), *Yale University, New Haven, Connecticut 06520*
Hong Zhunyan (213), *Beijing University, Beijing, China*
Ma Bin (213), *Economic, Technical, and Social Development Research Center, Beijing, China*
Barry Naughton (44), *University of Oregon, Eugene, Oregon 97403*
Richard Portes (64), *Birkbeck College, London WIP 1PA, England*
Bruce L. Reynolds (1, 189, 200), *Union College, Schenectady, New York 12308*
Anita Santorum (64), *Birkbeck College, London WIP 1PA, England*
T. N. Srinivasan (137), *Yale University, New Haven, Connecticut 06520*
David Sunding (154), *University of California, Berkeley, California 94720*
Wang Ziaoqiang (172), *China Economic System Reform Research Institute, Beijing, China*
Thomas B. Wiens (82), *The World Bank, Washington, DC 20433*
Christine P. W. Wong (95), *University of California, Santa Cruz, California 95064*
Wu Jinglian (19), *Economic, Technical, and Social Development Research Center, Beijing, China*
Xu Jing-an (219), *China Economic System Reform Research Institute, Beijing, China*

Zhao Renwei (19), *Economic Research Institute, Chinese Academy of Social Sciences, Beijing, China*
Zhou Xiaochuan (109), *China Economic System Reform Research Institute, Beijing, China*
Zhu Li (109), *The Commission on Economic System Reform, Beijing, China*

JOURNAL OF COMPARATIVE ECONOMICS **11**, 291–294 (1987)

Introduction

BRUCE L. REYNOLDS

Union College, Schenectady, New York 12308

Discussion of economic reform by Chinese economists began, like that in Eastern Europe and the USSR, in the late 1950s and early 1960s, in the works of Xue Muqiao, Sun Yefang, and others. The Cultural Revolution, beginning in 1966, and the succession crisis which followed, both obscured and muted the reform debate. But after the death of Mao Zedong in 1976, reform rapidly returned to the agenda. The December 1978 Third Plenum of the Chinese Communist Party Central Committee forged a political consensus for reform, and the first reform documents began to emerge from the State Council in mid-1979. Now, after more than 8 years of implementation, a comprehensive review and evaluation of economic reform in China is possible.

To undertake such a review, 32 scholars came together in October 1986, at the Arden House Conference Center in Harriman, New York, under the auspices of the Association for Comparative Economic Systems and Union College (and with the generous financial support of the Ford and Rockefeller Foundations). Half the group came from the People's Republic of China, representing two research units of the State Council, the Chinese Academy of Social Sciences, and Beijing University. Of the remaining participants, 12 were American and 4 were European. The conference papers, revised in light of 3 days of discussion, are presented here.

Economic reform can be defined in terms of institutional change—change in the planning process, for example, such that industrial enterprises gain greater discretionary power over fixing their production plans, or change in the institutions governing income distribution. As the term is used in socialist economies, reform refers to institutional changes whose net effect is to leave detailed decision-making power less centralized than before. Economic reform in these countries is also often used more loosely to refer to any introduction of market mechanisms. By these criteria, reform has been widespread throughout the Chinese economy since 1978.

An alternative definition might read: economic reform is a process of institutional change which serves to increase the rate of growth of total factor

CHINESE ECONOMIC REFORM

1

ISBN 0-12-587045-0

productivity. This approach focuses, not on the mechanisms of reform, but on the avowed objectives of the reformers. For the most successful market economies, up to half of economic growth comes from productivity growth. For planned economies, the proportion is significantly lower. For China, the most telling single statistic from the prereform period is that total factor productivity growth in the years 1952–1975 was at best stagnant, and most probably *declined* at a rate of roughly 0.5% per year. It is the difficulty of sustaining acceptable growth rates in the face of this phenomenon, coupled with the diagnosis that overcentralization is to blame, which fires reformist zeal.

By this criterion, reform in China has been very successful in agriculture, and a dismal failure in industry. Agricultural output has grown at unprecedented rates despite negligible increases in land and labor and a sharp decline in investment. In industry, growth rates have been high for output, but also for capital stock and other inputs. Total factor productivity declined sharply in the 4 years after 1978. In China's roughly 90,000 state-owned enterprises, and in particular the 8000 large-scale enterprises which have traditionally been under direct central government control, reform has brought major changes in the way work proceeds, but it has not achieved its objective. The October 1984 Decision of the Central Committee, which proposed to focus the full force of reform efforts on the urban sector, was implicit recognition of this experience.

Why has reform in industry fallen short of the mark? It is analytically useful, in searching for an explanation, to consider the four separate components which any economic system, whether plan or market, must include: power, information, motivation, and constraint. Any set of institutions for making economic decisions must specify who has decision-making power, must provide decision-makers with information about scarcity, and must motivate decision-makers to act while constraining them from overexpansion. In a market economy, information about scarcity is generated by markets and conveyed by prices. Monetary restraint, expressed through the interest rate, constrains excessive expansion. And private ownership disposes tidily of the problems of decision-making power and motivation: the owner of an enterprise makes the allocative decisions and gains the (residual) reward from decisions which are efficient.

In combination, these four components, whatever their other failings, have generated sustained growth in factor productivity (technological progress) in the market economies. In their attempt to replicate that result, through a reformed socialist economic system in industry, the Chinese have successfully experimented with using market prices to inform producers about scarcity. Linking profit to incomes has effectively motivated enterprises to raise output—but not to produce more efficiently. Meanwhile, attempts to further decentralize decision-making power, in 1979–1980 and again in 1984–1985, have generated unacceptable macroeconomic instability due to unconstrained expansion.

These 16 papers address this experience from several perspectives. The 5 papers in Part I explore the reformed price system and the macroeconomic mechanism. Papers by Byrd and by Wu and Zhao analyze the dual pricing system in industry, under which a significant portion of major commodities, such as steel, coal, and trucks, is allowed to flow onto a free market, where price is sharply higher than the price at which the state rations out these commodities. Both papers explain China's success with this new form by pointing to the substantial history of extra-plan pricing in China prior to 1978; and both argue that the dual system is unstable and can only be transitional. Byrd stresses the usefulness of the system in generating efficient behavior; because the market-generated prices determine producers' decisions *at the margin,* their impact is great despite a small "market" share. Wu and Zhao stress the drawbacks of the system, in particular illegal arbitraging and the growth of inefficiently small-scale producers.

The remaining three papers in Part I deal with the Chinese macroeconomy. Naughton presents a model within which he estimates a household saving function for 1957–1978, finding a very low saving rate. For the post-1978 period, Naughton traces the rapid growth in money income and in the government deficit, and comes to the startling conclusion that households and enterprises in China have accommodated government–sector imbalance through a voluntary increase in saving. The other two papers in this section represent diametrically opposed approaches to modeling a "planned macroeconomy." Chow shows that traditional econometric techniques provide a very good fit; indeed, his estimated relationship between price level, money supply, and GNP is more stable for Chinese than for U.S. data. Portes and Santorum obtain comparable results using the disequilibrium macroeconomics approach.

Part II presents sectoral and cross-country studies by Wiens, Wong, Zhou and Zhu, Balassa, and Srinivasan. Wiens reminds us that agricultural reform still has a considerable unfinished agenda. Wong makes it clear that the substantial role of local governments in industry is a major impediment to economic change. The shortcomings of China's banking system as an effective tool for monetary control are made manifest by Zhou and Zhu. Balassa and Srinivasan set Chinese reform in relief against the experience of Hungary and India, generating useful policy implications for China.

The papers in Part III measure the impact of reform. Adelman and Sunding find that rural income inequality increased between 1978 and 1983, but that total inequality decreased markedly due to a narrowing urban/rural income gap. Chen et al. present the results of a massive 1985 survey of reform in industry, spearheaded by the Economic Reform Research Institute. They chart

significant successes, but raise concerns about inflationary pressure and irrational investment allocation. Reynolds, using a World Bank input–output
table for China, generates evidence that China's pattern of foreign trade shifted
between 1981 and 1985 in a "job-creating" direction.

Part IV turns to the fundamental issue of ownership in industry. At one
extreme, Xu argues that a stock share system will resolve many of the outstanding difficulties in industrial reform, and is urgently needed. At the other,
Ma and Hong argue that wage goods provide sufficient incentive to motivate
industrial workers; a private capital market is inappropriate to China's present
conditions. Fei and Reynolds take a middle ground, arguing that opening a
capital market is a necessary part of constructing a reformed economy, but
that this change can only come gradually and in the context of broader changes
in culture and values in China.

Recent months have seen clear setbacks for reform in China. What do these
papers say about its future? Evsey Domar likes to remark that technological
change is nothing more than the net effect of millions of small decisions by
individuals who are trying to be more productive. But an analysis within
which the individual is the lynchpin presents problems, both technical and
ideological, to a socialist reformer. How shall that individual be empowered
and motivated to produce efficiently, short of private property? How can
direct control be replaced by indirect monetary restraint, in a highly politicized
banking system? And how can socialist values be made consistent with an
emphasis on individual gain?

These are difficult problems. But a common theme throughout the papers
presented here is the ability of China to find unique solutions: the production
responsibility system, the two-tier price system, and so on. This innovativeness
and pragmatism, and willingness to stretch ideological constraints, reflects
China's strong, deep-rooted nationalism—a sense of national and cultural
identity which enables China to say: We will define, and create, Chinese socialism.

JOURNAL OF COMPARATIVE ECONOMICS 11, 295–308 (1987)

The Impact of the Two-Tier Plan/Market System in Chinese Industry[1]

WILLIAM A. BYRD

The World Bank, Washington, D.C. 20433

Byrd, William A.—The Impact of the Two-Tier Plan/Market System in Chinese Industry

There has been a great expansion in the role of the market mechanism in the distribution of industrial goods in China since the late 1970s. A two-tier system, whereby part of total production of each good is allocated by various kinds of directive plans, part by markets, has emerged. It is argued that the two-tier system has resulted in the demise of the direct role of mandatory planning in the allocation of industrial goods, and that the inherent dynamic tendencies of the system are leading to a continual increase in the share of the market over time. *J. Comp. Econ.,* September 1987, **11**(3), pp. 295–308. The World Bank, Washington, D.C. 20433. © 1987 Academic Press, Inc.

Journal of Economic Literature Classification Numbers: 052, 113, 124.

This paper will try to make a strong case that China is well on its way toward becoming an economy where the allocation of goods is determined primarily by the market, rather than by directive plans and administrative controls. It will also sketch out an analysis of how this transition is occurring, with primary focus on the two-tier plan/market system of resource allocation. The subject matter will be limited to production and trade in industrial goods (mainly producer goods), although the same points could be made even more forcefully for agriculture. The paper will start by discussing the origins and development of the two-tier plan/market system that has emerged in Chinese industry since the late 1970s. The static and particularly the dynamic impacts of the system will be analyzed. Then actual developments in the 1980s will be briefly reviewed, primarily through case studies of coal, trucks, cement, and steel products.

[1] The views, findings, interpretations, and conclusions set forth in this paper are those of the author and should not be attributed to the World Bank or to its affiliated institutions. This paper has benefited from information gathered as part of World Bank Research Project RPO 673-14. Comments from Janos Kornai, Bela Balassa, Bruce Reynolds, and other participants of the conference are gratefully acknowledged.

CHINESE ECONOMIC REFORM

5

THE TWO-TIER PLAN/MARKET SYSTEM:
ORIGINS AND DEVELOPMENT

Plan and market can be combined in several different ways. Some goods could be subject to plan allocation, while others are allocated by the market. The bifurcation between plan and market could also be along enterprise lines, with some firms' inputs and outputs regulated by plan, others by market. Alternatively, the demarcation could cut across inputs and outputs of particular enterprises, which would have part of total supply/demand for each input and output subject to plan, part allocated by market. This last alternative is the most general one and corresponds closely to present Chinese practice.

Formally, under the two-tier system each enterprise faces a vector of output plan targets, targets for compulsory procurement of output, and input allocations; input purchases, production, and output sales above these target levels occur through the market at flexible prices. All types of mandatory production planning, compulsory procurement of outputs, and administrative allocation of supplies are included in the "plan" part, while the market portion is only that part which is genuinely subject to market allocation on a voluntary basis, at market-determined prices. Market prices are assumed to be higher than plan prices.

Prereform roots of the two-tier system. These included (1) cost-based multiple pricing for different enterprises and localities; (2) multiple planning and supply channels; and (3) a fringe of market and market-like activities which remained underdeveloped. These were all related to the decentralized, autarchic industrialization policy of the Cultural Revolution period (Wong, 1985, pp. 574–576), which brought a proliferation of small, high-cost plants, coexisting with the larger ones built in the 1950s and later under central or provincial auspices.

The limitations of these prereform roots of the two-tier system are readily apparent. Prices remained administratively controlled, even though such control may have been exerted at lower levels of government, which were just as inflexible in their pricing practices as the central government. Second, goods flows were subject to local government direction; even the transactors were often government units rather than enterprises. Finally, the share of the more market-like of the prereform allocation channels in total economic activity remained small. Prereform practices did create potential and a springboard for later development of the two-tier system, however.

Patterns of adjustment to buyers' and sellers' markets. There has been a basic asymmetry in price pressures and price adjustments as between a buyers' market and a sellers' market (Byrd, 1987b, pp. 261–262). In the former, downward pressure is exerted on the price of the entire supply of the good concerned. Buyers need not accept high-priced goods allocated to them through the plan, since a lower price can be obtained on the open market. In this kind of situation, the tendency is for planning to break down and market allocation and pricing to take over.[2]

In the case of chronic sellers' markets, market-oriented reforms exacerbated the strong pressures for price increases already present, which interacted with the existing system to create the two-tier system, with market allocation at the margin. In a sellers' market, users with access to plan allocations will not willingly give them up and would oppose any price increase. But would-be purchasers without allocations as well as those who need more than they are allocated would be willing to pay market prices for what they cannot get through the plan, which of course would also be of benefit to sellers. Thus there is a strong tendency for some part of output, particularly incremental output, to be sold at a higher price. The multiple pricing and allocation system already in place lent itself to this transformation, since the market could simply be added as another channel of goods distribution among many.

A key contrast between adjustment to a sellers' market and to a buyers' market is that in the case of the former, the existing multiple allocation and pricing system remained in place and evolved into the two-tier system by developing an additional channel of market distribution. A strong buyers' market, on the other hand, tended to erode the system of multiple allocation channels and prices (if it was present in the first place[3]), by putting downward pressure on the price of the entire supply of the good concerned. There was no chance for a two-tier system to emerge, since if state prices were higher than market equilibrium prices, users would refuse plan input allocations.

In sum, the two-tier system emerged in China since the late 1970s as a result of market-oriented reforms in a chronic sellers' market situation. The response of the system to market forces was to provide a "safety valve" at the margin, which could absorb some of the pressure of excess demand, while maintaining low plan prices for purchasers with plan allocations.

Government pricing policies. A number of pricing policy reforms have helped promote the two-tier system.[4] *Floating prices* were introduced relatively early, though initially only in a downward direction, except for some better-quality products. *Negotiated prices* have proliferated since the late 1970s, especially for consumer goods. A major reform in early 1985 was the general decontrol

---

[2] The pattern of adjustment to a buyers' market is clearest in the case of consumer durables like watches and bicycles. See Byrd and Tidrick (1984) for a discussion of the watch industry. There have also been buyers' markets for machinery and temporarily for basic industrial goods like steel when adjustment policies generated temporary excess supply in 1980–1981.

[3] For many consumer goods, particularly consumer durables, there was no multiple pricing system during the prereform period. Prices were set very high to tax consumption, so even the highest-cost producers could still make profits and multiple pricing on cost grounds was unnecessary.

[4] Price reform in Chinese industry is treated in Chai (1986), which cites many useful Chinese sources on this topic.

of prices of industrial producer goods sold outside the plan (Shen and Han, 1986, p. 18), which consummated the two-tier system by freeing the market portion from price restrictions.

THE STATIC AND DYNAMIC IMPACT OF THE TWO-TIER SYSTEM

As the two-tier system established itself and came to affect a significant share of industrial output, its internal tendencies and dynamics influenced the pattern of resource allocation and the behavior of industrial decision makers. This in turn had an effect on its environment and on its subsequent development.

Static impact. If all enterprises are participating in the market for at least part of the supply of each of their inputs and part of the sales of each of their outputs, and furthermore if enterprises maximize profits, then not only will there be a meaningful short-run equilibrium solution, but that equilibrium will be Pareto optimal, given fixed enterprise endowments of factors of production, including labor (Byrd, 1987a, Ch. 6). While the assumptions required for this result undoubtedly do not hold in their entirety, they may not be too far off as "approximate" stylized facts. Table 1 indicates that the bulk of Chinese industrial enterprises engage in at least some market transactions on both input and output sides (though this is not necessarily true of every input and output for each enterprise). In any case, relatively minor departures from the assumption of complete penetration of the market to all enterprises and goods would not greatly affect the results. Enterprise objective functions other than profit maximization would still allow for the existence of an equilibrium but not its Pareto optimality.[5]

Static results are limited even if the required assumptions hold. Given the rigid factor allocation system in Chinese state-owned industry (Byrd and Tidrick, 1987), enterprise factor endowments are treated as exogenous and excluded from the analysis, but uneven factor endowments and the lack of a mechanism to reallocate factors over time are probably a much greater source of inefficiency than distortions in goods markets. Similarly, static efficiency results mean less in a situation of rapid structural and institutional change. Nevertheless, they do demonstrate the irrelevance of planning in short-term resource allocation, the central concern of this paper.

---

[5] An attractive alternative enterprise objective function is maximization of output value subject to a profit or "resource" constraint (see Baumol, 1959; Ames, 1965; and Portes, 1969). In this case changes in plan targets and plan prices have "income effects" on enterprise production decisions. The merits of different enterprise objective functions are discussed in Byrd (1987a, Ch. 5). There is considerable evidence that Chinese enterprise managers are increasingly concerned about profits (as opposed to fulfillment of plan targets or even quantity maximization) in their decision making (see CESRRI, 1986, pp. 178, 288).

TABLE 1

Market Input and Output Transactions for Industrial Enterprises, 1984–1985[a]
Percentage of Total Value of Purchases or Sales

Share of market transactions in total purchases or sales	Share of total number of sample enterprises	
	1984	1st half 1985
Input purchases		
0	9.6	6.5
0–20	49.6	41.9
20–40	16.8	21.5
40–60	9.1	10.3
60–80	3.2	4.7
80–100	11.7	15.0
Output sales		
0	14.9	16.2
0–20	20.1	15.7
20–40	16.4	12.0
40–60	6.7	10.7
60–80	8.2	7.2
80–100	33.7	38.2

[a] From a sample of 429 industrial enterprises in 27 cities. 279 enterprises were state owned, 131 were urban collectives, and 19 were township and village enterprises. 241 enterprises were classified as large or medium sized, 188 as small.

Source. CESRRI (1986, Tables 1.1 and 1.2, p. 46).

"Growing out of the plan." Turning now to the dynamic properties of the two-tier system, it is first assumed that agents behave as they are supposed to: producers always meet their plan targets for output and compulsory delivery at the state price, while commercial intermediaries and allocators resist the temptation to earn easy profits by diverting goods from plan to market channels. Even with these idealistic assumptions, there are strong tendencies working toward the expansion of the market share of output over time.

Incentives for investment in expansion are much greater for the market portion than for the plan portion, since the former earn higher financial returns. Profit-oriented enterprises might refuse to put their funds into projects for which output would have to be sold through the plan at a low price (unless they also get entitlements to low-priced plan-allocated inputs). Banks and even planners themselves also may be increasingly responsive to profitability criteria in deciding which projects to finance.

This tendency to grow out of the plan could be offset by state investment funds being ploughed into expansion of the planned sector. But the state budget now accounts for a much lower share of total investment than in the past. Moreover, many large projects are now jointly financed by the central government, local governments, and other entities; pressures from the more profit-oriented investors would require market pricing for at least part of the output generated by such projects. When investments are made to expand production at plan prices, these are usually special arrangements like compensation trade deals, which typically involve preassignment of output to users.

The "ideal" long-term equilibrium results that would be generated by assuming that agents follow the rules of the system require conditions that are much more stringent and unrealistic than in the static case. The conditions for static optimality must hold, and moreover there must be no ratchet effect or similar performance-based increases in plan targets. But the key issue is whether "income effects" from the two-tier system affect enterprise investment activity. The system generates "windfall' profits for some enterprises and artificially low profits (or even losses) for others. If these profit differentials affect investment in different sectors and industries, then the result is unlikely to be long-term Pareto optimal.

Incentives to undermine the system. Producers under the two-tier system "lose" potential profits because they have to sell part of their output at the low plan price. Thus they have an obvious incentive to divert output from plan to market channels, or to impose side payments or other costs on purchasers. Diversion can be accomplished in a number of ways, even in the face of a system which frowns on this kind of activity. In a relatively weak planning system like China's, such behavior is difficult to police. Even passive behavior by producers, for instance refusing to produce for plan delivery until state-allocated inputs have arrived, will tend to undermine the system, particularly if many are doing this. Commercial intermediaries trading in plan-allocated goods have the same incentives as producers to divert goods from plan to market channels.

Precarious forces in favor of stability. The linkage between planned input allocations and output/delivery targets should be a major factor in keeping the unstable compromise represented by the two-tier system from breaking down. If a producer (who is, after all, also a purchaser of inputs) knows that diverting goods from plan to market channels will cost him his low-priced input allocations, he may be deterred from doing so. But incentives to undermine the system are still present, if this can be done without jeopardizing future input allocations. Second, the linkage may be destabilizing if it operates in both upward and downward directions. Diversion of goods from plan to market channels means that "downstream" purchasers, who do not get all of their plan-based input allocations, can legitimately refuse to fulfill *their* output plans, and so on. Thus the linkage between input allocations and output/ delivery targets can be a two-edged sword.

Since provision of inputs must precede production, for the linkage to work there must be a downward ratchet effect at work: failure to fulfill the output target in one year must mean a lowering of the input allocation for the following year, since inputs for current-year production have already been provided and cannot be reduced *ex post*. Given the pervasive bargaining over plan targets and input allocations in China, this kind of ratchet probably would not work very well. Initial input allocations for the following year are often made before current year production is known, further attenuating any possible linkage. Planners in any case would be harming themselves if a reduction in input quotas in the following year were accompanied by a reduction in the compulsory procurement plan. On the other hand, authorities would find it difficult to force delinquent enterprises to produce a similar amount of output for compulsory procurement with a smaller supply of plan-based input allocations.[6]

The linkage between output targets and input allocations also can slip if enterprises shift production for the market forward within the year and production for the plan backward.[7] This means late output deliveries for the plan, which would bear any risk from lower-than-expected output (contrary to the way the "ideal version" of the system is supposed to work). Late plan deliveries in turn mean late arrivals of input allocations for other enterprises, which increases the danger of underfulfillment of targets at downstream stages of production.

The other main force with an interest in preventing a switch to market allocation is users with plan allocations. Many of these are also producers, while others are final users, most prominently the government investment budget and urban consumers. But as has already been noted, they are at least somewhat schizophrenic, in that they are willing to bid supplies away from other users if their quotas are insufficient or if they have no plan allocations.

Another factor is the extent to which monitoring and enforcement of the two-tier system is feasible. The complicity of buyers and sellers makes mon-

[6] The Mindong Electrical Machinery Corporation "borrowed" against future input plan allocations of rolled steel and silicon steel, but it is not clear whether and in what way these borrowings would be "repaid." The No. 2 Auto Plant had a major conflict with the material supply system over plan inputs that the factory had used to produce trucks for market sales in 1981, when orders through the plan were insufficient to fill production capacity. The enterprise's "debt" of trucks "owed" to the planning system was carried over for several years, but in the end was "settled" without anything near full "repayment" by No. 2 (interview information, October–November 1984).

[7] A good example is the Anshan Iron and Steel Plant's severe underfulfillment of its state pig iron delivery plan in the first half of 1985, reportedly because it was more profitable to sell pig iron at negotiated prices on the market. Ashan fulfilled only 23% of its state contracted supply of pig iron, even less for certain important customers. See Xinhua News Agency, 8/9/85, translated in BBC, 8/14/85, p. BII-11.

itoring and enforcement very difficult, because the benefits of diversion can be reaped through unreported side payments, barter deals, or other mechanisms that are very hard to detect. All in all, the incentives inherent in the two-tier system, combined with internal contradictions within the forces trying to uphold it and the difficulties of monitoring and enforcement, make it very precarious. Some aspects of the two-tier system and the behavior it engenders, combined with the economic interests of users in getting low-priced supplies, could provoke a political reaction, which might lead to the demise of the two-tier system and a return to command planning. But in China the dynamics have been working in the opposite direction.

EVOLUTION OF THE TWO-TIER SYSTEM IN THE 1980s

It remains to sketch out how the two-tier system has developed in practice in China over the past half decade. This will be done mainly with case studies.

Coal: Growing out of the plan. Coal is a good example of the tendencies for expansion of the share of output allocated by the market, even if the absolute amount flowing through the plan is not cut back. Table 2 shows the share of coal output produced by different types of coal mines in 1978–1984. These figures cannot be translated directly into plan and market shares, since large amounts of coal produced by locally controlled mines are subject to allocation through local or provincial plans. Nevertheless, at one extreme *tongpei* (unified-allocation) coal, subject to administrative allocation through the state plan, saw its share in total coal output decline from 55% in 1978 to 48% in 1984. This strongly suggests that the share of market allocation has gone up by at least a similar margin.[8]

The pattern of coal is broadly duplicated by other key basic raw materials, for which deliveries through state plan contracts have remained nearly constant in absolute terms over the past 5 years or so, even though production has increased by a considerable margin in many cases. The declining proportion of state plan allocation most likely has not been offset by a rise in the share of output allocated by local governments.

Trucks: Sharp decline in plan allocations. Direct marketing of trucks by producers started in 1981, when cutbacks in state investment left many units that had been allocated trucks in the plan with insufficient funds to pay for them. Market conditions later reverted to excess demand, but due to the strength of the largest truck producers, general proreform policies, and the shift in truck ownership toward rural individuals, producers were able to hold

---

[8] Indeed, the bulk of incremental coal output is accounted for by small coal mines run by townships and villages, a large share of whose production is subject to market allocation at flexible prices. Thus the share of the market may have risen by an even greater margin than the decline in the share of *tongpei* coal.

TABLE 2

SHARE OF COAL OUTPUT BY DIFFERENT TYPES OF MINES

	Share in total raw coal output (%)		
Year	Unified-allocation mines	Local state-owned mines	Nonstate mines
1978	55.3	29.1	15.6[a]
1979	56.3	26.7	17.0[a]
1980	55.5	26.2	18.3
1981	53.9	25.7	20.4
1982	52.5	25.6	21.9
1983	50.8 (52.5)[b]	25.4 (23.7)[b]	23.8
1984	47.9 (50.0)[b]	24.6 (22.5)[b]	27.5
Share of incremental output 1978–1984	21.2	8.4	70.4

[a] Based on the assumption that the ratio of total collective mine output to output by commune and brigade coal mines was the same in 1978 and 1979 as in 1980.

[b] Sichuan Province's provincially run state coal mines were put in the unified-allocation category in 1984, which results in overstatement of the share of unified-allocation mines in the official statistics for 1984 (in parentheses for that year). An adjustment was made for both 1983 and 1984, using actual output of the Sichuan provincial mines in 1983, and based on the assumption that their output grew at the same rate as that of national coal output in 1984. Thus the figures in parentheses for 1983 and 1984 include the Sichuan mines in the unified-allocation category.

Sources. Ministry of Coal Industry (1982, pp. 9, 16; 1983, p. 61; and 1985, p. 12) and Ministry of Agriculture (1981, p. 125; and 1982, p. 50).

onto substantial marketing rights. The linkage between compulsory procurement of trucks through the state plan and supply of inputs at state prices was made explicit, but producers were still forced to sell all their output at state prices, or could increase prices only to the extent that costs increased due to purchases of inputs outside the plan.

A secondary market in trucks arose, with the plan entitlement for a truck (not including the truck itself) being worth up to Y50,000 at one point, compared with a state price of Y20,000 plus for a typical medium-sized truck. This led to complaints by producers about the "middleman" profits being reaped. In response, the system legalized the market for trucks, setting up trading centers at which trucks could be bought and sold, and allowing producers to participate in them, getting at least part of the benefit of the higher market price. This generated a full-blown two-tier system.

There has also been a sharp decline in the share of trucks allocated through

TABLE 3

DIRECT MARKETING BY THE NO. 2 AUTO PLANT, 1980–1985

Year	Total production (units)	Share of national production (%)	Directly marketed production (units)	Share of direct marketing in total (%)
1980	31,500	14	0	0
1981	37,503	21	20,000	53
1982	51,171	26	30,000	59
1983	60,106	25	10,000	17
1984	75,000	24	20,000	27
1985	91,500	21	36,500	40

Sources. Interview information, October 1984 and August 1985; Xinhua News Agency, 6/8/85, in BBC, 6/19/85, p. A9, and 1/8/86, translated in BBC, 1/22/86, p. A17; State Statistical Bureau (1985, p. 340; 1986, p. 29).

the central plan, which was only 42% in 1985 (Xia, 1985, p. 4).[9] The rest was subject to allocation by both local governments and enterprises, but the experience of the No. 2 Auto Plant, China's largest truck producer, suggests that the share of enterprise marketing is substantial. As is shown in Table 3, No. 2's share of "self-sales" in total output was over 50% in both 1981 and 1982. In late 1982 the market shifted back to strong excess demand, and as a result self-sales fell sharply in 1983. In 1984, the combination of major general reforms and encouragement of sales of trucks to individuals led to a resurgence in self-sales, and in 1985 they further increased their share in fast-growing total output to over 40%.

Cement: Raising plan prices to near-market levels. Cement had a firmly established multiple pricing system in the prereform period, with local administratively fixed prices well above the state price. By 1984–1985 even higher, market-determined prices had emerged. At the end of 1985 the state price of cement was raised by over 60%; local fixed prices were kept roughly the same; and fees for packaging (which may have been used as a means of disguised price increases) were standardized. In principle there were to be no further increases in the state price (*Jingji Cankao,* 1/16/86, p. 4).

It is too early to ascertain the long-term results of this major price adjustment, and important questions remain about the degree of price flexibility and relative roles of plan and market in the future.[10] But what appears to

[9] This percentage is based on the initial production plan for 1985, which was exceeded by 22%. Thus the share of total realized output allocated by the central plan was probably even less than 42%.

[10] As early as January 1986 there were reports of increases in market prices for cement in some localities, attributed in part to the increase in the state price (*Jingji Cankao,* 1/16/86, p. 4).

have happened is the near demise of the two-tier system through the raising of plan prices to the point where embodied rents in plan-allocated goods are drastically reduced if not eliminated. In this situation any remaining price differential may be largely offset by the inconvenience of obtaining goods through the plan. Planning thus would seem to have lost its redistributional as well as its resource allocation role. In any case, the absolute amount of cement allocated by the central state plan has remained constant and its share in total output fell from 35% in 1980 to only 19% in 1985 (Ling, 1986, p. 2). Once the share of the state plan reached such a low level, a sharp price increase may have been relatively painless.

Rolled steel: Where the two-tier system survives. The two-tier system for rolled steel is still firmly entrenched. Very large amounts are still allocated through the plan at low prices, while at the same time there is an active market for the main varieties of rolled steel. Large steel plants can directly market 2% of within-plan output and all above-plan output, at increasingly flexible prices. The share of state plan allocations in total production of rolled steel fell from 74% in 1980 to 57% in 1985 (Ling, 1986, p. 2). Information from an investigation of 10 machinery plants in Shandong Province in 1985 (State Price Bureau, 1986) indicates that the share of rolled steel coming to typical users through the plan is already relatively low, only 41% on average.

The two-tier system seems more durable for rolled steel than for cement, timber, or trucks, perhaps in part because it is such a common input into production of other goods that large inframarginal price increases would exacerbate inflationary pressures. There were some adjustments in the state price of rolled steel in 1984, in response to steep price rises for its main material inputs (coke, iron ore, and pig iron). Prices have been increased for certain kinds of high-quality steels as well. But there have been no large across-the-board price adjustments, and the two-tier system at present survives. This situation may well change in 1987.

An example of monetization of embodied rents. The Shijiazhuang Material Supply Bureau in Hebei Province instituted experimental reforms in late 1984 and 1985. For a number of key producer goods, it made sales both within the plan and outside the plan at the same market prices. Holders of state plan input allocations were then separately given a sum of money to offset the difference between state and market prices for their plan allocations (*Jingji Cankao*, 1/20/86, p. 1). Under this system, rents have been "disembodied" from goods and transformed into pure rents separate from resource allocation. It is not clear how widespread practices like this are, but the Shijiazhuang experiment has received praise and is being further developed.

Key general policy changes. Government policies have been supportive of the trends for specific goods in a number of ways. Perhaps most important has been a progressive relaxation of controls over prices for transactions outside the plan (see above). This to some extent merely legalized behavior that was already pervasive, but it provided a needed stamp of approval for the two-tier system and allowed it to operate freely so that its dynamic tendencies could work themselves out.

Another key facet of overall government policy was the general refusal to pull back from the two-tier system (in the direction of comprehensive planning and controls), even when major problems arose. Rather than trying to restrict market sales and market pricing of cement, the government response was a sharp increase in state prices. In other cases increases in state prices were unspectacular, but nevertheless there was little backsliding. Finally, in some specific areas the government has made a conscious push for market-oriented reforms, seemingly independently from other considerations, for example the reduction of truck allocations through the central plan, even in the strong sellers' market of 1984.

CONCLUSIONS

The two-tier system appears to have worked, in the Chinese context, as an effective mechanism for the transition from a "command system" (albeit territorially and administratively decentralized) to a system where the market is coming to play a dominant role in the allocation of goods. This transition has not been completed for all products, and indeed may still be at a relatively early stage for many goods. But the general pattern and direction of the transition is clear.

Is there any continuing role for the two-tier system over the medium term? It appears to be on the way out for some of the main industrial producer goods. The two-tier system of producer prices in agriculture has been drastically modified. The system appears most entrenched in the case of urban consumer prices of basic agricultural commodities. These serve as a rent-transfer mechanism to the urban population, the bulk of which has access to low-price grain and edible oil. Their interests are relatively unified on this issue, in contrast with enterprises, whose access to state plan allocations is highly uneven. Finally, the state as commercial intermediary can insulate the producer and consumer price systems from each other, preventing or at least reducing the destabilizing incentives of the two-tier system for producers. This suggests that the places where the system is most likely to survive are those where (1) it is operating on the demand side but not on the supply side; and (2) the political interests of the beneficiaries are strong and relatively free from internal contradictions. In any case, where the two-tier system remains, planning plays a primarily redistributional rather than an allocative role.

Thus in an only partly conscious and largely undesigned manner, China has groped its way out of the system of directive planning and administrative allocation of industrial goods, in a period of roughly 6–7 years of reforms. Superficially, this would put it on the same footing that Hungary achieved with one stroke in 1968, which might lead to questions as to whether it took the long way about. But there are probably some major, possibly even essential benefits from the tortuous and prolonged path of transition taken by China. China has established and gained experience with functioning markets, where enterprises directly face periods of severe competition, major price fluctuations, etc. There has been a great increase in commercial channels and in the range of choice for selling output by enterprises, which appears to have been lacking in a country like Hungary, perhaps partly because the formal abolition of the command system was so "easy."

It is probably impossible to sort out the precise relative importance of the inherent dynamics of the two-tier system, the changing constellation of political forces, and central government policy in contributing to the articulation, change, and prospective demise of the two-tier system. But it is clear that the economic forces inherent in the two-tier system and strongly proreform central government policy reinforced each other. Both may have been essential for the transition to work.

A key feature of the two-tier system may be that it provides substantial and progressively increasing open expression of the economic power inherently held by sellers in a sellers' market situation. This is manifested in higher prices and more money for producers (if only at the margin initially). It also renders clearly visible the rents embodied in goods that flow through plan channels and creates the potential opportunity for their appropriation by producers and commerical intermediaries.

If the observations and arguments of this paper are correct, what are the implications for the future? At a fundamental level, the issues of market allocation and to a lesser extent price reform are becoming passé, and they no longer need to be the prime concern for reformers.[11] The focus of attention thus can shift to the next "level" of resource allocation—China's factor allocation system, which is full of rigidities and problems (see Byrd and Tidrick, 1987).

REFERENCES

Ames, Edward, *Soviet Economic Processes*. Homewood, IL: Richard D. Irwin, 1965.
British Broadcasting Corporation (BBC), *Summary of World Broadcasts: The Far East*.
Baumol, William J., *Business Behavior, Value and Growth*. New York: Harcourt Brace Jovanovich, 1959.

---

[11] There is still a lot of "cleaning up" to be done with prices of specific products, but the general direction is already clear, provided that the inherent dynamics of the two-tier system are judiciously reinforced by central government policy.

Byrd, William, "The Market Mechanism and Economic Reforms in Chinese Industry." PhD Dissertation, Department of Economics Harvard University, Cambridge, MA, 1987a.

Byrd, William, "The Role and Impact of Markets." In Gene Tidrick and Chen Jiyuan, Eds., *China's Industrial Reforms*, pp. 237–275. London: Oxford Univ. Press, 1987b.

Byrd, William, and Tidrick, Gene, "Adjustment and Reform in the Chongqing Clock and Watch Company." In Byrd, Tidrick et al., *Recent Chinese Economic Reforms: Studies of Two Industrial Enterprises*. World Bank Staff Working Papers, No. 652, 1984.

Byrd, William, and Tidrick, Gene, "Factor Allocation and Enterprise Incentives." In Gene Tidrick and Jiyuan Chen, Eds., *China's Industrial Reforms*, pp. 60–102. London: Oxford Univ. Press, 1987.

Chai, C. H., "Reform of China's Industrial Prices." Paper presented at Conference on China's System Reforms, Centre of Asian Studies, University of Hong Kong, March 17–20, 1986.

China Economic System Reform Research Institute (CESRRI), Comprehensive Investigation Group (Eds.), *Gaige: Women Mianling de Tiaozhan yu Xuanze (Reform: The Challenge and Choices We Face)*. Beijing: Zhongguo Jingji Chubanshe, 1986.

Jingji Cankao (Economic Information) daily newspaper.

Ling, Yuxun, "Duanzheng Dangfeng, Jianchi Gaige, Fazhan you Jihua de Shengchan Ziliao Shichang" [Rectify Party Methods, Support Reform, Develop a Planned Market for Means of Production]. *Wuzi Guanli (Materials Manage.)* 6:2–11, April 1986.

Ministry of Agriculture, *Zhongguo Nongye Nianjian (China Agricultural Yearbook)*. Beijing: Nongye Chubanshe, 1981 (1980 Yearbook), 1982 (1981 Yearbook).

Ministry of Coal Industry, *Zhongguo Meitan Gongye Nianjian (China Coal Industry Yearbook)*. Beijing: Meitan Gongye Chubanshe, 1982, 1983, 1985.

Portes, R. D., "The Enterprise under Central Planning." *Rev. Econ. Studies* **36,** 2:197–212, April 1969.

Shen, Yulao, and Han, Demin, "1985 Nian Zhuyao Wuzi Shichang Jiage Biandong Fenxi" [An Analysis of Market Price Movements for the Most Important Materials in 1985]. *Wuzi Jingji Yanjiu (Materials Econ. Res.)* **3:**18–19, March 1986.

State Price Bureau, Comprehensive Planning Office, Investigation Group, "Dui Shige Qiye de Gangcai Gongying he Kucun Qingkuang de Diaocha" [An Investigation of the Supply and Stockpiling of Rolled Steel in Ten Enterprises]. *Wuzi Guanli* **2:**18–19, February 1986.

State Statistical Bureau, *Statistical Yearbook of China*. Beijing: China Statistical Information and Consultancy Service Centre, 1985.

State Statistical Bureau, "Communique on the Statistics of 1985 Economic and Social Development." In *Beijing Review*, 3/24/86, pp. 27–33.

Tidrick, Gene, and Chen, Jiyuan, Eds. *China's Industrial Reform*. London: Oxford Univ. Press, 1987.

Wong, Christine, "Ownership and Control in Chinese Industry: The Maoist Legacy and Prospects for the 1980s." In US Congress, Joint Economic Committee, *China's Economy Looks Toward the Year 2000, Volume I: The Four Modernizations*, pp. 571–603. Washington: US Government Printing Office, 1986.

Xia, Junbo, "Guanyu Banhao Qiche Maoyi Zhongxin de Jige Wenti" [Several Questions Concerning Handling Well Vehicle Trading Centers]. *Wuzi Guanli* **4:**4–5, April 1985.

JOURNAL OF COMPARATIVE ECONOMICS 11, 309–318 (1987)

The Dual Pricing System in China's Industry

WU JINGLIAN

Economic, Technical, and Social Development Research Center, Beijing, China

AND

ZHAO RENWEI

Economic Research Institute, Chinese Academy of Social Sciences, Beijing, China

Wu Jinglian and Zhao Renwei—The Dual Pricing System in China's Industry

Since February 1985, China has permitted producer goods exchange at two different prices: a state-set price, for centrally rationed supplies, and a higher free-market price. The paper describes the origins of this system and its development from 1981 to 1985. The authors argue that its disadvantages outweigh its advantages, but that it is acceptable as a temporary, transitional device. *J. Comp. Econ.*, September 1987, **11**(3), pp. 309–318. Economic, Technical, and Social Development Research Center, Beijing, China; Economic Research Institute, Chinese Academy of Social Sciences, Beijing, China. © 1987 Academic Press, Inc.

Journal of Economic Literature Classification Numbers: 052, 113, 124.

A dual pricing system has evolved in the midst of China's economic reform: products allocated according to the central plan, on the one hand, follow a fixed pricing system, while the portion of its output that an enterprise produces on its own, as above-plan output, can be sold on the free market. This duality, which some people call a "two-track" system, has been the subject of much controversy in China. At the very beginning, as it took shape, enterprises which were barely breaking even under the set-price system welcomed it, while some economists worried about its negative consequences (Wu, 1984). In 1985, the debate became heated. Some held that the two components conflict with each other, and that in the long run the conflict would lead to chaos in the Chinese economy and doom reform (Gou et al., 1985). Their opponents believed that the marketed portion of production, despite its small share, not only gives the enterprise a better feeling of reward, but enforces a cost-consciousness on the enterprise, and also alleviates shortages of certain materials and generates reasonable prices. Advocates of the dual pricing system depict it as an approach to price reform which is uniquely Chinese (Hua and He, 1985; Liu, 1985): gradual expansion of the market portion in conjunction with adjustment of the state-set price hopefully will lead to a uniform pricing system based exclusively on the market.

An assessment of the dual pricing system is central to evaluating the strategy of economic reform and its rational sequence. It also bears on the evaluation of the performance of economic reform to date. This explains why it has become the subject of controversy.

THE EVOLUTION OF THE DUAL PRICING SYSTEM IN INDUSTRY

In command economies, strictly speaking, a "two-track" system has never been allowed, except for some agricultural products sold at country fairs. Although the existence of black markets in socialist countries, pejoratively called the "second economy," is well known, these have never occupied a significant place. China's industry is exceptional. The proportion of extra-plan pricing is larger than in other socialist countries. The main reasons are as follows.

First, strict centralized management of the economy by directives, as under the pure Soviet model, has never existed in China. The "decentralizing movement" which took place in 1958 and has been renewed from time to time ever since has eroded central planning and its power to control. There have always been a variety of transactions between regions and enterprises outside the planning system, a minor market economy, normally at prices higher than planned prices. These economic relations have been euphemistically called in China "cooperation relations," and the goods purchased in this fashion, "cooperation materials."

Second, the Chinese government is under pressure to find jobs for a rural population which has been crowded out of farming due to the scarcity of arable land. Consequently, there are a large number of small, inefficient industrial enterprises, which must sell their products at higher prices in order to cover higher costs. These enterprises would otherwise go bankrupt or require government subsidies. In 1958, when China launched the "Great Leap Forward," of which the "mass movement for smelting iron" was a part, the government promulgated a decision that "backyard" pig iron could sell at higher prices. A professor at Beijing University, attempting to rationalize this duality of prices, argued that under socialist conditions a product had two "value centers" (Fuan, 1959). The theory was forgotten soon after the failure of the "Great Leap Forward," but the practice has been maintained.

Nevertheless, the dual pricing system has only recently been expanded, acknowledged, and legitimized. The original plan for economic reform did not envisage this.

After the December 1978 3rd Plenum of the 11th Party Committee, the emphasis of urban reform was on experimental expansion of enterprise decision-making powers. But it was soon realized that if expanded decision-making on the part of enterprises was not coordinated with overall change in the pricing system, it could achieve little. As rightly pointed out by Premier Zhao in his report addressed to the People's Congress in 1981, "These reforms are still partial and exploratory in nature and our work has suffered from certain incongruities and from lack of coordination. The task before us is to sum up our experience in these reforms and, after careful investigation and study and repeated scientific confirmation, to draw up as soon as possible an overall plan for reforming the economy and carry it out step by step." For various reasons this "overall plan" has never been implemented. However, it has been generally recognized that in designing a policy mix for reform, price reform deserves special attention.

The steps recommended for price reform for the period 1980–1981 were very similar to the measures taken by Czechoslovakia in 1967–1968. First, adjust ex-factory prices throughout industry. Second, reform the existing price management by abolishing "pricing-fixing by directive" (except for a few items), and introducing a market-determined price system. Around 1981, the chief of the newly founded "Structure Reform Office of the State Council," Mr. Xue Muqiao, an influential Chinese economist, wrote a series of papers envisaging this process (Xue, 1984). In the same year the State Council set up the "Price Research Center," which embarked on an action plan for price reform.

Unfortunately, the 1981 action plan for price reform was not put into effect, because in 1982 a nationwide debate on the relationship between the planned economy and the market unfolded. In the debate, those who believed that commodity exchange was also an attribute of the socialist economy were criticized. For example, "Red Flag," a monthly magazine published under the auspices of the Central Committee of the C.C.P., prefaced its "Reader on Planned Economy and the Market Mechanism" by saying, "it is incorrect to think that planning applies only to macro-economic control, while the micro-economy, i.e., the enterprises' behavior, should be regulated by the market," and "that enterprises are independent in such decision-making as determining their production and transactions." It pointed out further, "to follow the mandatory plan is a basic element of the socialist economy and embodies socialist public ownership both in the organization of production and in management;" therefore, what we should do is to "include such economic levers as pricing, taxation and credit loans in the state plan and make them important parts of it" (Red Flag, 1983). Such an atmosphere made the implementation of the above-mentioned price reform impossible, in particular the recommendation to loosen the state's grasp on price management.

Under these circumstances, it was out of the question to carry out the envisaged reforms in the realms of production, investment, and distribution. Die-hard reformists had to live in the cracks of the mandatory plan, or seek leeway outside it. Consequently, the sphere of cooperation materials was further expanded. It was not until 1984, when the political atmosphere shifted to favor reform, that this more or less underground expansion of the free market attained legitimacy.

The decision of the State Council, in May 1984, "On Further Expansion of Decision Making Power on the Part of State Run Industrial Enterprises" (also called "Ten Regulations"), stipulated that there are two components of production, namely, planned economy and non-planned economy ("plan" denotes mandatory plan); that there are two types of material supplies for the enterprises, namely, state allocation and free purchase by individual enterprises; that, accordingly, the prices of the goods produced in the state quota system will be fixed by the state and the prices of the goods produced outside the state quota system can be manipulated within a range up to 20% higher or lower than state prices. In February 1985, the State Price Administration and the State Material Administration jointly cancelled the 20% limit. At that point, the dual pricing system was formally in place.

The adoption of "On the Reform of Economic Structure" by the Central Committee of the Chinese Communist Party at its 3rd Plenum of the 12th Congress was a breakthrough in this regard. It was crystal-clear: "The socialist economy is a commodity economy based upon public ownership." Obviously, to set up this institution presupposed a price system free from government intervention, reflecting production costs and shifts in supply and demand. After the October 1984 adoption of this document, judging that political preconditions were ripe for price reform, the leading economic authorities discussed at length how to do it and finally concluded that the task for 1985 was to reform the prices of agricultural products and non-staple foods (e.g., meats, eggs, and vegetables) and maintain the dual system for the remainder (mainly raw materials energy and other producer goods). Concerning producer goods, the national planning conference decided that the quantity of materials allocated to various departments and localities would be determined by (a) 1984 Plan parameters and (b) the priority of the particular projects.

What are the relative shares of planned prices and market prices in production and in distribution? There are no accurate data. What makes it worse is that when the state plan goes down through ministries and localities to the enterprises the plan tends to grow bigger, further confusing any attempt at calculation. Data from the National Conference on Material Flows in early 1986 indicates that the number of categories of materials controlled by the state was reduced from 256 to 23 in 1985, and that planned allocation of coal, timber, steel, and cement to enterprises fell to 50, 30.7, 56.9, and 19.4%, respectively. In 1985, free market purchase of steel, timber, and cement constituted 38, 46, and 61% of total consumption by industrial enterprises (*Eco-*

nomic Daily, February 1986). Of course, it varied in different regions and cities. For instance, Shanghai had a relatively higher percentage of allocated supply (steel, 72%; pig iron, 66%; and coal, 90%), while its neighbor Jiangsu Province registered a much lower percentage (steel, 35%; pig iron, 22%; and coal, 58%).

One ought to look at this data very cautiously because distortion is likely. For example, the volume of steel that was reported sold on the free market was 15–20% of the total steel production in the country, but the proportion of steel consumption said to have been bought on free markets by enterprises was about 40% of total steel consumption.

The market prices of some important materials can be a multiple of the allocation price set by the state. The ex-factory price of No. 6.5 steel wire is 610 yuan per ton, but its market price in 1985 reached 1500 to 2000 yuan per ton. The price of coal under the state plan in 27 yuan per ton while in the free market it was sold at 100 yuan per ton. Of course, this disparity varies in different regions and at different times.

ANALYSIS OF THE ADVANTAGES AND DISADVANTAGES OF THE DUAL PRICING SYSTEM

What benefits does the dual pricing system bring China's economic life, according to the advocates of the "two-track" system? First, it stimulates production and alleviates the pressure of excess demand. Industrial enterprises which formerly had to obey government production directives are given leeway to produce, for themselves, products that they can dispose of at prices set by themselves. They feel a great incentive to seek success and profit. Enterprise behavior is redirected toward tapping their potential resources, organizing technical renovation, and increasing production. As a result of that initiative the extent of shortage of some materials has been lessened. This market-supply response has been most evident in coal production, where an annual increase of 8.35% in each of the last 2 years is attributed to the establishment of a coal market. Coal prices in the free market in Jiangsu Province fell from 150–200 yuan per ton to 80–120 yuan per ton. The market mechanism helps break bottlenecks, partially because it helps get rid of the "production for the sake of production" model of socialism and interrelates production and demand.

Second, the new system encourages energy conservation and high-quality management. The old system, material supply by the state at a fixed price, gives no impetus to the enterprises to save energy, resulting in high coefficients of material consumption and energy consumption and a relatively low technology level. The prices of raw materials and energy in China are sometimes much lower than international prices. For example, washed coal is only 45% of the international market price, crude oil 30%, cast pig iron 70%, and plain carbon steel 60%. Their prices in the free markets are normally close to the international ones, if not higher. Therefore, the consumers must economize or look for substitutes. A survey of steel consumption by 300 industrial enterprises shows an 18% reduction in terms of "steel consumption for ten thousand yuan output value" in the 1984 fiscal year, indicating some of the enterprises tried to save steel consumption.

A third advantage of the new system was that it represented a compromise: preserve planned allocation, while drawing incremental output into a market system. As pointed out above, the major theme of the political debate from 1982 to 1984 was that it was a matter of basic importance to maintain the leading position of mandatory planning. The dual pricing system in China was intended, on the one hand, to keep preexisting economic interrelationships coordinated under the state plan, with an eye to avoiding further conflict among the already divided economic interests of the various sectors, while on the other hand drawing a growing part of production and distribution into new orbits within a market economy. (Some additional measures were needed to readjust interpersonal economic relationships. The low state prices of mineral products relative to manufactured goods have been raised so that those factories could earn profits. This change also lessens to some extent the bias in favor of state supplies.)

Last, the dual pricing system softens the risks of economic reform, by "changing a big earthquake into several small tremors." Mr. W. Bruce, who, based on the experience of East Europe, disagrees with the idea of partial economic reform, has nevertheless accepted the feasibility of China's approach. He was quoted (Liu, 1985) as saying, at the 1985 International Conference on Macroeconomic Management, that in the transition from an allocation system to an exchange system, China has adopted a dual pricing system for producer goods in addition to consumer goods; that the latter has been practiced by some other socialist countries; and that this may be a useful invention, a bridge that makes it possible for the new system to replace the old, in a smooth transition from direct control by commands to indirect control through the market.

Like everything else, the dual pricing system has its disadvantages. Premier Zhao's report addressed to the National People's Congress, "On the Seventh Five Year Plan," correctly pointed out, "in the reform of our country the replacement of the old by the new system is a gradual process and it takes time. When it is evolving the two systems are interacting upon each other. The fact that the new system cannot altogether replace the old system, whose functions still operate for a period of time to come, determines the very complex nature of the present situation." The dual system generates four problems, as follow.

First, hypocritical behavior by enterprises. On the one hand, they try to hide their production capacity so that they will get lower production quotas from the state, while on the other hand they strive to claim as large an allocation of material as they can from the state. Allocated materials tend to leak to the free market for profits. Contracts between enterprises in accordance with the state plan are sometimes not honored. In the first half of 1985, of 18 kinds of products under contracts, 16 were not fulfilled. For example, unfulfilled production quotas for steel and iron totalled 510,000 tons, coal 2.98 million tons, and cement 470,000 tons. This has greatly hampered the progress of some industrial enterprises on the priority list of the state and the progress of some priority projects. What is especially worrisome is that the situation is worsening.

Second, loss of objective standards for performance assessment by the state. State production quotas are based on past enterprise performance. Now, a well-managed enterprise that receives a larger production quota from the state is less able to produce extra for its own profit through the free market, while a less efficient factory is in a better position to profit in this way. One ton of steel provided at the state price is equivalent to a 1000 yuan subsidy. This shows how easily one can make a large profit. The enterprise need only elicit a high input quota and a reduced output quota, instead of improving managerial skill and reducing production costs. This indicates that, under the dual pricing system, the output value and profitability performance of different enterprises cannot be assessed using uniform standards and norms. Enterprises competing under these confused criteria may well experience anomie.

Third, induced smuggling in distribution. Knowing that profit can be made by reselling allocated materials, smugglers avail themselves of numerous wide-open loopholes. In 1985, when the price difference from trucks was highest, reselling just one 4.5-ton truck immediately created a "ten thousand yuan household" (a slang term for a *parvenu,* but in this case one engaged in unlawful activities). In the last few years the Chinese papers have reported many cases of smuggling groups which made as much as 100,000 yuan profit. In the period 1984–1985 there emerged some 200,000 companies that had neither resources and equipment nor a business orientation, but instead specialized in this field.

Fourth, irrational utilization of resources. The high prices and profits in the free market attract investment. The investment is flowing to the "right" industry, but the flow hatches a number of small and inefficient enterprises. This gives rise to irrational utilization of resources due to the loss of economies of scale. Undeniably, the development of a large number of township enterprises serves some purposes: increasing production, creating jobs for the rural population, and supplementing the output of state-run enterprises. But it is also evident that they are competing with the big enterprises for raw materials and energy. Therefore, one should not be surprised to see that occasionally the most well-equipped rolling mills or steel mills stand idle, while energy-consuming small township mills continue to produce, at much higher cost, simply because they have succeeded in obtaining raw materials and energy supplies. Mr. G. Tidrick, after having surveyed 10 industrial enterprises, concluded (*People's Daily,* June 4, 1985): "In summary, the Chinese multiple-price, multiple-channel allocation system has enhanced the flexibility of supply, but at a high resource cost. It has also increased enterprise autonomy and weakened central control over resource allocation without, however, providing an effective alternative market control mechanism."

It is our view that the dual system, as an interim measure, has its due place. But if it lasts longer than appropriate it can hinder future reform, because its defects will tend to grow. Pricing is a basic parameter in the commodity economy. If this parameter is not properly constructed it not only affects the whole economic system, because of no effective market control mechanism, but also affects the other parameters in the system, e.g., interest rate, tax rate, and exchange rate, essential instruments for macroeconomic control.

RECOMMENDED SOLUTIONS AND OUR ANALYSIS

How can this dilemma be solved? The alternative solutions can be grouped into three categories. (1) Allow a comeback for the old system while leaving a limited role for market price fluctuation. (2) Eliminate the remnants of the old system and set up a free price market system "at one stroke." (3) Gradually transform the old system into the new system, using the dual system as a transitional device. Although there has always been a danger of a restoration of the old system, no one at the present time openly advocates it. The second approach, seemingly impractical, is out of the question at least for the foreseeable future. Therefore, the only question is how to handle the problem of transition and at what speed. At present, there are two different opinions.

First, the "as fast as possible" scenario. Some people, for instance, believe that the dual system should not last long because the innate profound defects outweigh its advantages (Tidrick, 1987). Some argue that what prevails now is not an effective market control mechanism, which should be a result of a consistent policy mix. Therefore, "the only way out is to break the impasse and bring the role of the new mechanism into full play as soon as possible" (Zhao, 1986). Under today's circumstances, when the old system is only marginally eroded and will not automatically disappear, the new market control mechanism will not function effectively. Meanwhile, economic stagnation or other ills can be blamed on the ongoing reform, as an excuse to restore the old system. Aware of this danger, the reformers anticipate a breakthrough, such that the new mechanism will become the dominant force in the whole economy. "Domination" by the market control system will ensure, they hope, a mutually reinforcing relationship between economic development and economic reform. Suggesting an integrated policy mix, they seek (a) independent enterprises responsible for their own profit and loss, (b) a free-price market that encourages competition, and (c) an indirect control mechanism. To pave the way, according to their scenario, it is necessary to reform the price system by first adjusting, and then freeing, all the prices within a short period of time, while at the same time setting up a new government budgetary system and a new monetary system.

A large number of people do not agree with them, and label their scenario "over-optimism." In recognizing that China's market is underdeveloped and that the transition from a dual pricing system to a commodity economy takes time, the second scenario depicts the process of transition as "bit-by-bit, hands off," i.e., allowing an annual increase of 10–20% in materials whose prices are market determined and simultaneously adjusting the planned prices. Consequently, it is expected that 5 to 10 years will be needed to rationalize the price system.

The arguments in support of the second scenario are many. Of them, the main consideration is that the dual pricing system will have to continue for a due length of time before its function of increasing production and invigorating the market will have been exhausted. In the absence of a much better alternative to it, the "wash our hands of it" approach in price reform is not desirable. We feel, in addition, that the present economic situation does not permit such a major step in reform. As correctly pointed out by Mr. Liu Guoguang (Wu, 1986), "successful transition depends on macro-balance between aggregate demand and aggregate supply. Unless this can be solved it is impossible to put an end to the dual pricing system, based upon the dual planning system and dual material flow system." He continues, "if this predicament goes on, the length of the transition period will not be shorter than predicted by many Chinese and overseas scholars."

Liu's analysis reflects the reality of China's economy. What remains to be discussed is whether this macro-balance can be achieved or not. We know very well that in the traditional socialist economy, as pointed out rightly by Mr. Kornai, "expansion drive," "investment hunger," and "consumption hunger" are chronic disorders, and "swollen demand" and "shortage" are innate syndromes of the socialist economy. Nevertheless, we have had times in the past when the political and economic leaders succeeded in curing these illnesses by "economic adjustment," and a "national movement for production increase and frugality," although the cure did not last long. A recent example was in 1981, when China required only a month's time to change the seller's market into a buyer's market (Liu, 1986). What was lacking was a set of reform policies to take advantage of the favorable situation. The excessive growth of consumption and fixed-assets investment which took place in 1984 and still has not been fully curtailed is a mistake that is by and large manmade. That is, the decision-makers failed to handle the relationship between economic development and reform properly (although it should also be admitted that the tendency to "investment hunger" and "consumption hunger" did recur). If in the future, "priority is given to reform," "economic development is planned in such a way as to facilitate reform," and "a basic balance of aggregate supply and demand is always kept in mind with an appropriate ratio between saving and consumption," thus providing a better environment for economic reform, these mistakes can be avoided and are not doomed to failure.[1]

In summary, we suggest the following strategy: at present, efforts should be made to control the growth of aggregate demand and to initiate a product market, services market, and monetary market through price reform, finance, and tax reform, and monetary reform in order to put an end to the impasse of duality. Even when the market control mechanism has the upper hand, the remnants of the old system and the old institutions will still survive for a long time, because China is economically backward and vulnerable. It will take an even longer time for the new system to be fully operational and for the dual price system to expire.

REFERENCES

Fuan Hong, "On Socialist Commodity Production and Value: Their Laws." *Econ. Study J.* **2**, Feb. 1959.

Gou Shu-xing, Liu Ji-rei, and Quo Shu-fang, "An Overall Consideration Urgently Needed for Reform." *Comp. Study Socioecon. System* **1**, Jan. 1985.

Hua Cheng and He Hia-chun, "On Chinese Price Reform." *Econ. J.* **2**, Feb. 1985.

Liu Guo-guang, "China's Price Reform: Its Present Situation and Problems." *Finance Econ. J.* **5**, May 1986.

Liu Guo-guang, "Economic System Reform and Macro-Economic Management." *Econ. Study J.* **12**, Dec. 1985.

Red Flag Editorial Office, *Preface to the Reader on Planned Economy and the Market Mechanism*, Beijing: Red Flag Press, 1983.

Tidrick, G., "Planning and Supply in Chinese State Owned Industry." In Gene Tidrick and Chen Jiyuan, Eds., *China's Industrial Reforms*. London: Oxford Univ. Press, 1987.

Wu Jing-lian, "Economic Fluctuation and the Dual System." *Finance Econ. J.* **6**, June 1986.

Wu Jing-lian, "Invigoration of Enterprises: Key to Rural Reform." *World Econ. Herald* Sept. 24, 1984.

Xue Mu-qiao, "On Price Adjustment and Price Management Reform," and "The Price Society Ought to Study Laws Governing Price Fluctuation." In *Xue Mu-qiao On Economy*. Beijing: People's Press, 1984.

Zhao Lin-ru, "On Price Reform: Important Issues." *Ref. Econ.* **7**, July 1986.

---

[1] Cited from "On Suggestions for the Seventh Five Year Plan by the Central Committee of the Chinese Communist Party" October 1985, which has a good analysis of the relation between economic development and economic reform.

JOURNAL OF COMPARATIVE ECONOMICS **11**, 319–333 (1987)

Money and Price Level Determination in China[1]

GREGORY C. CHOW

Princeton University, Princeton, New Jersey 08544

Chow, Gregory C.—Money and Price Level Determination in China

The quantity theory of money provides a useful starting point in explaining the price level in China. The ratio of money supply to real output is an important variable in explaining the price level, but the elasticity is below unity, suggesting that velocity is not constant. A short-run model for changes in the price level explains the Chinese annual data from 1952 to 1983 better than the United States data from 1922 to 1953. This model is stable after 1979 and forecasts well in 1984. *J. Comp. Econ.* September 1987, **11**(3), pp. 319–333. Princeton University, Princeton, New Jersey 08544. © 1987 Academic Press, Inc.

Journal of Economic Literature Classification Numbers: 123, 134, 311.

INTRODUCTION

The possible effect of an increase in money supply on inflation became an important issue for the Chinese economic reform officials in 1985 when currency in circulation had actually increased by about 50% from the end of 1983 to the end of 1984, mainly as a result of the policy to allow individual banks the discretion to extend credit without having established a mechanism of monetary control by the central bank. The main purpose of this paper is to study the effect of money supply on the price level in China. This topic is not only of theoretical interest in economics, but is of relevance to the choice of different options in carrying out price reforms. To the extent that inflation is found to be a monetary phenomenon, there should be less concern over possible inflationary effects of decontrolling or adjusting prices of selected individual commodities. At the same time, to the extent that upward movements of prices of selected consumer goods require, for political reasons, and assuming downward price rigidity, certain adjustments in money wages which may lead to an increase in money supply, the inflationary effect of the policy can be quantitatively evaluated.

[1] The author thanks Josef Brada, John Fei, Dwight Jaffee, and Bruce Reynolds for helpful comments, The Garfield Foundation and the National Science Foundation for financial support.

CHINESE ECONOMIC REFORM   29   ISBN 0-12-587045-0

In Section 1, I discuss the theoretical issues in applying the quantity theory of money to explaining the price level in the Chinese institutional setting. In Section 2, long-run relations based on the quantity theory will be empirically established using Chinese annual data from 1952 to 1983. In Section 3, equations explaining short-run price changes from year to year will be estimated and tested. In Section 4, for comparison purposes, analogous equations for the long run and the short run will be estimated using data from the United States from 1922 to 1953. The similarities of results between the two countries are noteworthy. In Section 5, additional issues concerning short-run price determination will be addressed, including the possible direct effect of aggregate wage on the price level, a possible structural change after the economic reform began in 1979, and the use of the short-run model for forecasting inflation.

1. THEORETICAL AND INSTITUTIONAL ISSUES

Economists have suggested that the quantity theory of money may provide a crude explanation of the price level. It is of interest to ascertain how well this theory can explain the price level in China from 1952 to 1983, and to compare the results with those obtained for the United States using similar data three decades earlier. To do so, it is necessary to specify the theory more precisely and discuss its relevance in the Chinese setting.

The quantity theory of money is based on the quantity equation

$$Mv = Py \qquad (1)$$

where M is the stock of money, P is the price level, y is national income in real terms, and v is income velocity. The quantity Eq. (1) can be interpreted merely as an identity which defines the velocity v as the ratio of national income Py in money terms to the stock of money M. If so interpreted, it cannot serve as an explanation of P. However, if v is nearly constant through time and if changes in y are largely independent of changes in M, and these are big ifs, then a change in M will lead to a proportional change in P. The quantity theory of money is derived from Eq. (1) on the condition that these two presuppositions are roughly valid. Under this condition, the theory provides an explanation for the price level P.

There are many reasons the constancy of v is at best a rough approximation to reality. A well-known one is the Keynesian argument that when prices are rigid an increase in M will lead to a downward movement in the rate of interest and a reduction in v, rather than a rise in P. How good is the assumption of the constancy of v? This question has been answered both theoretically and empirically mainly by reinterpreting (1) as a demand equation for money,

$$\frac{M}{P} = ky \qquad (2)$$

where $k = v^{-1}$. If the demand for real money balances, M/P is approximately proportional to real income y, or if (2) is a good approximation to reality, k or its inverse v can be treated approximately as a constant. Theoretically, it is known that the demand for M/P depends also on the rate of interest, and that the income elasticity of demand for money does not have to be unity as (2) implies. These two considerations aside, it is still worthwhile to observe how well Eq. (2) fits the data.

However, assuming that Eq. (2) fits the data reasonably well by some standard, one cannot thereby conclude that an increase in M, given y, will lead to a proportional increase in P. To demonstrate this point, suppose hypothetically that the data for M and y satisfy the relation $M = ky$, or

$$\log M = \log k + \log y.$$

Suppose also that $\log P$ is generated as an independent, identically distributed random variable ϵ. Under these two hypothetical assumptions, the data will satisfy

$$\log(M/P) = \log k + \log y - \epsilon.$$

A regression of $\log(M/P)$ on $\log y$ may yield a coefficient of unity and possibly a high R^2, supporting the hypothesis (2). Yet, by the way the data on P are constructed, changes in M do not affect changes in P. Hence by studying the demand for real money balance through Eq. (2), one learns little about how well money supply explains the price level. Nevertheless, the demand for money is itself a subject of interest.

To apply the quantity theory of money to explain the price level P, we rewrite (1) as

$$P = v(M/y). \qquad (3)$$

If v were close to being constant, regressing $\log P$ on $\log(M/P)$ would yield a coefficient of unity and a good fit. If v itself is negatively associated with (M/y), changes in P will be less than proportional to changes in (M/y). As long as an increase in (M/y) is not completely offset by a proportional reduction in v, it will have a positive effect on P. The question of how good the assumption of a constant v is should be answered differently depending on the variable one wishes to explain. A constant k may be satisfactory when Eq. (2) is used to explain M/P. A constant v may be more or less satisfactory when Eq. (3) is used to explain P. A more relevant question for the purpose of this paper is how well the theoretical framework suggested by (3) can explain the price level P in China. We will try to answer this question in Section 2, and study the short-run dynamics of changes in P in Section 3. Before proceeding, let us consider briefly the institutional setting of China and examine whether the theoretical framework above is applicable.

Three sets of issues have to be addressed when the quantity theory is applied to explain a general price index in China. First, prices of many producer and consumer goods have been controlled. Therefore these prices may not adjust to monetary forces as they would in a market economy. However, the theory could still provide a good explanation of the general price level if the remaining, uncontrolled prices were able to adjust sufficiently. Second, the quantity theory assumes that all income flows are associated with money payments. As in a less developed economy, some agricultural products in China are a part of national income but do not go through market transactions. Furthermore, as in a centrally planned economy, many producer goods are paid for by transfers of funds to and from bank accounts held by state enterprises. Bank deposits of state enterprises are often earmarked for specific purposes and cannot be used to finance general purchases. If these deposits are excluded from our definition of money supply, certain flows of producer goods will be excluded from both sides of the quantity equation. The theory may be applicable if we confine ourselves to expenditure flows paid by consumers provided that the variables M, P, and y are defined accordingly. Third, related to the choice of variables is the accuracy of Chinese official statistics which will be used to test the theory. The quality of these data has been subject to question by scholars. I have discussed this issue in Chow (1986). It suffices to point out here that these data have been found reasonable when used to estimate simple economic relationships, including those reported in Chow (1985b, pp. 123, 129, 165–166, and 263; and 1985a). By using these data to test economic hypotheses as in this paper, one learns more about their quality.

Bearing in mind that the stock of money M has to be defined consistently with the output y being purchased at an average price level P, I have decided to confine my attention to retail purchases by consumers. The main price index to be explained is a general index of retail price. The relevant stock of money is currency in circulation. In China consumers do not use checks and demand deposits by consumers are nonexistent. However, saving deposits exist and could be included in the definition of money. Concerning the output variable y, one may choose to include only those products that are related to final purchases by consumers and to exclude producer goods purchased by state enterprises. I have decided to use a more comprehensive measure of output, namely, national income available as reported in Chinese official statistics. This measure will be appropriate if it is highly correlated with final purchases by consumers. It is interesting to find out how well such a measure which is usually employed in testing the quantity theory can perform in the Chinese context, realizing that the measures of P and M are more narrowly defined. To employ a more narrowly defined measure of y would make the theory less powerful because such a measure itself has to be explained.

2. LONG-RUN EXPLANATIONS OF THE PRICE LEVEL

The general index of retail prices is one of the five price indices regularly published in the *Statistical Yearbook of China*. In the 1981 edition of the *Yearbook* (pp. 519–520), the following explanations are given:

In China there are several ways in pricing commodities, including list prices of the state-owned commercial departments and the free markets (fair trade), the negotiated price and the purchasing price of the surplus farm and sideline products. Therefore, apart from the indexes of the list price, it is important to compile the general retail price index and the general index of the cost of living of the workers and staff members, both of which include the list retail price and the negotiated retail price and the retail price in free market, as well as general purchasing price indexes for farm and sideline products that include the list purchasing price, negotiated purchasing price and the purchasing price of surplus farm and sideline products. The actual value of sales and purchases based on different prices is taken as the weights for calculating the general indexes.

(1) The index of the list retail price is calculated by the formula of weighted arithmetic mean. The weights used are adjusted annually based on the data on actual retail sales. The markets and items of commodities selected for calculation have been on the increase. At present more than 140 cities and 230 county towns are selected as the basic units for data collection; 450 items of commodities in the cities and 400 in the county towns are included in the calculation. The price of a standard commodity from each item of products is adopted in the calculation.

Almost identical explanations are found in the 1984 edition (pp. 569–579) and the 1985 edition (p. 672). This is the main price index to be studied. Annual data are available, presumably referring to the middle of the year or to an average within the year.

The stock of money is measured by currency in circulation reported in a table on "bank credit receipts and payments" of the *Statistical Yearbook*. The data are for the end of each year, although for our purpose the unavailable mid-year figures would be more appropriate. The chosen measure of output is national income available. In Chinese official statistics, it is the sum of consumption and capital accumulation, government expenditures being included in either of the two. Some service items are excluded from Chinese national income figures. "National income available" differs from "national income" by including imports minus exports and a statistical discrepancy. To obtain a measure of national income available in real terms, I have deflated it by an implicit deflator which is the ratio of national income in current prices to national income in constant prices (the last two series being found on pp. 29 and 30, respectively, of *Statistical Yearbook of China, 1984*).

Annual data from 1952 to 1983 on the general index of retail price P, currency in circulation M, national income available in real terms y and in nominal terms Y are given in Table 1. In this section, we will examine how well the quantity theory of money can provide a framework for explaining the demand for money and the level of retail prices in China, without regard to the short-run dynamics of annual changes. To get some preliminary idea about the possible constancy of income velocity v in the context of the demand for money, I have exhibited the ratio $k = v^{-1}$ of M to Y in the last column of Table 1. Observe that the ratio k changes somewhat from year to year, with large increases occurring in 1960 and 1961 and falling to about normal levels in 1964, smaller but still significant increases in 1967 and 1968, and taking higher values in the 1980s than before. The large increases in k during

GREGORY C. CHOW

TABLE 1

PRICE LEVEL AND ITS DETERMINANTS

Year	Index of retail price (P)	Currency in circulation (100,000 yuan) (M)	Real national income available (100,000 1952-yuan) (y)	Nominal national income available (100,000 yuan) (Y)	Ratio M/Y (k)	Total wage (100,000 yuan) (W)
1952	1.118	38.55	607.0	607.0	0.0635	68.78
1953	1.156	39.60	688.5	727.0	0.0545	90.15
1954	1.183	41.19	726.5	765.0	0.0538	99.79
1955	1.195	40.13	773.9	807.0	0.0497	110.44
1956	1.195	57.03	868.2	888.0	0.0642	161.56
1957	1.213	52.80	928.0	935.0	0.0565	188.44
1958	1.216	67.59	1098.7	1117.0	0.0605	200.62
1959	1.227	74.98	1241.0	1274.0	0.0589	262.73
1960	1.265	96.10	1215.6	1264.0	0.0760	300.82
1961	1.470	125.67	838.7	1013.0	0.1241	289.87
1962	1.526	106.66	791.0	948.0	0.1125	265.32
1963	1.436	89.76	893.6	1047.0	0.0857	265.22
1964	1.383	80.26	1009.6	1184.0	0.0678	281.59
1965	1.346	90.82	1129.7	1347.0	0.0674	295.49
1966	1.342	108.25	1316.8	1535.0	0.0705	305.48
1967	1.332	121.97	1212.2	1428.0	0.0854	313.57
1968	1.333	134.12	1175.4	1409.0	0.0952	317.72
1969	1.318	137.29	1338.6	1537.0	0.0893	328.61
1970	1.315	123.56	1690.7	1876.0	0.0659	342.78
1971	1.305	136.23	1795.4	2008.0	0.0678	367.42
1972	1.302	151.02	1836.1	2052.0	0.0736	412.43
1973	1.310	166.33	2010.8	2252.0	0.0739	428.91
1974	1.317	176.36	2041.3	2291.0	0.0770	450.62
1975	1.319	182.70	2218.8	2451.0	0.0745	469.47
1976	1.323	203.82	2202.5	2424.0	0.0841	490.14
1977	1.350	195.37	2313.4	2573.0	0.0759	514.95
1978	1.359	212.27	2638.3	2975.0	0.0714	570.09
1979	1.386	267.71	2861.2	3356.0	0.0798	651.62
1980	1.469	346.20	3037.0	3686.0	0.0939	776.93
1981	1.504	396.34	3144.8	3887.0	0.1020	818.76
1982	1.533	439.12	3448.1	4256.0	0.1032	879.79
1983	1.556	529.78	3812.8	4731.0	0.1120	931.51

the political–economic crises of 1960–1961 and 1967–1968 may be attributed to the reductions in national income in the denominator. The higher values in the 1980s may signify the effect of economic reforms leading to an increase in the demand for money. In spite of these changes in velocity, can the quantity theory provide a crude explanation of the demand for money and of the price level?

To investigate the demand for money, we take natural logarithms of both sides of Eq. (2) and explain $\ln(M/P)$ by $\ln y$ in the following regression using annual data from 1952 to 1983,

$$\ln(M/P) = -3.927 + 1.162 \ln y \qquad R^2 = 0.9083 \qquad (4)$$
$$\quad\;\;(0.492)\quad(0.067) \qquad\qquad s = 0.1971$$
$$\qquad\qquad\qquad\qquad\qquad\qquad DW = 0.7847$$

where the standard errors of the regression coefficients are put in parentheses, s stands for the standard error of the regression, and DW for the Durbin–Watson statistic. This demand for money equation appears reasonably good except for the facts that the coefficient of $\ln y$, or the income elasticity of demand for money, is larger than unity, contradicting the quantity theory, and that the Durbin–Watson statistic is low, signifying positive serial correlation in the residuals. Both of these characteristics have been found in demand for money equations estimated using data for the United States (see Eq. (4A) of Section 4). A simple way to account for the positive serial correlation in the residuals is to assume that $\ln y$ explains only the equilibrium level of $\ln(M/P)$, and that the actual change in $\ln(M/P)$ is only a fraction of the difference between this equilibrium level and the actual level, leading to the equation, for 1953–1983,

$$\ln(M/P) = -1.322 + 0.3504 \ln y + 0.7409 \ln(M/P)_{t-1} \quad R^2 = 0.9749 \quad (5)$$
$$\qquad\;\;(0.394)\quad(0.0966)\qquad\;\;(0.0813)\qquad\qquad\quad s = 0.1024$$
$$\qquad\qquad\qquad\qquad\qquad\qquad\qquad\qquad\qquad DW = 2.101$$

The positive serial correlation in the residuals is eliminated in Eq. (5) as seen from the Durbin–Watson statistic. For our purpose, it is important to note that the quantity theory as formulated in Eq. (2) provides a reasonable first approximation in explaining the demand for money in China.

To find out how well the price level can be explained, we take logarithms of both sides of (3) and regress $\ln p$ on $\ln(M/y)$ using annual data from 1952 to 1983, obtaining

$$\ln P = 0.9445 + 0.2687 \ln(M/y) \qquad R^2 = 0.8217 \qquad (6)$$
$$\quad\;\;(0.0567)\quad(0.0229) \qquad\qquad s = 0.0363$$
$$\qquad\qquad\qquad\qquad\qquad\qquad DW = 1.003$$

Equation (6) shows that the ratio M/y does provide a good explanation of the price level P, as the quantity theory predicts. The t statistic for the coefficient of $\ln(M/y)$ is $0.2687/0.0229$ or 11.76, and the R^2 is fairly high. However, the coefficient of $\ln(M/y)$ is only 0.2687 and very much below unity, contradicting the quantity theory. The conclusion is that although the ratio M/y can explain the price level P fairly well, changes in M/y lead to less than proportional changes in P. This can happen if v is negatively associated with M/y so that when M/y increases, its effect is partly absorbed by the reduction in v and only partly reflected in an increase in P. A second shortcoming of Eq. (6) is the low Durbin–Watson statistic, a subject to be studied in Section 3. Before concluding this section, we will check whether the variables M and y should enter Eq. (6) separately or as a ratio as implied by the quantity theory. Regressing $\ln P$ on $\ln M$ and $\ln y$ separately yields

$$\ln P = 0.6219 + 0.2388 \ln M - 0.2046 \ln y \quad \begin{aligned} R^2 &= 0.8566 \\ s &= 0.0331 \\ \text{DW} &= 0.9546 \end{aligned} \quad (7)$$
$$(0.1320) \quad (0.0237) \qquad (0.0319)$$

The coefficient of $\ln y$ turns out to be approximately equal to the negative of the coefficient of $\ln M$. To test the null hypothesis that the coefficient of $\ln y$ indeed equals the negative of the coefficient of $\ln M$, we compare the sum of squared residuals of the restricted regression (6), or 0.039577, with the corresponding sum of the unrestricted regression (7), or 0.031834. The ratio of their difference 0.007743 to the latter sum is only 0.2432, far from being significant as a statistic from the $F(1,29)$ distribution and supporting the hypothesis that $\ln(M/y)$ is an appropriate variable to use in explaining $\ln P$.

3. SHORT-RUN DYNAMICS OF PRICE CHANGES

In Eqs. (6) and (7) we have found that the price level P can be reasonably explained by the ratio M/y as suggested by the quantity theory, although velocity is not constant, resulting in less than proportional changes in P. It is often easier to explain the levels of economic variables than their changes. How well can the theoretical framework of Eq. (6) explain annual changes in $\ln P$? To answer this question two common approaches are taken. The first is to introduce the lagged dependent variable $\ln P_{t-1}$ in Eq. (7), as we did in Eq. (5), and use the resulting equation to explain $\Delta \ln P$ by subtracting $\ln P_{t-1}$ on both sides. The second is to take the first difference of Eq. (6) and try to explain $\Delta \ln P$ by $\Delta \ln(M/y)$, allowing for more complicated lag structures.

Pursuing the first approach we find

$$\Delta \ln P = 0.5167 + 0.1491 \ln(M/y) - 0.5054 \ln P_{t-1} \quad \begin{aligned} R^2 &= 0.6824 \\ s &= 0.0199 \\ \text{DW} &= 1.341 \end{aligned} \quad (8)$$
$$(0.0656) \quad (0.0201) \qquad (0.0708)$$

The coefficient of $\ln P_{t-1}$ is significant. To use Eq. (8) for explaining the level $\ln P$ rather than the difference $\Delta \ln P$, the coefficient of $\ln P_{t-1}$ would be $(1 - 0.5054)$ or 0.4946, and R^2 would be higher. Although (8) is an improvement over (7), it still leaves a positive serial correlation in the residuals as seen in the Durbin–Watson statistic.

To pursue the second approach, we attempt to explain $\Delta \ln P$ by $\Delta \ln(M/y)$. Using the simplest lag structure, we find

$$\Delta \ln P = 0.00747 + 0.1266 \ \Delta \ln(M/y) \qquad R^2 = 0.4647 \qquad (9)$$
$$ (0.00461) \quad (0.0252) \qquad\qquad s \ = 0.0254$$
$$\text{DW} = 1.723$$

The result shows that $\Delta \ln(M/y)$ is a significant variable in explaining $\Delta \ln P$. R^2 is lower in Eq. (9) than in Eq. (8), but the Durbin–Watson statistic shows less positive serial correlation in the residuals. To establish a more satisfactory lag structure, we employ the modeling techniques of error correction and cointegration. Engle and Granger (1987) provide an exposition of these techniques. I will review briefly the essential ideas before applying them to the Chinese data.

Supppose that one is interested in establishing a dynamic relationship between the first differences Δy_t and Δx_t of two economic variables and that the levels y_t and x_t of these variables are believed to satisfy certain stable relationships in the long run. In our problem, we may believe that the levels of the variables $\ln P$ and $\ln(M/y)$ satisfy certain long-run equilibrium relationships as estimated by Eq. (6), and we are interested in constructing a dynamic model for $\Delta \ln P$ and $\Delta \ln(M/y)$. If one were not concerned with the long-run relationship, one might choose the model

$$\Delta y_t = \beta \Delta x_t + \epsilon_t. \qquad (10)$$

However, if the ϵ_t are independent and identically distributed, Model (10) implies a nonstationary relationship between the levels y_t and x_t. To convert (10) to a relation between the levels, we use the identity

$$y_t = \sum_{s=1}^{t} \Delta y_s + y_0 \qquad (11)$$

and substitute the right-hand side of (10) for Δy_s in (11), yielding,

$$y_t = \sum_{s=1}^{t} (\beta \Delta x_s + \epsilon_s) + y_0 = \beta \sum_{s=1}^{t} \Delta x_s + \sum_{s=1}^{t} \epsilon_s + y_0$$

$$= \beta x_t + y_0 - \beta x_0 + \sum_{s=1}^{t} \epsilon_s. \qquad (12)$$

The residual $\sum_{s=1}^{t} \epsilon_s$ in the regression of y_t on x_t is not only serially correlated but has a variance increasing linearly with time.

To allow for a stable long-run relationship $y_t = \alpha x_t$ between y_t and x_t in a model explaining Δy_t by Δx_t, one may introduce an error correction mechanism by using the lagged deviation $(y_{t-1} - \alpha x_{t-1})$ from the long-run relationship as an additional variable in (10). The model becomes

$$\Delta y_t = \beta \Delta x_t - \gamma(y_{t-1} - \alpha x_{t-1}) + \epsilon_t. \qquad (13)$$

The rationale is that if in the last period y_{t-1} is above its long-run equilibrium level αx_{t-1}, the change in y_t during the current period should be smaller, and vice versa. The error correction model (13) has two desirable characteristics. It is stationary. The long-run change in y_t associated with a permanent unit change in x_t is α. Both can be easily shown by converting (13) into an equation in the levels of the variables:

$$y_t = (1 - \gamma)y_{t-1} + \beta x_t - (\beta - \alpha\gamma)x_{t-1} + \epsilon_t. \tag{14}$$

When $0 < \gamma < 1$, the coefficient $(1 - \gamma)$ is smaller than one, giving a stationary model for y_t. The long-run relation between y and x is given by

$$[1 - (1 - \gamma)]y = [\beta - (\beta - \alpha\gamma)]x, \tag{15}$$

which is obtained by collecting all the coefficients of the y and x variables while ignoring the time subscripts. From (15), we have $y = \alpha x$, which is the long-run relationship.

These two desirable characteristics remain when the error correction term $\gamma(y_{t-1} - \alpha x_{t-1})$ is added to a more complicated distributed lag relation between Δy_t and Δx_t than (10), such as

$$\Delta y_t = \beta_1 \Delta x_t + \beta_2 \Delta x_{t-1} + \beta_3 \Delta y_{t-1} + \epsilon_t. \tag{16}$$

An error correction model is a special case of a dynamic model for the first differences of variables in which the variables are "cointegrated;" i.e., the levels of the variables (obtained by integrating the differences) satisfy certain long-run relation or relations.

To construct an error correction model to explain $\Delta \ln P$ by $\Delta \ln(M/y)$, we allow the short-run dynamics to be as complicated as in Eq. (16) and add an error correction term. The error correction term can be estimated as the difference between $\ln P_{t-1}$ and the regression of $\ln P_{t-1}$ on $\ln(M/y)_{t-1}$, i.e., as the lagged residuals u_{t-1} in the regression Eq. (6). Using annual data from 1954 to 1983, this model is estimated to be

$$\Delta \ln P = \underset{(0.00380)}{0.00445} + \underset{(0.0217)}{0.1364} \ \Delta \ln(M/y) + \underset{(0.0328)}{0.0267} \ \Delta \ln(M/y)_{-1}$$

$$+ \underset{(0.1447)}{0.1415} \ \Delta \ln P_{-1} - \underset{(0.1478)}{0.3086} \ u_{t-1} \qquad \begin{array}{l} R^2 = 0.7247 \quad (17) \\ s = 0.0195 \\ DW = 1.895 \end{array}$$

The coefficient -0.3086 of the error correction term has the correct sign and is statistically significant. The residuals of the regression do not show a significantly positive serial correlation. The lag structure, however, is more complicated than necessary in that both the coefficients of $\Delta \ln(M/y)_{-1}$ and of $\Delta \ln P_{-1}$ are not significant. If the weakest variable $\Delta \ln(M/y)_{-1}$ is dropped, the result is

$$\Delta \ln P = \underset{(0.00376)}{0.00422} + \underset{(0.0201)}{0.1430} \ \Delta \ln(M/y) + \underset{(0.1098)}{0.2176} \ \Delta \ln P_{-1}$$

$$- \underset{(0.1209)}{0.3771} \ u_{t-1} \qquad \begin{array}{l} R^2 = 0.7174 \quad (18) \\ s = 0.0193 \\ DW = 2.068 \end{array}$$

Equation (18) is a satisfactory error correction model. All three coefficients have the right signs and are statistically significant. The Durbin–Watson statistic indicates the lack of positive serial correlation in the residual. The equation explains about 72% of the variance of $\Delta \ln P$. Engle and Granger (1987) suggest seven tests of the null hypothesis that a long-run relation between the levels of the variables do *not* exist. One such test is to examine the DW statistic of the regression (6) and accept the null hypothesis if it is close to zero. Since the DW statistic is as high as 1.003, we reject the null hypothesis and conclude that a long-run relation between $\ln P$ and $\ln(M/y)$ does exist, as suggested by the quantity theory. The short-run dynamic relation between $\ln P$ and $\ln(M/y)$ is satisfactorily given by Eq. (18).

4. COMPARABLE ANALYSES OF U.S DATA

It is interesting to find out how well the statistical models of Sections 2 and 3 can explain a comparable set of data for the United States. To do so I have selected a sample of annual data of the same length from 1922 to 1953, used in my study of the demand for money (1966), and estimated equations analogous to (4), (5), (6), (7), (8), (9), (17), and (18). The selection of this sample period is somewhat arbitrary. The period includes the Great Depression and World War II, providing variations in the data comparable to those occurring after the Great Leap Forward movement in China. Our main purpose is to see whether the explanatory power of the theoretical framework is different and how different. For the U.S. equations, P is a price index of consumer expenditures, M is currency and demand deposits adjusted in the middle of the year, and y is net national product deflated by the above consumer price index, as referenced in Chow (1966, pp. 128–129). For ease of comparison, the equations are given the same numbers as before, except with an A added.

The demand for money equation corresponding to (4) is

$$\ln(M/P) = -3.912 + 1.241 \ln y \qquad R^2 = 0.9216 \qquad (4A)$$
$$(0.801) \quad (0.066) \qquad\qquad s = 0.1428$$
$$DW = 0.4070$$

After the lagged dependent variable is added, it becomes

$$\ln(M/P) = -0.5942 + 0.1908 \ln y + 0.8487 \ln(M/P)_{-1} \qquad R^2 = 0.9856$$
$$(0.4570) \quad (0.0954) \qquad (0.0735) \qquad\qquad s = 0.0616$$
$$DW = 1.141$$
$$(5A)$$

The similarities between these equations and the corresponding Eqs. (4) and (5) are striking. Equation (5A) is slighly less satisfactory than (5) in having a smaller t ratio for $\ln y$ and a lower DW statistic.

The equations explaining ln P corresponding to (6) and (7) are

$$\ln P = 0.4699 + 0.6334 \ \ln(M/y) \qquad R^2 = 0.7324 \qquad (6A)$$
$$\quad (0.1031) \quad (0.0699) \qquad\qquad s \ = 0.1239$$
$$\qquad\qquad\qquad\qquad\qquad\qquad\qquad DW = 0.2381$$

$$\ln P = -0.7472 + 0.5385 \ \ln M - 0.4493 \ \ln y \qquad R^2 = 0.7376 \quad (7A)$$
$$\quad (1.6106) \quad (0.1437) \qquad\quad (0.2531) \qquad\quad s \ = 0.1248$$
$$\qquad\qquad\qquad\qquad\qquad\qquad\qquad\qquad\qquad DW = 0.1806$$

To test whether the coefficient of ln y equals the negative of the coefficient of ln M, we compare the sum of squared residuals of (6A) 0.46026 with the sum for (7A) 0.45134. Their difference divided by the latter sum is 0.0198, not at all significant as an $F(1,29)$ statistic and supporting Eq. (6A). However, the DW statistics of (6A) is very low, requiring further modeling of the dynamics of Δ ln P as in (8) and (9).

The corresponding results from the U.S. data are

$$\Delta \ln P = 0.1632 + 0.1450 \ \ln(M/y) - 0.1313 \ \ln P_{-1} \quad R^2 = 0.2950 \ (8A)$$
$$\quad (0.0443) \quad (0.0442) \qquad\qquad (0.0632) \qquad\quad s \ = 0.0457$$
$$\qquad\qquad\qquad\qquad\qquad\qquad\qquad\qquad\qquad DW = 0.9079$$

$$\Delta \ln P = 0.0116 + 0.1773 \ \Delta \ln(M/y) \qquad R^2 = 0.0563 \qquad (9A)$$
$$\quad (0.0097) \quad (0.1347) \qquad\qquad\qquad s \ = 0.0520$$
$$\qquad\qquad\qquad\qquad\qquad\qquad\qquad DW = 0.8414$$

Both equations are not as good as the corresponding equations for China, in terms of the lower t statistics for the coefficients of ln(M/y) and Δ ln(M/y), higher standard errors of the regression, and less satisfactory DW statistics.

Attempts to construct a suitable error correction model using the residuals u_t from (6A) have produced

$$\Delta \ln P = 0.0038 - 0.0322 \ \Delta \ln(M/y) + 0.0072 \ \Delta \ln(M/y)_{-1}$$
$$\quad (0.0073) \quad (0.1144) \qquad\qquad (0.1144)$$

$$\qquad\qquad + 0.6886 \ \Delta \ln P_{-1} - 0.1578 \ u_{t-1} \qquad R^2 = 0.5814 \quad (17A)$$
$$\qquad\qquad\quad (0.1398) \qquad\qquad (0.0622) \qquad\qquad s \ = 0.0371$$
$$\qquad\qquad\qquad\qquad\qquad\qquad\qquad\qquad\qquad\qquad DW = 1.506$$

$$\Delta \ln P = 0.0034 + 0.6758 \ \Delta \ln P_{-1} - 0.1575 \ u_{t-1} \qquad R^2 = 0.5836 \ (18A)$$
$$\quad (0.0068) \quad (1.242) \qquad\qquad (0.0548) \qquad\quad s \ = 0.0358$$
$$\qquad\qquad\qquad\qquad\qquad\qquad\qquad\qquad\qquad\qquad DW = 1.564$$

For explaining Δ ln P in (17A), neither Δ ln(M/y) nor Δ ln$(M/y)_{-1}$ are significant. After both terms are dropped, we are left with Δ ln P_{-1} and the error correction term u_{t-1} in (18A), both being significant. The long-run effect of

$\ln(M/y)$ on $\ln P$ implicit in (18A) is still given by the coefficient 0.6334 of Eq. (6A). Equation (18A) is of the form

$$\Delta y_t = \beta \Delta y_{t-1} - \gamma(y_{t-1} - \alpha x_{t-1})$$

and can be rewritten as

$$y_t - (1 + \beta - \gamma)y_{t-1} + \beta y_{t-2} = \gamma \alpha x_{t-1}, \qquad (19)$$

which implies a long-run relationship $\gamma y = \gamma \alpha x$ or $y = \alpha x$.

By (19) we see that (18A) amounts to explaining $\ln P_t$ or $\Delta \ln P_t$ by $\ln P_{t-1}$, $\ln P_{t-2}$ and $\ln(M/y)_{t-1}$. By adding the variables $\ln(M/y)_t$ and $\ln(M/y)_{t-2}$ in the regression of $\Delta \ln P_t$ on the above variables, we have found them to be very insignificant, with t ratios of -0.097 and 0.083, respectively. Dropping these variables, the regression becomes

$$\Delta \ln P = \underset{(0.0430)}{0.0990} + \underset{(0.1496)}{0.4803} \ \ln P_{-1} - \underset{(0.1405)}{0.6357} \ \ln P_{-2}$$

$$+ \underset{(0.0412)}{0.1135} \ \ln(M/y)_{-1} \qquad \begin{array}{l} R^2 = 0.5900 \\ s = 0.0362 \\ DW = 1.538 \end{array} \quad (18B)$$

Note that (18A) and (18B) are less satisfactory than Eq. (18) for China in having lower R^2's, larger standard errors of the regression, and DW statistics further away from 2. The DW statistic of (6A) is low, failing to reject the null hypothesis that a stable long-run relation between $\ln P$ and $\ln(M/y)$ does not exist.

In summary, we have found $\ln(M/y)$ to be a significant variable in explaining $\ln P$ in both China and the United States, but the short-run dynamics are harder to model and the long-run relationship may be less stable for the United States.

5. ADDITIONAL ISSUES

Two additional issues are addressed in this section. First, does total wage affect the price level? Second, does our Eq. (18) remain stable after the economic reforms from 1979 on and how well does it forecast for 1984? To answer the first question, a wage variable W is constructed as the sum of total wage of state enterprises (*Statistical Yearbook of China, 1984*, p. 458) and total wage of collective enterprises. The latter equals the number of staff and workers in collectives (*Yearbook, 1984*, p. 110) times their average wage rate, which is assumed to be the average wage rate in state enterprises divided by 1.2752. 1.2752 is the ratio prevailing in 1978 (*Yearbook, 1984*, p. 455). Data for W are also given in Table 1. The addition of $\ln W$ to Eq. (6) gives

$$\ln P = \underset{(0.1221)}{0.5297} + \underset{(0.0266)}{0.2010} \ \ln(M/y) + \underset{(0.0117)}{0.0430} \ \ln W \qquad \begin{array}{l} R^2 = 0.8786 \\ s = 0.0305 \\ DW = 0.9543 \end{array} \quad (20)$$

The coefficient of ln W is statistically significant, but the effect is small, having an elasticity of only 0.043. If ln W_t and ln W_{t-1} are added to equation (18), their coefficients have t statistics of 0.309 and −0.164 and the coefficients of the other three variables are hardly affected. It can be concluded that the effect of money supply on the price level is much more important than that of the wage bill, and that Eq. (18) remains valid in ignoring the possible effects of total wage.

To see whether Eq. (18) is subject to a structural change after 1979, we perform the standard F test by dividing the data into two periods, the first from 1954 to 1978 and the second from 1979 to 1983. The sum of squared residuals of the two separate regressions is 0.008217 with 30 − 8 or 22 degrees of freedom. The sum of squared residuals of the pooled regression (18) is 0.009731 with 30 − 4 or 26 degrees of freedom. The test statistic is the ratio of (0.009731 − 0.008217)/4 to 0.008217/22, or 1.013, much smaller than the 10% right-tail critical value 2.22 for the $F(4,22)$ distribution. We thus accept the null hypothesis that the four coefficients of Eq. (18) did not change after 1979.

If Eq. (18) remains valid after the economic reforms began in 1979, it can be used to forecast the retail price index P. The first post-sample year, 1984, provides a good opportunity for observing how well Eq. (18) can forecast since there was a rapid increase in the amount of currency in circulation M from 529.78 hundred-thousand yuan at the end of 1983 to 792.11 at the end of 1984, while the index of real national income increased by a much smaller percentage of 13.9 (see *Statistical Yearbook of China, 1985*, p. 34). To perform the forecasting experiment for 1984, we rewrite Eq. (18) as an equation explaining ln P by ln P_{-1}, ln P_{-2}, ln(M/y) and ln$(M/y)_{-1}$,

$$\ln P = 0.360428 + 0.840422 \ln P_{-1} - 0.217564 \ln P_{-2}$$
$$+ 0.143004 \ln(M/y) - 0.0416556 \ln(M/y)_{-1}. \quad (21)$$

Data for P_{-1}, P_{-2}, and $(M/y)_{-1}$ are given in Table 1. M is 792.11; y is 4342.79, or 13.9% higher than the 1983 figure given in Table 1. Using these data, Eq. (21) yields a forecast of 0.477928 for ln P or 1.6127 for P in 1984. The actual value of P in 1984 is 1.600 (see *Yearbook, 1985*, p. 530). The error in forecasting ln P is −0.0079, even smaller than the standard error of regression 0.0193 for Eq. (18). Hence Eq. (18) stands up very well when it is used to forecast the retail price index in 1984.

In this paper I have found that the quantity theory of money provides a useful starting point in constructing a model to explain the index of retail prices in China. The ratio of money supply to real output is an important variable in explaining the price level, as the quantity theory implies. However, the elasticity of the price level with respect to this ratio is smaller than unity, suggesting that velocity is not constant. The assumption of constant velocity may serve as a satisfactory first approximation in explaining the demand for money, but not necessarily in explaining the price level. The success in one case does not carry over to the other. The theoretical framework suggested in this paper is somewhat more successful in explaining the Chinese data from 1952 to 1983 than the United States data from 1922 to 1953. The model for short-run changes in log price is more satisfactory, and the stability of a long-run relation between the price level and the money-output ratio is better established for China than for the United States. Total wage is found to assert little or no additional effect on price. The model for price change is stable after 1979, and forecasts well in 1984.

REFERENCES

Chow, Gregory C., "A Model of Chinese National Income Determination." *J. Polit. Econ.* **93**, 4:782–792, August 1985a.

Chow, Gregory C., "Chinese Statistics." *The Amer. Statistician* **40**, 3:191–196, August 1986.

Chow, Gregory C., "Development of a More Market-Oriented Economy in China." *Science,* 295–299, January 16, 1987.

Chow, Gregory C., "On the Long-run and Short-run Demand for Money." *J. Polit. Econ.* **74**, 2: 111–131, April 1966.

Chow, Gregory C., *The Chinese Economy.* New York: Harper & Row, 1985b.

Engle, Robert F., and Granger, C. W. J., "Co-integration and Error Correction: Representation, Estimation and Testing." *Econometrica* **55**, 2:251–276, March.

State Statistics Bureau of the People's Republic of China, *Statistical Yearbook of China, 1981; 1984; 1985.* Hong Kong: Economic Information & Agency, 1982, 1985, 1986.

JOURNAL OF COMPARATIVE ECONOMICS 11, 334–353 (1987)

Macroeconomic Policy and Response in the Chinese Economy: The Impact of the Reform Process

BARRY NAUGHTON[1]

University of Oregon, Eugene, Oregon 97403

Naughton, Barry—Macroeconomic Policy and Response in the Chinese Economy: The Impact of the Reform Process

The paper presents a macroeconomic model of the Chinese economy, which is then used to estimate a household saving function for 1957–1978, showing a 3% saving rate. Applying the model to the post-1978 period, the author concludes that the rapid growth in the government budget deficit was accommodated in part by voluntary saving by households and enterprises. *J. Comp. Econ.,* September 1987, **11**(3), pp. 334–353. University of Oregon, Eugene, Oregon 97403. © 1987 Academic Press, Inc.

Journal of Economic Literature Classification Numbers: 124, 311, 322.

As part of the economic reform process in China, production enterprises and commercial units have been given greater freedom of operation, and the role of the market has increased. As a result, techniques of macroeconomic control that depend for their efficacy on the direct allocative authority of planners must be replaced by indirect instruments of control, similar to the monetary and fiscal policy familiar in market economies. This fact is well recognized in China, and great importance has been attached to the reform of the banking system, and to the gradual adoption of new macroeconomic instruments.

Whatever instruments are employed to affect macroeconomic variables, they depend for their efficacy on a specific environment made up of different economic agents, characterized by certain behavioral regularities, and linked by certain identities. While the need for change in the instruments used is widely acknowledged, it is less widely appreciated that the behavior of most economic agents in China has been changing rapidly as a result of reforms,

---

[1] The author is Assistant Professor of Economics, University of Oregon. The author thanks the participants at the ACES/Union College Conference on Chinese Economic Reform for numerous helpful comments. Christine Wallich also provided valuable comments on a later draft. The analysis was suggested by Montias (1968).

44

CHINESE ECONOMIC REFORM

and that these changes have affected the macroeconomic response of that economy in fundamental ways.

In the following, I describe the operation of the Chinese economy through the interaction of three classes of agents: households, enterprises, and government, which includes both the budgetary and banking authorities. Since the initiation of reform in 1978, the behavior of each of these classes of agents has changed markedly in response to the reform-induced changes in the economic environment. Macroeconomic policy—the behavior of the governmental sector—has become much more stimulative, with large budget deficits combining with an acceleration in the rate of credit creation. However, both households and enterprise have responded to government dissaving by increasing their own saving propensities. This response—which I argue is predominantly a voluntary response to expanded economic opportunity—has largely mitigated the negative results of governmental policy that might otherwise be considered excessively expansionary. At the same time, the drastic shifts in behavior have made it difficult to determine adequate guidelines for the implementation of a stable and effective macroeconomic policy. I emphasize throughout that from 1978 to the present, the changes in behavior of the three classes of agents have been of much greater significance than the relatively modest movement made thus far toward the adoption of new instruments of control.

In the first section of the paper, I present a set of simple identities that link the three classes of agents through financial flows. I then show that these identities can be used to characterize macroeconomic policy in any centrally planned economy. In the second section, I build on this framework to examine the experience in China since the initiation of reforms, stressing the differences that separate the prereform experience from the more recent period. Much of the analysis makes use of the consolidated balance sheet of the Chinese banking system. In the final section, I draw some conclusions and show that the progress of Chinese economic reforms has been crucially influenced by the changes in behavior and overall macroeconomic response with which this paper has been concerned.

NOMENCLATURE

A Agricultural procurements
C Outlays for consumption goods
I_f Fixed investment in state units
I_f^g Fixed investment in state units funded by the government budget
I_i Inventory investment in state units
I_i^g Inventory investment in state units funded by the government budget
I^h Investment funded by households
L_e Loans to the enterprise sector (new lending: a flow variable)

L_h Loans to the household sector (new lending: a flow variable)
M Household financial assets, current and saving deposits (stock)
R Gross enterprise revenues
S^e Enterprise balances with the banking system (stock)
S^g Government balances with the banking system (stock)
t Tax rate on enterprise net revenues
W Aggregate wage bill
X Index of consumer good shortage
Y Household income received in money form
$m(.)$ Household saving function
$s(.)$ Enterprise saving function
$i(.)$ Rate of warranted inventory accumulation
$\wedge$ Indicates amount of change in a stock variable

1

Four simple identities can be used to describe the financial flows between sectors. In their initial form, these are accounting relationships only. For the household sector

$$W + A + L_h = C + I^h + \hat{M}. \tag{1}$$

W represents the wage bill, A is agricultural procurements, and L is loans extended. The subscript indicates the recipient of a financial flow, L_h indicating loans received by the household sector. C is purchases of consumption goods, I^h purchases of investment goods by households, and $\hat{M}$ increments to currency balances and savings deposits. There are no direct taxes on households. The government budget identity is given as

$$t(R - W - A) - \hat{S}^g = I_f^g + I_i^g. \tag{2}$$

Government revenues derive from a fixed proportion tax, shown by t, on the net revenues of enterprises. That net revenue is defined as the difference between gross revenues, R, and production costs which equal the wage bill plus agricultural procurements. The government budget surplus, which equals the increment in budgetary deposits with the banking system, is shown as $\hat{S}^g$. I_f^g and I_i^g represent fixed and inventory investment, respectively, which are financed by budgetary allocations. The enterprise sector balance is

$$R + I_f^g + I_i^g + L_e = W + A + I_f + I_i + t(R - W - A) + \hat{S}^e. \tag{3}$$

New credits to the enterprise sector are represented by L_e, and $\hat{S}^e$ is the increment to enterprise bank balances. I_f and I_i are total fixed and inventory investment, respectively, in the state sector. The other symbols have already been explained. The bank balance sheet is given as

$$\hat{M} + \hat{S}^g + \hat{S}^e = L_h + L_e. \tag{4}$$

Increments to bank liabilities equal increments to assets. $\hat{S}^g$ will be interpreted to include additions to the banking system's owned capital, while $\hat{M}$ includes increments to currency and savings deposits of the population.

Equations (1) through (4) are simple accounting identities expressed in nominal values. In order to give meaning to the problem that faces macroeconomic policy-makers, it is necessary to introduce three other relationships over which policy-makers have limited influence. The first is the saving propensity of households:

$$\hat{M} = m(A, W, M_{t-1}, \cdots). \tag{5}$$

The desired increment in monetary assets held by households is determined by current household income as well as other current and lagged variables. Enterprises also have a "saving propensity" that is determined by their desire to hold monetary balances for transactions or investment purposes:

$$\hat{S}^e = s(R, I_f, \cdots). \tag{6}$$

Finally, total inventory accumulation is determined by a complex of factors, of which the most important is the growth of production and retail sales, but which may also include the quality of production and the fit between output assortment and consumers' needs. There is thus a "warranted" rate of investment in inventories:

$$I_i = i(R, C, \cdots). \tag{7}$$

Equations (5) through (7) describe desired additions to monetary balances, and warranted additions to inventories. Macroeconomic policy, however, can cause these values to deviate from their desired or warranted values. For instance, if income growth is excessive, monetary holdings of households may exceed desired levels, and inventories may fall below warranted levels. Both of these phenomena would reflect macroeconomic imbalance in a predominantly fixed price environment, corresponding to increased shortages and frustration of consumer choice. Conversely, macroeconomic balance will prevail when all of these schedules are at their warranted or desired values.

Policy-makers must have some knowledge of these schedules, either through simple "rules of thumb" derived from experience managing the economy, or through indications of imbalance (shortages or price increases) that can be monitored. Equation (4), originally an identity, can therefore be rewritten as a rule for macro-policy:

$$L_h + L_e - \hat{S}^g = m(.) + s(.). \tag{8}$$

Equation (8) states that a balanced macro-policy implies that the sum of new credit extension and the budget deficit (minus the surplus) equals the desired increase in money holdings of the household and enterprise sectors. This simple reformulation has a number of advantages. First, it enables us to define a stimulative macro policy as one that increases the value of the left-hand side of the equation, and thereby increases the growth of the money supply. Second, it shows that in a centrally planned economy, just as in a market economy, the impact of monetary and fiscal policy always depends on the interaction of the two. Any increase in the rate of credit creation can be offset by a sufficiently large budget surplus, and vice versa. Third, as I will demonstrate below, consistent data are available from China in the categories used in Eq. (8): by examining the consolidated balance sheet of the banking system, we can characterize macroeconomic policy during different time periods, and see how that policy has changed with the advent of economic reforms.

The preceding framework can be used to clarify the role of monetary and fiscal policy in a traditional centrally planned economy. It is commonly said that such policy is "passive," in the sense that monetary flows accommodate planned commodity flows and play no independent role in determining the allocation of resources (Garvy, 1966; 1977). This statement is an adequate summary of CPE reality, but it is impossible for monetary flows to be completely insignificant in an economy that has prices, profits, and monetary incentives, and in which planners are subject to limitations of knowledge and judgement. Unanticipated shocks to the production and distribution process will always cause some deviations between plan and reality and between physical and monetary balances. Rather, the passivity of macroeconomic policy in traditional CPEs should be understood as the outcome of specific policy formation rules that guide planners.

In a traditional CPE, there is no bank financing of fixed investment; moreover, credit policy is not autonomous but rather adapts passively to enterprise needs to finance inventory accumulation. Since enterprises are operating under the authority of the plan, the banking system is compelled to provide them with loans essentially on demand. In that case

$$L_e = I_i - I_i^g. \tag{9}$$

Substituting (9) and (7) into (8) yields

$$\hat{S}^g + I_i^g = i(.) - m(.) - s(.) + L_h. \tag{10}$$

Setting aside L_h, which is very small in traditional CPEs, Eq. (10) says that when bank credits adapt passively to enterprise needs for inventory accumulation, the sum of the budget surplus and budgetary allocations for inventory accumulation must adapt to provide macroeconomic balance. The budget surplus by itself is insufficient to characterize macro policy if budgetary allocations for inventory accumulation cannot be taken as constant.

Moreover, in a traditional CPE, the money demand schedules of both the enterprise and household sectors take on a characteristic form. Consider the case in the enterprise sector when an enterprise acquires an unanticipated monetary balance, either through its own economizing behavior, or because of an external shock. In the Soviet Union, planners will generally intervene to confiscate the "free balances" that the enterprises possesses (Birman, 1981). A determination will be made that the unanticipated balances are not part of the planned incentive fund of the enterprise, and they will be appropriated as part of budgetary revenues. The monetary effects will be minimal, but this does not happen automatically. Rather, the activist policy of planners neutralizes the impact of monetary shocks by regularly draining the enterprise sector of unanticipated liquidity. The enterprise "saving function" (Eq. (6)) reflects planners' preferences rather than enterprise preferences, and a kind of "forced dissaving" is imposed on the enterprise sector. Effective demand for money balances by enterprises is modest. At the same time, households in traditional CPEs generally have modest saving propensities. This generalization, although counter to impressions of "forced saving" in CPEs, is nonetheless well supported by all empirical work (Rudcenko, 1979; Pickersgill, 1980). This is also true in China in the prereform period, as I show below.

Because of these characteristics, macro policy in traditional CPEs can be accurately characterized in terms of Eq. (10). The values of $m(.)$ and $s(.)$ which enter the right-hand side with minus signs are small in absolute value. The value of inventory accumulation, $i(.)$, is regularly larger in absolute value than $m(.)$ plus $s(.)$. This yields the rule of thumb, subsequently elevated to dogma in both the Soviet Union and China, that the budget should be "basically balanced, with a slight surplus." This is an adequate rule of thumb, given stable low saving propensities in the household and enterprise sectors, a regular rate of inventory accumulation, and passive extension of bank credit. It is equivalent to asserting that a regular proportion of the total volume of credit extended should be sterilized by the budget surplus in order to keep monetary growth rates below the growth of credit extended. However, when saving propensities shift and the rate of credit extension diverges from the rate of inventory accumulation, the rule of thumb is no longer adequate as a guide to macro policy. When those changes do occur—as in China since the initiation of economic reform—new principles must be found to guide macro policy regardless of what instruments are used to implement that policy.

2

Discussion of China's macro policy requires a data base organized in consistent and meaningful categories. Budgetary data are inadequate because inconsistencies of definition and retrospective revisions make the data impossible to interpret. Moreover, budgetary authorities can increase government holdings at the bank through any of the following channels, all of which are equivalent from a macroeconomic standpoint: they may run a current surplus, depositing that with the bank; they may allow the bank to retain revenues; or they may allocate funds directly to the bank to serve as a credit fund. The Chinese have used all three of these channels, and the amounts are not known.

TABLE 1

CONSOLIDATED BANK BALANCE SHEET

Liabilities	Billion yuan			
	Households	Enterprises	Government	Total
End 1978	54.5	43.6	102.6	200.7
	(21.7%)	(27.2%)	(51.1%)	(100%)
Increment 1978–1983	101.3	83.0	20.4	204.7
	(49.3%)	(40.5%)	(10.0%)	(100%)
Increment 1983–1985	118.6	92.0	27.9	238.5
	(49.7%)	(38.6%)	(11.7%)	(100%)
Loans outstanding	Circulating capital	Fixed investment	Rural economy	Total
End 1978	182.9	2.5	15.5	200.9
	(91.0%)	(1.2%)	(7.7%)	
Increment 1978–1983	130.6	31.6	22.2	184.4
	(70.8%)	(17.1%)	(12.0%)	(100%)
Increment 1983–1985	164.8	36.5	40.2	241.5
	(68.2%)	(15.1%)	(16.6%)	(100%)

The alternative is to use the consolidated balance sheet of the banking system as a source of information. The Chinese publish "national credit balances" for the years since 1979, but these figures are not fully consolidated. Loans and deposits of the Construction Bank and the Rural Credit Cooperatives are first netted out, and only deposits are shown, and the classification of rural deposits and lending is arbitrary and misleading. These problems can be rectified through a tedious process of data collection and collation, although some errors may remain in estimation of Construction Bank assets and liabilities. The results of this process are shown in Tables 3 and 4.[2] Table 1 shows a summary version of the consolidated bank balance sheet for three benchmark periods, organized in categories that correspond to those in Eq. (8). Household assets are defined broadly to include assets of agricultural collectives and share capital of Rural Credit Cooperatives as well as savings deposits and currency in circulation. Enterprise deposits include those of rural enterprises held at the Agriculture Bank and Credit Cooperatives. Government assets are the sum of budgetary deposits and those of governmental organi-

---

[2] A data appendix, describing the sources of data, and procedures followed in the reconstruction, is available from the author on request.

zations, as well as the owned capital of the banking system. These figures are net of loans to the budgetary authority from the bank, and include unspecified "other" liabilities of the banking system.

The balance sheet for 1978 shows the cumulative result of Chinese macro policy in the prereform years. Over 50% of bank liabilities were held by the government. Enterprises held 27% and households 22% of total bank liabilities. Alternately stated, the budgetary authorities had sterilized over 50% of the extension of credit, so growth in the money supply amounted to less than half of credit creation. At this stage, China's financial structure was that of a traditional CPE. This structure was reflected on the asset side as well, in that over 90% of loans outstanding were the traditional category of loans for circulating capital, overwhelmingly to state-run enterprises. Lending for fixed investment already existed, but accounted for only 1% of lending, while loans to the rural sector (agriculture and rural enterprises) accounted for 8% of total lending. Lending differs from total assets by the net amount of foreign and "other" assets held.

The slow growth of the money supply, relative to credit creation, can also be examined by considering the household saving function, Eq. (5) above. In the years through 1979, the household saving function has a stable form which can be estimated using a Houthakker–Taylor form,

$$\hat{M}_t = -0.571 + 0.216 \ dY_t + 0.882 \ \hat{M}_{t-1} \qquad (11)$$
$$(0.267) \quad (0.061) \qquad (0.151) \qquad \qquad R^2 = 0.8426$$

where $\hat{M}_t$ is additions to household financial assets in the years 1957 through 1978; dY_t is the increase in household money income in the current year; and $\hat{M}_{t-1}$ is an instrumental variable representing the previous year's predicted saving. Figures in parentheses are standard errors. For details of the estimation process, see Naughton (1986).

Given the relatively slow growth of household income in China during the prereform period, the above relationship yields a low average saving rate, amounting to 2.4% of household income in the years 1970–1978. There is no evidence of structural change in the saving relationship through 1978, but when the relationship is extended beyond 1978, it substantially underpredicts actual household saving. A low household saving propensity is a characteristic of China in the prereform period, and in this respect as well, China resembles the traditional CPE pattern.

It is not possible to perform a similar exercise for enterprise asset accumulation in the prereform period. The data are insufficient, and there is no clear available theory to predict enterprise demand for financial assets. There is some incidental evidence that enterprises in China were more liquid than their counterparts in other CPEs prior to the initiation of reform. Enterprises were allowed to retain funds for the renovation and replacement of fixed assets, and this resulted in enterprises holding several billion in unspent financial assets at year-end (Hu and Wang, 1980). Nevertheless, the evidence of the bank balance sheet shows that enterprise holdings were modest relative to total credit creation.

The financial pattern that China shared with other traditional CPEs interacted with specifically Chinese realities to produce a unique pattern of macroeconomic interaction during the prereform period. Although household money income grew slowly, there is evidence that the rate of growth was constrained by the slow growth in the availability of consumption goods. That is, the problem of assuring macroeconomic balance, as defined in Eq. (8), became one of assuring that the growth rate of household income was consistent with available supplies of consumption goods. Planners were forced to adjust the growth of investment in order to remain within the constraint set by the availability of consumption goods.

I have constructed a variable which expresses the shortfall (positive or negative) in the supply of consumption goods in a given year with effective demand for consumption goods. This variable is a leading indicator of changes in investment:

$$dI_f/I_f = 52.76 - 1.04 \ t - 0.21 \ X_{t-1} \qquad\qquad (12)$$
$$(16.49) \quad (0.89) \quad (0.05) \qquad R^2 = 0.4679$$

The percentage growth of investment is regressed on a time trend, t, and an index of the relative degree of shortage of consumption goods in the preceding year (Xt_{-1}), for the years 1956–1978. The shortage index was the only time series found which predicted changes in investment: tests of agricultural production or procurement, energy supply, and foreign trade balance failed to provide any predictive power. See Naughton (1986; pp. 106–111, 168). This test indicates that conditions on consumption goods markets have been a crucial determinant of investment fluctuations, either because planners allow investment to grow rapidly when supplies of consumption goods are abundant, or because emerging shortages in the consumption sector bring expansionary episodes to a halt.

In the prereform economy, macroeconomic policy had the limited objective of maintaining household income growth within the limits set by consumption goods availability. Since household financial saving rates were low, increases in household income translated directly into demand for consumption goods. There may also have been disequilibria in the enterprise sector (shortages of producers goods, uncompleted construction projects) that contributed to limiting expansionary periods, but there is inadequate time series evidence of these phenomena. The Chinese experience before 1978 displays many examples of unsustainably rapid expansionary periods—macroeconomic policy was often excessively stimulative—and shortages of consumption goods were a major factor compelling the termination of these periods.

With this background in mind, I now examine China's postreform experience. The reform period can be usefully divided into two subperiods, one extending from 1979 through 1983, and a second from 1983 through 1985. Although the two subperiods share certain important characteristics, they also differ in important respects. I concentrate initially on the first subperiod.

The beginning of the reform period coincides with a striking shift in macroeconomic policy, and particularly in the behavior of the budgetary authorities. The Chinese budget was in deficit every year between 1979 and 1983, with a cumulative deficit of about 40 billion yuan, or just over 2% of national income. Moreover, Chinese fiscal policy became even more stimulative than this figure indicates, because Chinese budgetary practices conceal important changes in the structure of revenues and expenditures. The most obvious anomaly in Chinese accounting practices is that borrowing is included as current income: a cumulative total of 31.47 billion yuan in domestic and foreign debt is classified as budgetary income between 1979 and 1983. While proper accounting practices dictate adjustment of the deficit to include new borrowing, this particular adjustment is of little significance to the current analysis: domestic debt can be considered as a tax in the short run, while foreign borrowing has no immediate impact on the domestic economy.

However, even without including government debt, fiscal policy has become more stimulative than the figures on the deficit indicate. Referring to Eq. (10) above, we are reminded that for a given rate of inventory accumulation, reductions in budgetary allocations for inventory investment have the same macroeconomic impact as an increase in the budgetary deficit. Such allocations have declined substantially: averaging 5% of budgetary outlays in the late 1960s and 1970s, they declined steadily after 1978 and amounted to only 1% of budgetary outlays in 1983. In absolute terms, budgetary financing of inventories declined from 6.7 billion yuan in 1978 to 1.3 billion yuan in 1983. Not only has the budget deficit increased, but budgetary outlays cover a smaller proportion of the investment needs of the economy. This places a greater burden on the banking system, so that credits extended will grow more rapidly, *ceteris paribus,* and overall macroeconomic policy will be more stimulative.

This effect is reinforced by the entry of the banks into new types of lending on a large scale. Bank financing of fixed investment rapidly became significant after 1979, and lending to the rural economy also grew faster than traditional forms of lending. Whether this is considered compensation for a reduced role of the budgetary authorities in this area, or simply as an additional source of stimulus, the shift of macro policy is greater than that indicated by examining the budgetary deficit alone. These changes are reflected in the changes in the bank balance sheet shown in Table 1. Of the increment to bank liabilities between 1978 and 1983, only 10% were acquired by the government (fiscal and banking authorities combined; budgetary obligations to the banking system have been netted out of both assets and liabilities). Fifty percent of the new liabilities were held by households, and 40% by enterprises. Fully 90% of the increase in credit outstanding was translated into increases in the money supply. At the same time, household money income grew at an extraordinarily rapid pace, 16% per year through 1983, compared to 5% per year between 1957 and 1978. At first glance, it would appear that this phase carried all the characteristics of an unsustainably rapid expansionary phase, characterized by excessively expansionary macro policy.

However, important changes in the behavior of the household and enterprise sectors dramatically changed the response of the economy to macroeconomic stimulus. Household saving rates increased sharply; when the saving function reported as Eq. (11) is extended into the 1980s, it predicts household saving will increase to 4.5% of income in 1980–83, due to the more rapid growth of income. In addition, households could be expected to save another 1 to 1.5% of income to compensate for the drawing down of financial assets held by the agricultural collectives. (Extrapolating previous trends, the expansion of agriculture from 1978 through 1985 would have required additional balances of 26 billion yuan, while collective balances actually declined by 1.6 billion yuan.) Thus, household saving could have been expected to increase to between 5 and 6% of income, but actual saving in 1980–1983 amounted to just under 10% of income. This rapid increase in household saving rates is reminiscent of the similar change that occurred in Taiwan during the 1960s.

Enterprise behavior changed in equally dramatic fashion. Between 1979 and 1983, enterprise deposits increased 118%, while industrial production and retail sales increased by 36 and 58%, respectively (in current prices). Decentralized investment (including that financed by retained funds and by bank loans) increased by 127%, or slightly more than the increase in enterprise deposits. Clearly, enterprises are becoming more liquid as they take on additional responsibilities as part of the reform process. The picture of macroeconomic performance can be completed by examining Table 2. State retail

TABLE 2

GROWTH OF PRODUCTION, SALES, INVENTORIES, AND CREDIT[a]

	1965–1979	1979–1983	1983–1985
State-owned enterprises			
Retail sales	7.8	6.6	10.9
Commercial inventories	7.7	8.1	2.4
Industrial production	7.8	6.6	14.7
Industrial inventories	10.9	3.9	12.1
Total circulating capital loans to			
state units	9.0	11.4	22.4
Total credits extended to all sectors	9.0	14.8	27.5

[a] Annual percentage growth in current prices.

sales and industrial production both decelerated slightly during the 1979–1983 period, in part because non-state enterprises played an increasing role. Growth in commercial inventories accelerated slightly, while industrial inventory growth decelerated rather dramatically. As a result, the rate of credit creation accelerated quite modestly from 9% annually to 14.8%, with most of the acceleration coming as a result of expansion of nontraditional forms of lending. Although the banking system was forced to take a greater role in investment financing, part of the expansionary impact was mitigated by more economical use of inventories in the industrial system.

Thus, during the 1979–1983 period, macro policy shifted to an extremely stimulative position, and household income increased rapidly. At the same time, output growth accelerated only in the agricultural sphere, and industrial output growth actually declined. But the impact of expansionary policy was largely absorbed by increased savings by the household and enterprise sectors. Reduced rates of industrial inventory accumulation also contributed to an amelioration of expansionary pressures, by holding down the rate of acceleration of credit creation.

However, the preceding description needs to be further questioned. We know from Eq. (8) that the combination of an increased budget deficit and accelerated rates of credit creation must be accompanied by accelerated growth of the money supply, since the expression is an identity. As a result, an obvious question arises: to what extent does the increased liquidity of the household and enterprise sectors represent "forced saving," as households and enterprises are unable to locate consumer and producer goods they desire? Do increased shortage phenomena lie behind the redistribution of financial assets in China? In the household sector, there are numerous reasons to believe that the increased saving propensities represent voluntary adaptation to a changed economic environment, and no good evidence of increased shortage. While a full discussion of the problem of forced saving is beyond the scope of this paper, I believe we can confidently assert that the increase in household saving through 1983 is not a reflection of forced saving. Partial evidence that supports this view includes:

1. The number of formally rationed goods has declined drastically since 1978, while the observed quality and variety of goods available has improved markedly.

2. Prices in the farmers' markets, not subject to state controls, have remained stable, and in a roughly constant ratio to state prices.

3. Consumption good inventories at state commercial units have increased more rapidly than retail sales, contrary to the expectation that they would be reduced if excess demand were growing.

4. Most of the increased saving has been in the form of saving deposits, often fixed-term deposits. If households were searching for sporadically available consumption goods, we would expect them to hold larger stocks of cur-

rency in order to maximize the likelihood they would be able to purchase goods that were available, but this has not occurred. (For theoretical and empirical justification of this argument, see Naughton, 1986, pp. 102–117.)

None of these arguments is conclusive taken by itself, since changes in the structure of demand with rising income levels will influence each of them. Taken together, however, they make a strong case for the absence of forced saving. Moreover, there is no evidence *for* an increase of forced saving, unless one believes that the increase in saving rates is in itself such evidence. But comparable increases in saving rates have been observed in the past in Taiwan and Japan, and there are additional reasons to expect a rapid increase in saving in China in the specific years when saving rates increase. These reasons include (1) increased availability of "lumpy" consumer items (especially housing) which require preliminary periods of saving; (2) the shift of income to the countryside, where saving rates are higher; (3) a dramatically changed economic environment, with vastly greater opportunities for individual businesses, stimulating household investment. Of course, there is no doubt that shortages continue to exist in China for particular goods (especially high quality, "name brand" items), and shortages may intensify during brief periods. But there is no evidence that the sustained increase in saving can be explained by a corresponding sustained increase in shortages. The change in household behavior must be seen as a voluntary adaptation to a radically altered economic environment. Because of economic reform and income growth, household opportunities both for consumption and for investment in productive activities have expanded rapidly, and these increased opportunities lead to increased saving.

In the enterprise sector, the question is more complex, in part because there is no theory of enterprise saving comparable to that which can be drawn on to describe household behavior. Conceptually, enterprises require financial balances both for traditional transactions purposes, and as part of their investment activity. This second requirement may involve enterprises in saving behavior that resembles that of households. This is particularly true in China, since enterprises bear predominant responsibility for construction of housing and collective welfare facilities for their workers, who generally enjoy lifetime employment with the enterprise. Therefore, it would not be surprising to find enterprises engaged in long-term accumulation of assets in order to improve the future environment of the work force. Indeed, the Chinese financial system reflects precisely this kind of activity through two specific types of enterprise deposits. Enterprises can now hold fixed-term deposits, although such deposits were only 1.2 billion in 1982, the only year for which a figure is available (Jiang, 1985, p. 240). Similarly, enterprises deposit funds in the Construction Bank which are earmarked for worker housing construction; when such funds exceed 50% of the value of the housing project, they can be matched by specialized loans from the Bank (Liu, 1981).

However, there is no clear way to separate enterprise demand for transactions balances from enterprise demand for other types of accumulation. We have already noted that overall enterprise balances have grown at approximately the same rate as decentralized investment, and much more rapidly than enterprise sales. But if total enterprise balances are composed of both transactions and "investment" balances, that would imply that investment balances have grown more rapidly than investment. This suggests that enterprises have become more liquid even in relation to the rapidly growing enterprise investment activity.

Such an impression may also be corroborated by examining the rate of price increases of construction materials. These grew at a rate of 9.7% annually between 1978 and 1983, substantially more rapidly than the overall price level. This may be an indication of excess demand in this area, although it should be noted that price controls in construction are much weaker than those in other sectors. There is, therefore, some evidence of excess demand in the enterprise sector, but it cannot be considered conclusive. Part of the problem involved in making more definite statements is the difficulty of determining exactly what behavioral regularities underlie enterprise actions. If Chinese enterprises are characterized by soft budget constraints of the type made familiar by Kornai—and there is substantial evidence that this is the case—we would expect them to be characterized by an "insatiable" demand for investment goods, so that excess demand would be pervasive in this sphere in any case. The evidence presented here merely suggests that whether or not enterprise budget constraints are "soft," there is also some evidence that they are "slack."

Yet even if enterprises hold financial balances that they would prefer to spend for investment goods or wage increases, the saving may be voluntary in the sense that enterprises would prefer to retain the claim on future benefits which possession of the balances implies. In that sense, the promise of future consumption induces the enterprise to hold larger balances in the present; its more forward-looking behavior again cushions the impact of the rapid growth of the money supply. Finally, it may be appropriate to explain the slow growth of industrial inventories by improved enterprise incentives in the reform period: in disposing of useless inventories and economizing on the remainder, enterprises may have been responding to new inducements created by the greater importance of profitability since reforms began.

The second subperiod, extending from 1983 to 1985, resembles the first in the continuation of stimulative fiscal policy. A slight budget surplus in 1985 was offset by the larger deficit in 1984, and budgetary allocations for inventory investment remained very low. As shown in Table 1, government held only 12% of the increase in banking system liabilities from 1983 to 1985, while households again accounted for almost exactly 50% of those liabilities. The major difference between the two subperiods lies in the much more rapid growth of credit creation in the second. Excessive credit creation is manifestly evident in the final months of 1984. Enterprise deposits at year-end 1984 had increased 54% (while decentralized investment grew only 27%); household assets increased nearly 40%, and currency in circulation nearly 50%. It is clear that a major breakdown in state control over the banking system occurred.

The rapid expansion of lending in late 1984 swelled household income and created serious temporary excess demand. Open inflation in urban areas surged to 14% in 1985, and inventories in the commercial system grew by only 2.4% annually. Although some of the inflation actually reflects a calculated decision to allow state nonstaple food prices to rise closer to free market prices as a part of reforms of the distribution system, there is no doubt that the loss of control over aggregate demand obstructed the smooth implementation of price reforms, and undermined political support for further relaxation of price controls.

Macroeconomic policy shifted to a contractionary stance in mid-1985, under the impetus of an emerging foreign exchange shortage. For 1985 as a whole, enterprise deposits increased only 12%, while decentralized investment grew 52%. Enterprises worked off their excess balances during the year, and were sharply restricted in their access to new credits. One result of this shift in policy was a sharp, though short-lived, contraction in economic activity in the opening months of 1986.

Clearly macro policy cannot receive the same qualified approval during the second subperiod that it is entitled to during the first. Yet it is important to note that many of the forces that ameliorated the impact of stimulative policy in the earlier period continued to operate in the latter. Household savings rates continued to increase, and average slightly over 15% for 1984–1985. Indeed, the striking fact about this period is that extremely reckless credit policy did as little damage to the economy as it did. The problems encountered in 1985 are evidence of the immaturity of the institutions designed to implement macro policy in the future, as well as the resilience of the Chinese economy in the face of inappropriate macro policy at present.

3

Widespread behavioral changes have characterized each sector of the Chinese economy since 1978. These behavioral changes are all basically attributable to the change in economic environment induced by the economic reform process. The shift of the budgetary authority to substantial deficit has essentially occurred because the budgetary authorities have surrendered control over a significant portion of their prereform revenues. This has occurred through an increase in agricultural procurement prices, a reduction in the effective tax rate on enterprise net revenue, and, to a lesser extent, through an increase in the wage rate. Since the fiscal authorities have been unwilling or unable to reduce their outlays in a fashion commensurate with the reduction in revenue generation, the result has been substantial budget deficits. However, the negative consequences of those deficits were almost entirely offset by changes in the behavior of the enterprise and household sectors, who were themselves responding to the changed incentives created by the reform process. The willingness of the governmental authorities to permit households larger incomes and greater freedom in the disposition of those incomes resulted in voluntary household decisions to save a greater proportion of income, and enterprises responded in a similar fashion. In a sense, government dissaving led to a "crowding in" of private saving, since it was accompanied by a relaxation of government controls over the economy.

This simple fact has been of great importance to the Chinese reform process. Higher household saving rates have reduced the pressure on consumption goods supply, even as that supply has been augmented by accelerated agricultural growth. Increased asset-holding by households and enterprises has allowed the government to incur repeated deficits with minimal negative affect on the economy. In China, as in other countries, a budget deficit is a way of reconciling competing claims on society's output, satisfying current claimants at the expense of future claimants. This has meant that sectors in China which have no particular stake in the reform process have been able to receive at least minimally acceptable budgetary allocations, so that they do not actively oppose the reform process. For instance, the military has received reduced allocations, but apparently considers its current level of allocations acceptable. Thus, the economic reform process has been met with changes in the behavior of households and enterprises that in turn create a "breathing space" for reform, and allows the reform process to continue, in spite of obvious problems and mistakes. Observers of the East European reform experience have suggested that tendencies are created within that process that lead to the curtailment or elimination of reforms. The Chinese experience suggests that the reform process also creates tendencies that facilitate further reforms, and provide some room for a trial and error search for appropriate reform strategies.

At the same time, the redistribution of financial assets which is one of the most striking changes in China in recent years is a mixed blessing. The accumulation of assets by enterprise and households facilitates the emergence of the banking system into a central role in the management of the economy, and this is in itself one of the central objectives of economic reform. But if this accumulation is excessive—if enterprise budget constraints are "slack," as I suggest above—it will be almost impossible for the bank to function effectively as the main regulator of the economy. In particular, reform of the investment system, which must rely on the use of interest rates and credit extension determining by economic returns, cannot be gradually implemented if enterprises are highly liquid. In this situation, the need to control aggregate investment will require the repeated reinstatement of quantitative controls,

TABLE 3

CONSOLIDATED BANK BALANCE SHEET: I. LIABILITIES (BILLION YUAN)

	1978	1979	1980	1981	1982	1983	1984	1985
I. Enterprise deposits								
A. At PBC[a]	36.8	46.9	57.3	67.4	71.8	84.1	133.4	149.5
B. At CB	5.0	8.0	12.0	21.0	27.0	34.3	49.3	57.6
C. Rural enterprises (At AB and RCCs)	1.8	3.2	4.5	5.1	5.7	8.2	12.4	11.5
Subtotal	43.6	58.1	73.8	93.5	104.5	126.6	195.1	218.6
II. Household assets								
A. Currency	21.2	26.8	34.6	39.6	43.9	53.0	79.2	98.8
B. "Urban" savings deposits	15.5	20.3	28.2	35.4	44.7	57.3	77.7	105.8
C. RCC savings deposits	5.6	7.8	11.7	17.0	22.8	32.0	43.8	56.5
D. Deposits of agricultural collectives	8.5	10.2	11.0	11.7	12.6	9.5	9.3	7.5
E. RCC share capital plus "other" deposits	3.7	3.5	4.2	2.7	3.1	4.0	4.0	5.8
Subtotal	54.5	68.6	89.7	106.4	127.1	155.8	214.0	274.4
III. Budgetary and banking system								
A. PBC budgetary and organization deposits; banks capital; "other" liabilities, net of claims on budget	86.0	79.9	80.6	89.2	97.3	99.7	106.5	126.4
B. CB budgetary deposits and bank capital	16.6	18.9	21.8	22.8	28.8	23.3	25.3	24.5
Subtotal	102.6	98.8	102.4	112.0	126.1	123.0	131.8	150.9
Total liabilities	200.7	225.5	265.9	311.9	357.7	405.4	540.9	643.9

[a] Abbreviations used: PBC, People's Bank of China; CB, Construction Bank; AB, Agriculture Bank; RCC, Rural Credit Cooperatives.

TABLE 4

CONSOLIDATED BANK BALANCE SHEET: II. ASSETS (BILLION YUAN)

	1978	1979	1980	1981	1982	1983	1984	1985
Loans for circulating capital								
A. Industrial and commercial	168.2	183.7	210.5	237.0	255.5	284.5	346.7	419.5
B. Construction	9.4	9.8	10.5	9.4	11.9	13.1	17.4	26.7
C. Urban collective	5.3	5.8	7.8	12.1	13.3	15.9	29.5	32.1
Subtotal	182.9	199.3	228.8	258.5	280.7	313.5	393.6	478.3
Loans for fixed investment								
A. At PBC[a]	0	0.8	5.6	8.3	15.2	19.6	29.0	43.3
B. At CB	2.5	4.0	6.0	11.5	15.4	14.5	23.9	27.3
Subtotal	2.5	4.8	11.6	19.8	30.6	34.1	52.9	70.6
Loans to rural enterprises	3.3	4.0	8.4	10.0	11.6	14.1	29.4	34.5
Loans to collective and individual agriculture (from state banks and RCCs)	11.6	13.3	15.6	16.3	18.7	21.1	34.5	37.5
Loans to state farms	0.6	0.7	0.9	1.4	2.0	2.5	5.1	5.9
Total domestic loans	200.9	222.1	265.3	306.0	343.6	385.3	515.5	626.8
Net foreign assets	?	3.3	0.6	5.9	14.1	20.0	19.9	11.4
"Other" assets	0	0	0	0	0	0	5.6	5.6
Total assets		225.4	265.9	311.9	357.7	405.3	541.0	643.8

[a] See Table 3 for abbreviations.

and the reassertion of the primacy of the plan. Indeed, precisely this happened in 1985, along with contractionary credit policies.

Finally, changing behavior at the household and enterprise level makes the task of macroeconomic management more difficult, simply because it is more difficult to interpret the information reaching policy makers. Endless debates occur in China on the topic of whether household saving or currency in circulation is "excessive," and no clear standard has emerged. Indeed, the relative absence of harmful effects following stimulative fiscal policy in 1979–1983 may have led to an overly sanguine attitude toward stimulative credit policies in 1984. Similarly, it is possible that the unexpectedly sharp contraction in economic activity in early 1986 was the result of a misinterpretation of data on enterprise money-holdings. The velocity of circulation of enterprise balances was purposely suppressed in 1985 by a requirement that deposits had to be made in the Construction Bank at least 6 months prior to the disbursement of funds for investment purposes. The contraction of 1986 may have been partially due to an attempt to reduce the growth rate of enterprise money to approximate the growth rate of underlying economic activity at a time when other factors were forcing the velocity of circulation down. This would be especially serious if price increases for producers goods were significant, and inadequately considered by policy makers (there are no official price indices for producers goods). We need only recall the difficulties imposed on policy makers in the United States by the changing behavior of M1: the problem is much more severe in China because monetary data are among the few accurate aggregate data which are quickly available to policy makers in China. There has been extensive debate in China about the appropriateness of macro policy in late 1985 (See Song and Zhang, 1986, and Wu, 1986 for opposing views), and the data available to an outsider are not sufficient to allow a final judgement.[3]

Drastic fluctuations have characterized the Chinese economy for many years. While the character of those fluctuations has changed—with energy and foreign exchange limitations replacing consumer goods as the factors which limit growth in the short run—their magnitude has not declined much since the initiation of reform. If reforms are to continue, macroeconomic management must be placed on a more stable footing, particularly if policy makers are to gradually gain experience with new instruments of macroeconomic guidance. This will require more detailed collection and processing of

---

[3] The institution of a sharply contractionary credit policy in late 1985, followed by reductions in economic activity, may indicate that excess liquidity in the enterprise sector has been eliminated. However, this is not necessarily the case. Enterprises may seek to protect the funds they have set aside for investment and worker bonuses, at the cost of creating shortages in funds for current transactions needs. They can then present their pressing current needs to the banking system, with an urgent request for new credits. Song and Zhang (1986) argue that this is in fact the case.

data, and a greater effort to understand the behavorial changes that are some of the most striking results of the reform process thus far.

REFERENCES

Birman, I., *Secret Incomes of the Soviet State Budget.* The Hague: Nijhoff, 1981.

Garvy, George, *Money, Financial Flows and Credit in the Soviet Union.* Cambridge, MA: Ballinger, 1977.

Garvy, George, *Money, Banking and Credit in Eastern Europe.* New York: Federal Reserve Board of New York, 1966.

Hu Jing, and Wang Chengyao, "On Problems of Renewal and Reconstruction in Old Factories," *Gangye Jingji Guanli Congkan,* 3:6-15, March 1980.

Jiang Qiwu, Ed., *Yinhang, Xindai Guanli Cankao Ziliao (Reference Materials on Banking and Credit Management).* Beijing: Zhongyang Guangbo Dianshi Daxue, 1985.

Liu Lixin, "Suggestions for Improving Methods of Raising Capital." *Caizheng* 11:8-10, Nov. 1981.

Montias, J. Michael, "Bank Lending and Fiscal Policy in Eastern Europe." In G. Grossman, Ed., *Money and Plan,* pp. 38-56. Berkeley: Univ. of California Press, 1968.

Naughton, B. "Saving and Investment in China: A Macroeconomic Analysis." Yale University Ph.D. thesis, New Haven, 1986.

Pickersgill, Joyce, "Recent Evidence on Soviet Household Saving Behaviour." *R. E. Stat.* 62: 628-33, 1980.

Rudcenko, S., "Household Money Income, Expenditure and Monetary Assets in Czechoslovakia, GDR, Hungary and Poland, 1956-1975." *Jahrbuch der Wirtschaft Osteuropas* 8:431-50, 1979.

Song Guoqing, and Zhang Weihuan, "Several Theoretical Questions of Macroeconomic Balance and Macroeconomic Control." *Jingji Yanjiu* 6:23-35, June 1986.

Wu Jinglian, "Economic Fluctuation and Two Types of Economic Systems." *Caimai Jingji* 6: 1-8, June 1986.

JOURNAL OF COMPARATIVE ECONOMICS 11, 354–371 (1987)

Money and the Consumption Goods Market in China[1]

RICHARD PORTES and ANITA SANTORUM

Birkbeck College, London W1P 1PA, England

Portes, R., and Santorum, A.—Money and the Consumption Goods Market in China

This paper studies the relations between money and other macroeconomic variables as well as excess demand in the consumption goods market in the case of China, 1954–1983. We explicitly recognize the endogeneity of money in the CPE and do not impose (but instead test) some common restrictive assumptions; we assess the extent of aggregate excess demand (supply) in a macroeconomic disequilibrium model; and we allow at the macro level for the possible coexistence of micro markets in different states of excess demand or supply (shortages or slacks). We find bidirectional causality between money and income; that M_0 behaves in a manner more suited to building simple, conventional models than does M_2; and that there has been a mixed pattern of excess supplies and demands over the three decades. *J. Comp. Econ.,* September 1987, **11**(3), pp. 354–371. Birkbeck College, London W1P 1PA, England. © 1987 Academic Press, Inc.

Journal of Economic Literature Classification Numbers: 124, 130, 311.

1. INTRODUCTION

As Chow (1985a) and Peebles (1983) have stressed, basic monetary and macroeconomic data for China are now available for a sufficiently long period to permit serious quantitative analysis. Pioneering work of this kind is already appearing, taking into account some of the special characteristics of the Chinese economy (Chow, 1985b; Feltenstein and Farhidian, 1987; Feltenstein et al., 1986).

It is not surprising that this work deals with questions of macroeconomic disequilibrium familiar from the recent literature on East European centrally

[1] R. Portes is Professor of Economics at Birkbeck College, University of London, and Director of the Centre for Economic Policy Research; A. Santorum is a Ph.D. candidate at Birkbeck. The authors thank Chris Martin, Apostolis Philippopoulos, Ron Smith, Aris Spanos, and David Winter for advice and help. R. Portes owes his initial interest in the macroeconomics of China to Gong Zhuming. He gratefully acknowledges the Ford Foundation and Gregory Chow for introducing him to the Chinese economy in July 1985 and students and colleagues at the People's University of Beijing for stimulating his interest further. A. Santorum acknowledges with thanks support for her research and conference participation from the Istituto Bancario San Paolo di Torino. A first version of this paper was presented to the Arden House Conference on Chinese Economic Reform in October 1986, and it has benefited from the comments of participants, in particular the discussant, Gregory Chow.

64

CHINESE ECONOMIC REFORM

planned economies (CPEs). We report here some preliminary results on money and the consumption goods market in a framework with several distinctive characteristics: we explicitly recognize the endogeneity of money in the CPE and do not impose some common restrictive assumptions, we assess the extent of aggregate excess demand (supply) in a macroeconomic disequilibrium model, and we allow at the macro level for the possible coexistence of micro markets in different states of excess demand or supply (shortages and slacks).

We emphasize that this is an initial, exploratory effort. The work on money and on the consumption goods market is not yet fully integrated. Nor have we yet been able to deploy the full array of available tests for the specifications we have tried. Nevertheless, we find the results suggestive and promising, and we believe they raise questions which should be addressed by further work.

2. THE DEMAND FOR MONEY

Disequilibrium macroeconomics typically assumes both that the money stock is exogenous and that the demand for money is purely an asset demand, unaffected by transaction requirements. These assumptions seem to hold particularly well for CPEs. In the absence of a bond market, money balances at the end of the period may be identified with forced saving.

Kornai (1982) goes much further and does not even consider money in his model because, he argues, it is not a budget constraint for firms, while for households only real income and real consumption matter. According to Kornai, "a semi-monetized economy in which prices and money do not genuinely influence the macrovariables of production, investment and employment cannot properly be described in terms of its money being stable or inflated, or price increases being repressed or permitted."

We disagree with this statement, and we shall also query the exogeneity of the money stock in both its narrower and broader definitions. Price and interest rate shocks as well as changes in expectations about future constraints on the consumption and labor markets might affect the demand for money. On the other hand money holdings might affect future consumer decisions. An unstable demand for money could cause problems for the planners (see Portes, 1983).

The definition of money in a planned economy is still a controversial issue. Since cash is used only for retail sales, wages, and state purchases of agricultural products, we identify two monetary circuits: one where cash plays the role of means of exchange and another, restricted to government and production units, where most payments are made by bank transfer. Enterprises and production units in general can keep just a limited amount of cash for unpredictable transactions.

The literature stresses the cash circuit, generally looking for inflationary pressures on the consumption market. Currency is held by households and, in limited amount, by agricultural production units and enterprises.

Households can save income in only two forms of assets: cash and saving deposits; there is no bond market. It is worth noting that in China in 1977 (before the economic reform), currency was 50% of the money stock (defined as M_2, currency plus saving deposits). Only after 1979 did saving deposits increase considerably, reaching 60% of the money stock by 1982. About 82% of currency in circulation was held by households (Naughton, 1986) and the remaining by agricultural units and enterprises; this percentage has remained very stable over time.

The monetary system and monetary policy in China are discussed by Byrd (1983), Bortolani and Santorum (1984), and de Wulf and Goldsbrough (1986). As in other CPEs, before 1984, China had a monobank system; the People's Bank (PB) functioned both as central bank and as commercial bank and firmly controlled all the other banks. The Agricultural Bank (AB) and the Construction Bank had to keep at the central bank some reserves in proportion to their deposits, but apparently the proportion was not fixed, nor did the authorities admit to using them as reserve requirement. There was and still is no discounting operation; therefore the central bank has virtually no means of controlling the money stock, except by changes in the interest rate on savings deposits in order to reduce the currency in circulation.

Currency is put in circulation by the central bank through other banks, state enterprises (directly), and government units, and it is withdrawn through the same institutions. Eighty percent of the currency outflow is due to wage payments (42%) and state procurement of agricultural products (38%). On the other hand, retail sales account for 70% of the cash inflow (People's Bank of China, 1983).

In this kind of financial system, the mechanistic multiplier approach does not work properly; even if banks keep cash as reserve asset and we think of households having a fixed desired ratio in which they hold currency and bank deposits, the multiplier effect is limited to that part of bank loans which are cash loans.

The central bank determines the money stock on the basis of the credit plan used jointly with the cash plan (see Bortolani and Santorum, 1984). The balance of the People's Bank is something like the following:

Assets	Liabilities
	Enterprises' deposits
Loans to enterprises	Government deposits
Loans to government	Saving deposits
Loans to non-state sector (private	Currency
and agric. units)	Other banks reserves
Reserves (gold and foreign exchange)	Agricultural bank reserves

Only in the case of cash loans does a change in currency occur. The People's Bank cannot control total credit directly, since it is primarily determined by the economic plan and the government budget. Let us ignore for the moment loans to the non-state sector and the AB reserves, and as a further simplification assume fixed bank reserves.

Under a flow of funds analysis, changes in the money stock result as

$$\Delta CU = (\Delta L_E + \Delta L_G) - (\Delta D_E + \Delta D_G) - \Delta SD$$

$$\Delta CU = \underbrace{(\Delta L_E - \Delta D_E)}_{SEBR} + \underbrace{(\Delta L_G - \Delta D_G)}_{PSBR} - \Delta SD,$$

where CU = currency; L = loans, and D = deposits; subscripts E and G are, respectively, for enterprises and government units; SD = saving deposits; SEBR = State enterprises' net borrowing requirement; PSBR = public sector net borrowing requirement.

Thus

$$SEBR + PSBR > \Delta SD \;\rightarrow\; \Delta CU > 0$$

In principle both SEBR and PSBR are determined by the economic plan. The central bank has no power over them; it can just ensure that the borrowing requirement does not exceed the plan targets.

Only cash loans will produce changes in the money stock, since any other kind of loan is counterbalanced by a corresponding change in enterprise or government deposits. Cash loans are mainly for wage payments and purchases of agricultural products. They depend on the plan, the enterprises' economic performance (since bonuses have been introduced), and the unpredictable agricultural production. Interest rates on these loans did not have any incentive effects on enterprises or government units until perhaps 1985, when production units' performance became important and interest on loans finally became greater than the corresponding interest rate on deposits.

Now consider the complete balance sheet. The rural sector is very important: we can reasonably suppose that nearly half of the currency in circulation is in rural areas, where production units keep cash for payments to members of the brigade and purchases of various inputs, and peasants are paid just once or twice a year (even if only part of their income is in cash).

Unfortunately, the process of money creation in rural areas is not clear. The rural credit cooperatives (RCC) contributed in recent years to a very large savings deposit increase relative to rural areas, lending on the other hand less than one-third of the money they collected. The RCC deposit nearly all the collected savings (e.g., 70% in 1982) at the AB. The AB, in its turn, deposits at the PB a high ratio of its total deposits. This reserve is what in the balance sheet published by the PB is called "rural area deposits." How it is determined (a fixed ratio? of which items?) is virtually unknown.

Loans to the non-state sector should counterbalance savings deposits, giving a measure of the non-state sector net borrowing requirement (NSBR). Loans to the private sector are particularly important (both in size and effects) since the introduction of the responsibility system in agriculture and the growth of the free market. Since 1979–1980 people need and hold cash as working capital. Therefore the flow of funds identity should be read as

$$\Delta CU = SEBR + PSBR + NSBR,$$

where NSBR $= \Delta L_{NS} - \Delta SD$; here SD includes AB deposits at the PB. Thus

$$\Delta CU > 0 \quad \text{when} \quad SEBR + PSBR > -NSBR.$$

The substance is unchanged, but in this perspective, since NSBR is a variable particularly difficult to control, both total credit control and interest-rate policy acquire great importance when the central bank has an M_0 target. This is one reason why the question of exogeneity of M_0 (or M_2) is itself so important.

Before starting any experiment in general model building for the demand for money in China, we conducted two different investigations: first we looked for causality relationships among such key variables as the money stock (both in its narrower, M_0, and broader, M_2, definitions), disposable income, and prices; second, we have estimated a well-specified equation for the money stock and tested the restrictions of price homogeneity, income homogeneity, and nominal and real adjustment. The choice of the data series, so relevant for the construction of the statistical model, is explained in the Data Appendix.

We stress that we have had to use annual data, which preclude any short-run investigation. The sample used is 1954–1983 (30 observations); in evaluating the reported diagnostics, some attention should be paid to the limited number of degrees of freedom available.

For the purpose of investigating causality and lag ordering among the main variables we have carried out Granger causality tests (Granger, 1969) and the Cooley–Leroy test (Cooley and Leroy, 1985). In Tables 1 and 2, we report the results for money and real income interrelations; they are from the only well-defined model we were able to build. The tests we use are properly valid only in the context of a statistical model that has passed appropriate tests of its underlying assumptions (see Spanos, 1986), and we were unable to arrive at such a model for the relation between money and money income.

Using *nominal* income as a regressor we encountered autocorrelation and misspecification, while the price series is strongly nonstationary, which fundamentally affects the results of the Granger test. Regressing money on prices, however, we did get a relatively well-defined model, for which the results suggest that prices do not cause money (in both its definitions).

Considering Tables 1 and 2, we see that for M_2, both the Granger test and the Cooley–Leroy test are conclusive: M_2 causes real income and real income causes M_2, revealing as expected as bidirectional causality among the two variables. In other words, Chinese policy makers must recognize the importance of controlling the money stock, because it affects other macroeconomic variables.

There are some doubts, however, about the results relative to M_0: even if a certain degree of independence with respect to real income appears in the

TABLE 1

GRANGER CAUSALITY TEST, SAMPLE 1958–1983

$$X_t = \alpha_0 + \sum_{i=1}^{\lambda} \alpha_i X_{t-1} + \sum_{j=1}^{\lambda} \beta_j Z_{t-1} \qquad Z \text{ causes } X \text{ if } \beta_j \neq 0 \qquad \lambda = 4$$

	(1) M_0 on y	(2) M_2 on y	(3) y on M_0	(4) y on M_2
α_0	−1.19 (0.58)	0.81 (0.46)	0.11 (0.20)	0.05 (0.23)
α_1	0.94 (0.20)	0.91 (0.25)	1.35 (0.19)	1.50 (0.22)
α_2	−0.10 (0.31)	0.68 (0.37)	−0.45 (0.31)	−0.56 (0.36)
α_3	−0.42 (0.36)	−0.86 (0.39)	0.06 (0.26)	−0.06 (0.33)
α_4	0.21 (0.23)	0.08 (0.26)	−0.02 (0.16)	0.07 (0.19)
β_1	0.76 (0.58)	1.74 (0.45)	−0.27 (0.07)	−0.30 (0.12)
β_2	−0.65 (0.93)	−1.74 (0.74)	0.46 (0.10)	0.58 (0.18)
β_3	0.57 (0.77)	−0.05 (0.67)	−0.28 (0.12)	−0.46 (0.19)
β_4	−0.18 (0.48)	0.37 (0.39)	0.19 (0.08)	0.25 (0.12)
R^2	0.964	0.986	0.993	0.992
s	0.105	0.080	0.035	0.039
BJ(2)	0.42	0.64	1.74	0.31
LM1(1,16)	1.37	0.39	0.15	0.01
LM2(2,15)	0.93	2.09	1.08	2.20
$\xi^2(2,22)$	2.99	1.73	0.81	0.88
$\xi^3(2,22)$	0.18	0.30	1.22	0.30
F-test $H_1: \beta_j = 0$	2.81	4.55	9.98	7.10

Note. OLS has been used for estimation. BJ is the Bera–Jarques normality test, distributed χ^2 with 2 degrees of freedom; LM1 and LM2 are Lagrange multiplier tests against first-order and second-order autocorrelation; ξ^2 is a linearity test distributed $F(2,n\text{-}k)$ and obtained regressing the residuals on fitted values $\hat{u} = \lambda_0 + \lambda_1\hat{y} + \lambda_2\hat{y}^2 + \lambda_3\hat{y}^3$; ξ^3 is a homoskedasticity test, distributed $F(3,n\text{-}k)$, obtained regressing $\hat{u}^2 = \lambda_0 + \lambda_1\hat{y} + \lambda_2\hat{y}^2 + \lambda_3\hat{y}^3$. Restrictions are tested using the F-test. Standard errors are in parentheses. For the test of H_1, the critical value of $F(4,17)$ is 2.96 at the 5% confidence level. $T = 26$.

TABLE 2

COOLEY–LEROY TEST, SAMPLE 1958–1983

$$X_t = \alpha_0 + \sum_{i=1}^{\lambda} \alpha_i X_{t-1} + \theta Z_t + \sum_{j=1}^{\lambda} \beta_j Z_{t-j} \qquad \lambda = 4$$

X_t is predetermined if $\theta = 0$

X_t is strictly exogenous (in the C–L sense) if $\theta = 0$ and $\beta_j = 0$

	(5) M_0 on y	(6) M_2 on y	(7) y on M_0	(8) y on M_2
α_0	−1.32	−0.87	0.28	0.29
	(0.56)	(0.37)	(0.20)	(0.20)
α_1	1.24	1.29	1.24	0.97
	(0.27)	(0.24)	(0.19)	(0.25)
α_2	0.61	−0.06	−0.42	−0.03
	(0.43)	(0.38)	(0.30)	(0.34)
α_3	−0.11	−0.28	0.11	−0.04
	(0.40)	(0.37)	(0.26)	(0.27)
α_4	0.01	−0.23	−0.07	−0.04
	(0.25)	(0.23)	(0.15)	(0.16)
θ	1.12	1.26	0.17	0.30
	(0.69)	(0.41)	(0.07)	(0.10)
β_1	−0.75	0.15	−0.44	−0.58
	(1.09)	(0.71)	(0.09)	(0.13)
β_2	−0.14	−1.04	0.45	0.38
	(0.94)	(0.64)	(0.10)	(0.16)
β_3	0.50	0.02	−0.20	−0.20
	(0.73)	(0.55)	(0.12)	(0.18)
β_4	−0.15	0.28	0.16	0.22
	(0.46)	(0.32)	(0.07)	(0.10)
R^2	0.967	0.991	0.995	0.994
s	0.100	0.065	0.031	0.030
BJ(2)	2.99	0.23	0.18	3.01
LM1(1,15)	0.04	0.01	0.02	0.08
LM2(2,14)	1.71	2.04	1.69	2.65
$\xi^2(2,22)$	2.49	0.45	0.18	0.20
$\xi^3(2,22)$	1.21	0.85	0.57	0.59
$H_1: \theta = 0$	1.62	3.15	2.43	3.00
$H_2: \theta = 0; \beta_j = 0$	2.99	7.52	11.07	10.63

Note. The t-test was used for H_1 and the F-test for H_2. Critical values at the 5% level are $t(26) = 2.056$ and $F(5,16) = 2.85$. Also see notes to Table 1.

Granger test and predeterminedness (but not strict exogeneity in the Cooley–Leroy sense) is revealed, the income coefficients in equation (1) in Table 1 are quite big in their face value and seem to pick up a sort of cycle (as might reflect a control or adjustment rule), while in column (5), Table 2, the assumption of normality is very close to being rejected. We stress that these tests are not proper exogeneity tests; exogeneity can be tested only inside a well-defined simultaneous model, involving the specification of equations for each variable, and referring just to that particular model and the data series used (see, e.g., Engle et al. 1983). Nevertheless, our results do cast substantial doubt on whether M_0 or M_2 (especially the latter) could reasonably be viewed as exogenous.

As a second step, we carried out a less informal test of the hypotheses of income homogeneity, price homogeneity, nominal adjustment, and real adjustment, using a quite general specification of the money stock equation, in the form proposed by Hwang (1985).

According to Hwang, we can estimate the equation

$$m_t = \beta_0 + \beta_1 m_{t-1} + \beta_2(P_t - P_{t-1}) + \beta_3 y_t + \beta_4 P_t + \beta_5 R_t, \tag{1}$$

where all variables are in logs, and m is the real money stock, P is the retail sales price index, y is the real disposable income, and R is the nominal interest rate on 1-year saving deposits. We can then test the following linear restrictions upon the β_i's:

H_1:	nominal adjustment	$\beta_1 + \beta_2 = 0$
H_2:	real adjustment	$\beta_2 = 0$
H_3:	linear homogeneity in P	$\beta_4 = 0$
H_4:	linear homogeneity in y	$\beta_1 + \beta_3 = 1$

As a way to avoid the possibility that the lag coefficients were significant just because of the distinct temporal structure exhibited by both M_0 and M_2, we have first estimated

$$m_t = \beta_0 + \beta_1 m_{t-1} + \beta_2 y_t + \beta_3 y_{t-1} + \beta_4 P_t + \beta_5 P_{t-1} + \beta_6 R_t + \beta_7 R_{t-1} \tag{2}$$

then tested whether $\beta_3 = \beta_7 = 0$ (H_0) for M_0 and $\beta_3 = \beta_6 = 0$ (H_1) for M_2. H_0 is not rejected for M_0, while H_1 is rejected for M_2; in particular β_3 is different from zero.

According to the results in Table 3, we cannot reject the hypotheses of income homogeneity and price homogeneity with respect to M_0. For M_2, however, since we reject H_0: $\beta_3 = 0$, all four hypotheses are rejected against the more general model (2). Again, M_0 behaves in a manner more suitable to building simple, conventional models than does M_2. It is worth noting that we could not reject the hypotheses of real adjustment and price homogeneity

TABLE 3

HWANG TEST, SAMPLE 1955–1983

Coefficient	(1) $\hat{m}_0$	(2) $\hat{m}_0$	(3) $\hat{m}_2$	(4) $\hat{m}_2$
c	−2.07 (0.98)	−2.29 (0.49)	0.32 (0.66)	−1.16 (0.50)
m_{t-1}	0.42 (0.31)	0.35 (0.14)	1.17 (0.17)	0.79 (0.13)
y_t	0.81 (0.52)	0.73 (0.14)	1.46 (0.35)	0.50 (0.15)
y_{t-1}	−0.16 (0.78)		−1.51 (0.51)	
P_t	2.34 (0.74)	0.74 (0.44)	−0.07 (0.63)	−0.35 (0.41)
P_{t-1}	−1.75 (0.71)		−1.06 (0.52)	
ΔP		1.64 (0.52)		0.41 (0.54)
R_t	−0.17 (0.13)	−0.12 (0.06)	−0.21 (0.10)	−0.08 (0.10)
R_{t-1}	0.07 (0.14)		0.28 (0.09)	0.18 (0.10)
R^2	0.976	0.978	0.990	0.986
s	0.089	0.086	0.073	0.085
BJ(2)	1.86	0.97	0.50	0.09
$\xi^2(2,25)$	2.07	1.95	1.27	1.56
$\xi^3(2,25)$	2.15	3.03	1.03	3.66
LM1	0.30	0.58	2.08	0.40
LM2	0.20	0.31	1.01	0.80
CHOW ($T_1 = 15$; $T_2 = 14$)	2.44	2.03	2.56	2.73
F-tests				
H_1: nominal adjustment	5.01	16.03	8.11	5.66
H_2: real adjustment	3.15	9.96	4.68	0.57
H_3: P-homogeneity	0.94	2.80	4.80	0.74
H_4: y-homogeneity	0.56	1.08	16.16	14.82

Note. Diagnostics are as in Table 1. Restrictions are tested against each model using the F-test. OLS has been used for estimation. Standard errors are in parentheses. Critical F-values at the 5% confidence level are $F(2,21) = 3.47$, $F(3,21) = 3.07$, $F(4,21) = 2.84$ for column 1 and 3; $F(1,23) = 4.28$ and $F(2,23) = 3.42$ for column 2; $F(1,22) = 4.30$ and $F(2,22) = 3.44$ for column 4. $T = 29$.

conditional on $\beta_3 = 0$. This is a clear warning about imposing unwarranted restrictions on the lag structure of the variables, since we could end up with biased homogeneity tests and, in general, with models that are essentially not well defined.

The information collected from the tests above should then be used for the construction of a more general model, with the main purpose of questioning the degree of exogeneity of M_0 with respect to other major variables and the possibility of using M_0 as an instrument of economic policy.

A broader model should also take into account the disequilibria on the consumption goods market. In particular, when we estimate M_2, since households do not have any alternative investment to money balances and saving deposits, we are actually estimating a saving function, in a logarithmic form and under the implicit constraint

$$y_t = c_t + s_t$$

which implies equilibrium on the consumption market and no forced saving. The fact that $\Delta M_2 = y - c$ suggests that the causality tests are in fact picking up lagged consumption functions. It would seem that it only makes sense to have a monetary analysis within a macro model of consumption and production. Furthermore, as we discover in Section 4, the assumption of equilibrium on the consumption market should eventually be removed when dealing with a planned economy, without going to the other extreme by imposing the equally unwarranted constraint of continuous excess demand.

3. VIRTUAL PRICES

Our discussion of money in Section 2 did not explicitly model the possibility that with centrally controlled prices, the goods market might be in excess demand or excess supply at the aggregate level or in individual micro markets, and that the specification of money demand functions should be modified accordingly. Similarly, Chow (1985b) estimates a permanent income hypothesis without allowing for disequilibria of this kind. Feltenstein and Farhidian (1986; hereafter F–F) and Feltenstein et al. (1986; hereafter F–L–W) have sought to relax this assumption, the former in estimating the supply of and demand for money in China, the latter in estimating savings functions for the Chinese household sector.

F–F specify money supply and money demand equations and estimate them separately. In the latter, they suppose that prices are fixed exogenously and that if there are resulting aggregate-level disequilibria, there exists a "virtual price level" which causes consumers to hold voluntarily the amount of money they do actually hold given current official prices and possible shortages/surpluses.

Their chosen specification of this relationship is simply that the virtual price index stands in a constant log-linear relation to the official price index, so the inflation rate of the former is a constant multiple of the official inflation rate. In the course of estimating the modified demand for money function (adjusted for the virtual price level), this constant multiple is estimated by scanning over a grid of values to find that which maximizes the equation likelihood function. The result, on data from 1955–1981, was that the virtual rate of inflation was 2.5 times that of the official rate of inflation (the associated estimate of the true income elasticity of demand for real balances was 1.37).

The virtual price inflation rates so calculated are shown as FPI in Table 6, together with other indices of market tension—we shall discuss these jointly. Here we make only two points. First, whereas the F–F model includes a money supply equation in which wages and agricultural procurement payments (along with government deficits) determine the money supply—just as they form almost all of the income variable in the money demand equation—the equations are estimated separately, and results and simulations are discussed as if the government set the money supply exogenously. Second, the F–F specification, although perhaps necessarily crude, has the objectionable feature that it never permits that open inflation might eliminate excess demand. On the contrary, open inflation is in effect automatically magnified to show even more simultaneous repressed inflation, whereas one might expect the planners to change official prices in order to eliminate excess demand. Peebles (1986) draws this conclusion from his discussion of the association between official price changes and macroeconomic imbalances on the goods market.

This objection applies to the related work of F–L–W. They test various savings functions using a similar virtual price index to deflate nominal savings and then to include a real interest rate. The construction of the virtual price index is here backed by a theoretical derivation from an intertemporal model with goods rationing. The index derived relates the ratio of the virtual and actual price levels inversely to the velocity of money. Different estimates give different values for the elasticity, and we have chosen that from the equation which appears to give the best results on statistical criteria. The corresponding annual inflation rates are shown in Table 6 as WPI. The use of this index related to velocity as an indicator of tensions on the consumption goods market provides an appropriate transition to the final section of this paper.

4. THE CONSUMPTION GOODS MARKET

The theory and measurement of macroeconomic disequilibrium in CPEs, with primary attention to the consumption goods market, are surveyed in Portes (1986). Our own approach, applied to the East European economies, is set out in several papers cited individually in the references. Despite the caution of Peebles (1983), we thought it worthwhile using similar techniques on the Chinese data now available, simply to see whether one could establish empirical regularities and obtain results not obviously inconsistent with prior information.

Portes and Winter (1980; hereafter P–W) estimated a "canonical" disequilibrium model (Quandt, 1982), without a price or plan adjustment equation, for the consumption goods markets of four East European CPEs. There are equations representing the aggregate demand for and supply of consumption goods as well as the "minimum condition" requiring that actual consumption equal the minimum of supply and demand. The demand function was a simple transformation of the Houthakker–Taylor savings function; the supply function was a somewhat ad hoc representation of planners' behavior, justified from the CPE literature. The three equations are estimated jointly using maximum likelihood methods. The particular specifications are discussed extensively in P–W and other references cited, and we shall simply state them below, without wishing to defend them with excessive vigor. Note that although plan variables play an important role in our analysis, we do not have independent data on plans in China, like those used by Portes et al. (1987) for Poland, so we cannot add a plan adjustment equation like theirs, and we must use a constructed series for plan variables as in the original P–W paper.

Following criticism by Kornai (1980, 1982) of any such aggregative macroeconometric work on CPEs, in which both "shortages and slacks" (excess demands and supplies) might coexist at the micro level, Burkett (1987) sought to implement Kornai's implied research proposal. P–W had themselves anticipated the criticism with a heuristic "smoothing by aggregation" argument, but Burkett rightly recognized that this had to be tested empirically against Kornai's assertion. He developed an ingenious method to take account of simultaneous micro-level excess demands and supplies while using aggregate data, rather than going to the explicit submarkets model, as we may do in future work (Martin, 1986). Burkett applied his method to the East European countries studied by Portes and associates, using the same specification of demand and supply function for consumption goods. The model arrives at a simple equation with an additive error term,

$$C = (1/2)(\alpha x + \beta y) - (1/2)[(\alpha x - \beta y)^2 4\gamma^2(\alpha x)(\beta y)]^{1/2} + u \qquad (3)$$

where for our purposes here we may write

$$CD = \alpha x = a_1 S1 + \alpha_2 DYD + \alpha_3 YD1 \qquad (4)$$

$$CS = \beta y = \beta_1 CT + B_2 CYX + \beta_2 RNFA + \beta_4 IFX \qquad (5)$$

The variables are defined as follows: C = observed consumption; CD = household desired expenditure on consumption goods and services in the current period; CS = supply of consumption goods and services in the current period; $S1$ = household saving in the previous period; DYD = change in disposable income, previous to current period; YD1 = disposable income in the previous period; CT = fitted second-order exponential time trend in C; CYX = (CT/NMPT) (NMP-NMPT); NMPT = fitted second-order exponential time trend in national income; RNFA = deviation of household net financial assets from second-order exponential time trend; IFX = (IT/NMPT) (NMP-NMPT); IT = fitted second-order exponential time trend in investment.

Burkett estimates the single Eq. (3) with the minor modification that his representation of βy = CS omits the fourth term. In Burkett's model, it can

TABLE 4

PORTES–WINTER MODEL, 1954–1983

$$CD = \alpha_1 S1 + \alpha_2 DYD + \alpha_3 YD1 + u_1$$

$$CS = \beta_1 CT + \beta_2 CYX + \beta_3 RNFA + \beta_4 IFX + u_2$$

$$C = \min(CD, CS)$$

	(1) Unconstr.	(2) $\alpha_3 = 1$	(3) $\beta_1 = 1$	(4) $\alpha_3, \beta_1 = 1$
a_1	−0.6685 (0.081)	−0.5796 (0.088)	−0.6282 (0.097)	−0.3105 (0.189)
a_2	0.6582 (0.0357)	0.7252 (0.035)	0.5790 (0.0409)	0.8271 (0.068)
a_3	1.0119 (0.0039)	1.000	1.0208 (0.0049)	1.000
s_1	1.143 (0.092)	1.239 (0.098)	0.946 (0.095)	1.129 (0.111)
b_1	1.0501 (0.005)	1.0505 (0.006)	1.000	1.000
b_2	0.2003 (0.040)	0.1993 (0.039)	0.3261 (0.112)	0.2075 (0.094)
b_3	0.2840 (0.046)	0.2815 (0.047)	0.6176 (0.105)	0.7252 (0.088)
b_4	−0.3923 (0.043)	−0.3920 (0.043)	−0.5601 (0.122)	−0.4750 (0.136)
s_2	0.805 (0.118)	0.812 (0.117)	1.895 (0.218)	1.907 (0.192)
Log L	−46.40	−50.68	−59.27	−64.53

Note. Numbers in parentheses beneath parameter estimates are asymptotic standard errors. s_1 and s_2 are the equation standard errors. GQOPT (Goldfeld–Quandt) is used for estimation. Optimum is reached in all models.

be shown that a test of the hypothesis that $\gamma = 0$ is a test of the aggregative discrete switching model used by P–W, which can be written

$$CD = \alpha x + u_1 \tag{6}$$

$$CS = \beta y + u_2 \tag{7}$$

$$C = \min (CD, CS). \tag{8}$$

We have estimated both the P–W and the Burkett models for China over the period 1954–1983. The results are shown in Tables 4 and 5. They appear to be remarkably good. All estimated coefficients satisfy the a priori sign restrictions (and lie in prescribed intervals, where required), and they are quite well determined. In each case, we report estimates with and without the constraint $\beta_1 = 1$; this was imposed by Portes et al. (1987) but not by Burkett. We also report estimates with the constraint $\alpha_3 = 1$, imposed by Burkett but not by Portes et al.; and with both coefficients constrained. On the whole, likelihood ratio tests reject the restriction $\beta_1 = 1$ and accept $\alpha_3 = 1$; but some other features of the constrained estimates are preferable. The implied household and planners' behavior is reasonable and very similar to that shown in the earlier work on Eastern Europe. Moreover, in the Burkett test of P–W, the estimated γ is tiny and insignificantly different from zero, so that we can accept the P–W discrete switching model. Its coefficient estimates are in fact quite close to those found with the Burkett technique.[2]

So much for the technical background. The economically interesting output is in Table 6. Here we find comparisons of various indicators of tension on the consumption goods market: the official rate of inflation PI, the F–F virtual price rate of inflation FPI, the F–L–W virtual price rate of inflation WPI, Burkett's index of relative shortage BSH, and the P–W index of percentage excess demand PWXD. We have added for comparison the index of percentage shortage calculated by Naughton (1986), using quite different methods and data.

Recall that Burkett's index BSH measures the shortage only, without netting out slack, and is therefore nonnegative by definition. In that light, the only apparent inconsistencies between BSH and the P–W index of excess demand appear in 1963 and possibly 1965–1986 and 1972–1973; in 1963, the P–W estimates show excess supply and the Burkett index shows shortage, while in

---

[2] Burkett's equation relies on a very specific form for the excess demand/supply relationship. Proper tests of the functional form would be ideal. It should be possible to construct a score test for this purpose, treating tests of the restrictions on the coefficients as tests of omitted variables. It should also be possible to devise score tests for the nonlinear models and test for normality, serial correlation, and heteroskedasticity in both the Burkett model and the Portes–Winter model. However, the limited number of observations could represent a partial problem, since these tests tend to be far too large in small samples, giving massive over-rejection. Still, it might be useful to try them.

TABLE 5

BURKETT MODEL, 1954–1983

Estimated equation:

$$c = \frac{(\alpha x + \beta y)}{2} - \frac{1}{2}[(\alpha x - \beta y)^2 + 4\gamma^2(\alpha x)(\beta y)]^{(1/2)} + u$$

$$\alpha = (\alpha_1, \alpha_2, \alpha_3)$$

$$x = (S1, DYD, YD1)$$

$$\beta = (\beta_1, \beta_2, \beta_3, \beta_4)$$

$$y = (CT, CYX, RNFA, IFX)$$

	(1) Unconstrained	(2) $\alpha_3 = 1$	(3) $\beta_1 = 1$	(4) $\alpha_3, \beta_1 = 1$
a_1	−0.6302 (0.072)	−0.5511 (0.059)	−0.9053 (0.060)	−0.4200 (0.313)
a_2	0.6576 (0.032)	0.7111 (0.030)	0.6566 (0.052)	0.7251 (0.072)
a_3	1.0096 (0.003)	1.000	1.0170 (0.001)	1.000
b_1	1.0493 (0.004)	1.0481 (0.007)	1.000	1.000
b_2	0.2548 (0.073)	0.2227 (0.036)	0.3301 (0.066)	0.2942 (0.088)
b_3	0.2541 (0.059)	0.2778 (0.064)	0.6118 (0.063)	0.6332 (0.076)
b_4	−0.4168 (0.034)	−0.3632 (0.047)	−0.4567 (0.036)	−0.4663 (0.088)
g	0.4×10^{-8} (0.000)	0.4×10^{-5} (0.001)	0.1×10^{-5} (0.001)	0.3×10^{-11} (0.003)
Log L	−45.24	−49.38	−65.90	−67.08

Note. Numbers in parentheses beneath parameter estimates are asymptotic standard errors. GQOPT (Goldfeld–Quandt) is used for estimation. For Models 1 and 2, we approach convergence (the optimum is approximated but not reached); for Model 3, the gradient of α_3 differs from zero; for Model 4, the optimum is reached.

the other periods, P–W show excess demand and Burkett shows no shortages. Lest it be thought that P–W or Burkett tend systematically to underestimate excess demand, note that Naughton shows much more excess supply than either.

TABLE 6

PRICES AND EXCESS DEMAND

Year	PI	FPI	WPI	PWXD	BSH	NSI
1955	1.1	0.8	5.8	−1.7	0.0	n.a.
1956	0.0	−0.2	38.1	4.2	2.7	2.6
1957	1.5	6.6	4.1	2.8	1.9	−12.1
1958	0.2	−2.7	54.3	8.1	5.6	−2.9
1959	0.9	0.8	2.0	−0.3	0.0	−8.3
1960	3.0	6.5	13.7	2.5	0.6	9.2
1961	16.2	45.4	69.5	−2.6	0.0	3.6
1962	3.8	9.8	−29.4	−4.3	0.0	−7.0
1963	−5.9	−14.2	−19.7	−1.1	0.6	−3.4
1964	−3.7	−9.0	−11.7	0.7	1.0	−3.6
1965	−2.6	−3.0	20.3	0.6	0.0	−3.6
1966	−0.2	−3.0	13.2	0.9	0.0	−3.6
1967	−0.7	−1.6	1.3	1.0	0.9	2.9
1968	0.0	0.2	25.6	−1.9	0.0	−2.7
1969	−1.1	2.4	−10.9	−2.2	0.0	0.3
1970	−0.2	0.0	−15.1	0.6	0.0	−7.7
1971	−0.7	−0.2	8.5	2.0	0.7	−7.0
1972	−0.2	0.4	5.5	1.1	0.0	−2.1
1973	0.6	0.2	8.1	1.4	0.0	−7.1
1974	0.5	1.6	6.5	0.0	0.0	−3.0
1975	0.1	1.1	−2.8	−0.7	0.0	−3.4
1976	0.3	0.7	7.6	2.3	2.0	0.8
1977	2.0	6.9	−2.4	−4.5	0.0	−7.7
1978	0.7	1.7	8.3	−1.8	0.0	−8.6
1979	2.0	4.7	23.4	0.8	0.0	n.a.
1980	6.0	19.9	31.4	7.2	4.5	n.a.
1981	2.4	6.4	22.7	3.7	2.7	n.a.
1982	1.9	5.2	23.5	5.5	4.2	n.a.
1983	1.5	5.1	21.7	5.1	3.5	n.a.

Note. PI = percentage change of official price index. FPI = percentage change of virtual consumer price index proposed by Feltenstein and Farhidian (1987). WPI = percentage change of virtual consumer price index proposed by Feltenstein et al. (1986) calculated according to the estimates of equation (c), page 26 of their paper. PWXD = Portes and Winter (1980) percentage of excess demand $[100(\hat{C}D - \hat{C}S)/C]$, from Model 4 estimated in Table 4 (α_3 and β_1 constrained). BSH = Burkett (1987) index of relative shortage $[100(\hat{C}D - \hat{C})/\hat{C}]$, from Model 4 estimated in Table 5 (α_3 and β_1 constrained). NSI = Naughton (1986) index of percentage shortage (column 4 of his Table III-2, p. 109). n.a. = not available.

Thus the picture these measures give is fairly consistent. It suggests excess demand in 1956–1958, 1960, 1964, 1967, 1971, 1976, and 1980–1983. There is a clear relation with the Great Leap Forward, the Cultural Revolution, the stormy year of Mao's death, and the economic reforms. The price indices are much more erratic. One must conjecture that in years like 1961–1962, for example, the open inflation was sufficient to eliminate excess demand within the period. Conversely, in 1964 deflation may have created excess demand. In any case, *none* of these indices suggests that excess demand dominated the entire period—and *all* suggest significant excess demand under the recent reforms.

DATA APPENDIX

Data from the *Statistical Yearbook of China, 1984* (English edition):

net material product (current prices), p. 29

personal consumption (current prices), p. 33

investment in fixed assets (capital construction) from state-owned units, p. 301

retail price index, p. 425

Saving deposits and currency are from Byrd (1983) and the *Statistical Yearbook.*

The chosen rate of interest is the 1-year saving deposit interest rate, taken from Hsiao (1971), from Byrd (1983), and, for recent years, from the BBC bulletin *Summary of World Broadcasts,* Part 3, The Far East.

M_0 is equal to currency.

M_2 is equal to currency plus personal savings deposits.

Disposable income (at current prices) has been constructed adding current year changes in net financial assets to personal consumption. Real income is this series deflated by retail price index.

REFERENCES

Bortolani, Sergio, and Anita Santorum, *Moneta e banca in Cina.* Milano: Finafrica, 1984.

Burkett, John, "Slack, Shortage and Discouraged Consumers in Eastern Europe: Estimates Based on Smoothing by Aggregation." *Rev. Econ. Studies,* forthcoming, 1987.

Byrd, William, *China's Financial System.* Boulder, CO: Westview Press, 1983.

Chow, Gregory, *The Chinese Economy.* New York: Harper & Row, 1985a.

Chow, Gregory, "A Model of Chinese National Income Determination." *J. Polit. Econ.* **93,** 782–92, 1985b.

Chow, Gregory, "Money and Price Level Determination in China." *J. Comp. Econ.* **11,** 319–333, 1987.

Cooley, T. F., and Leroy, S. F., "Atheoretical Macroeconomics." *J. Monet. Econ.* **16,** 283–308, 1985.

de Wulf, Luc, and Goldsbrough, David, "The Evolving Role of Monetary Policy in China." *IMF Staff Papers* **33,** 209–42, 1986.

Engle, Robert F., Hendry, David F., and Richard, Jean-Francois, "Exogeneity." *Econometrica* **51,** 277–304, 1983.

Feltenstein, Andrew, and Farhidian, Z., "Fiscal Policy, Monetary Targets and the Price Level in a Centrally Planned Economy: An Application to the Case of China." *J. Money, Credit, Banking* **19,** 137–156, 1987.

Feltenstein, Andrew, Lebow, D., and van Wijnbergen, Sweder, "Savings, Commodity Market Rationing and the Real Rate of Interest in China." CPD discussion paper No. 1986-27, World Bank, 1986.

Granger, C. W. J., "Investigating Causal Relations by Econometric Models and Cross Spectral Methods." *Econometrica* **37**, 424–438, 1969.

Hsiao, Katherine H., *Money and Monetary Policy in Communist China.* New York: Columbia Univ. Press, 1971.

Hwang, Haeshin, "Test of the Adjustment Process and Linear Homogeneity in a Stock Adjustment Model of Money Demand." *Rev. Econ. Stat.* **67**, 689–692, 1985.

Kornai, Janos, *The Economics of Shortage.* Amsterdam: North-Holland, 1980.

Kornai, Janos, *Growth, Shortage and Efficiency.* Berkeley: Univ. of California Press, 1982.

Martin, Chris, "General Linear Rationing Models." Birkbeck discussion paper No. 184, 1986.

Naughton, Barry J., "Saving and Investment in China: A Macroeconomic Analysis." PhD dissertation, Yale University, 1986.

Peebles, Gavin, "Inflation, Money and Banking in China: In Support of the Purchasing Power Approach." *ACES Bull.* **25**, 2:81–103, 1983.

Peebles, Gavin, "Aggregate Retail Price Changes in Socialist Economies: Identification, Theory and Evidence for China and Soviet Union." *Soviet Studies* **38**, 477–503, 1986.

People's Bank of China, *Survey of Banking* (Jinrong Goikuang). Beijing: China's Banking Publishing House, 1983.

Portes, Richard, "Central Planning and Monetarism: Fellow Travellers?" In P. Desai, Ed., *Marxism, Central Planning and the Soviet Economy.* Cambridge, MA: MIT Press, 149–65, 1983.

Portes, Richard, "The Theory and Measurement of Macroeconomic Disequilibrium in Centrally Planned Economies." Centre for Economic Policy Research discussion paper No. 91, 1986.

Portes, Richard, and Winter, David, "The Demand for Money and for Consumption Goods in Centrally Planned Economies." *Rev. Econ. Stat.* **60**, 8–18, 1978.

Portes, Richard, and Winter, David, "Disequilibrium Estimates for Consumption Goods Markets in Centrally Planned Economies." *Rev. Econ. Studies* **47**, 137–159, 1980.

Portes, Richard, Quandt, Richard, Winter, David, and Yeo, Stephen, "Macroeconomic Planning and Disequilibrium: Estimates for Poland, 1955–80." *Econometrica* **55**, 19–41, 1987.

Quandt, Richard, "Econometric Disequilibrium Models." *Econ. Rev.* **1**, 1–63, 1982.

Spanos, Aris, *Statistical Foundations of Econometric Modelling.* Cambridge: Cambridge Univ. Press, 1986.

JOURNAL OF COMPARATIVE ECONOMICS 11, 372–384 (1987)

Issues in the Structural Reform of Chinese Agriculture[1]

THOMAS B. WIENS

The World Bank, Washington, D.C. 20433

Wiens, Thomas, B.—Issues in the Structural Reform of Chinese Agriculture

Starting in 1979, China carried out a structural reform of rural institutions which led to greatly increased farm production and income. A second stage of reforms is intended to lead to a market-oriented farm economy. However, urgent problems of both a transitional and long-term nature still require attention. The author gives his views on the remaining problems and the directions of reforms in output, price, tax, and legal structure required to complete the transition. *J. Comp. Econ.,* September 1987, **11**(3), pp. 372–384. The World Bank, Washington, D.C. 20433 © 1987 Academic Press, Inc.

Journal of Economic Literature Classification Numbers: 124, 713, 715.

The series of reforms in the agricultural sector between 1979 and 1985 was so comprehensive and successful in increasing production and marketing that many observers in China and abroad have regarded the rural reform process as essentially complete, and turned attention to the problems of urban and industrial reform. However, problems which emerged in 1985–1986 suggest that the rural reforms remain incomplete and failure to follow through is leading, not merely to a slowdown in agricultural growth rates (which is inevitable) but also to instability or declines which may erase some of the progress made to date. This paper will briefly review the achievements of rural reform in the 1979–1985 period, as well as the new problems which have emerged, and discuss the structural issues which must be resolved if the Chinese government is to maintain the role of the agricultural sector in sustaining or promoting economic growth.

RURAL REFORMS, 1979–1986

Beginning with experimental abolition of collective farming in the more impoverished areas, the Chinese Government has moved swiftly since 1979

---

[1] The views, findings, interpretations, and conclusions set forth in this paper are those of the author and should not be attributed to the World Bank or to its affiliated institutions. Statistical information cited is derived from the yearbooks of China's State Statistical Bureau.

CHINESE ECONOMIC REFORM

to implement a comprehensive restructuring of rural institutions. The reforms, a major feature of which is implementation of the "production responsibility system" (PRS), were designed to improve incentives and management at all levels of the rural economy. By 1983 the farm household had become the fundamental unit of management and production in the agricultural sector, within a framework of collective or state ownership of land and major fixed assets. The process of reform was then directed at reinforcing the new structure, dismantling redundant collective institutions, and facilitating a higher degree of commercialization and specialization.

The PRS is based on a system of contractual relationships which define the rights and responsibilities of owners (state, collective, or private) and managers of assets. The contract system is also applied to define vendor–consumer or supplier–producer relationships. It is intended to provide scope for increased, albeit constrained, independence of decision making and encourage relationships based on negotiation rather than administrative fiat. A wide variety of contractual forms have been tried, and in agriculture one system has become nearly universal: *bao gan dao hu* (BGDH). Loosely translated, this means "contracting all actions to the household." In BGDH, management of collectively owned land was contracted to households, usually in proportion to household size or labor force. Other collective assets were divided up, sold, or contracted to individuals or groups willing to manage them. The household was obligated to pay taxes, make contributions to collective welfare funds, provide its share of state procurement requirements, and contribute labor to maintain or construct public infrastructure. All remaining output could be retained by the household.

Reform of the farm price structure to provide higher incomes and greater incentives for production, and reduce the need for administrative control over production decisions, was a precondition for success of the PRS. A major price adjustment in 1979 increased average procurement prices by about 25% for grains, 40% for oilseeds, 17% for cotton, and 37% for pigs; and created a differentiated procurement price system whereby price premiums (50% for grain and oilseeds, 20% for bast fibers, and 30% for cotton) were offered for production in excess of quotas, and all minor products and a growing proportion of major products were procured at negotiated prices pegged at close to free market price levels. The scope of permissible free market activities was simultaneously enlarged.

A further series of reforms beginning in 1984 enlarged the scope of private activities in procurement, transport, and marketing of agricultural products, specifically allowing licensed merchants to cross county and provincial lines in their marketing of most agricultural products, including livestock, aquatic products, and processed foods. Private or joint investment in capital goods, such as trucks and tractors, has been encouraged and has grown rapidly. It has been recognized that development of the rural commercial and service sector required legalization of individually or jointly owned enterprises, and access to official as well as private sources of loan capital. As part of the trend toward a reduced role for administrative bodies in economic management, higher level institutions are also undergoing restructuring. The commune has been transformed into the township (*xiang*) and the brigade into the village (*cun*), with their economic roles confined largely to fostering township and village enterprises (TVEs; formerly commune and brigade enterprises).

A major objective of the policy reforms is to encourage specialization and commercialization, thereby reversing the past self-sufficiency orientation of Chinese collective agriculture. This ultimately requires markets in labor, land, and other inputs, and outputs. One precondition for input market development was establishment of lengthy land tenure under the PRS system; at present, land contracts typically provide 15 years of tenure. To encourage labor mobility, farmers are now allowed to hire labor at negotiated wage rates and to surrender or subcontract land use rights in order to engage in off-farm activities. While outmigration to major cities and towns is still highly restricted, rural market towns are encouraged to develop into centers of commerce and services through absorption of surplus labor.

A means of mobilizing growing rural private savings was also necessary. Reforms of the rural financial system have raised interest rates on deposits and loans from Agricultural Bank of China (ABC) and the Rural Credit Co-operatives (RCC) to more reasonable levels. RCCs are supposed to have some freedom to set their own deposit and loan rates according to local investment opportunities, although implementation of this reform has lagged. The formation of private credit societies and the resumption of private moneylending, a spontaneous development, has received official blessing.

A series of good harvests, climaxed by an extraordinary record harvest of grain, cotton, and most other crops in 1984 provided convincing proof of the efficacy of these policies. The 1984 harvest also brought a new problem—the management of surpluses, which in turn stimulated a "second stage" of reform. Marketing increased faster than the harvest, partly because on-farm storage was saturated, and a declining free market price differential had reduced the incentive for farmers to hold stocks. As a result, the government procured some 20–30 million tons more grain than necessary to meet urban, industrial, export, and strategic reserve requirements. Surpluses of cotton similarily turned China from major importer to major exporter.

The intention of the second stage of reforms is to gradually remove most administrative control over procurement of agricultural products, and replace it with a market-oriented agricultural sector subject mainly to indirect control via the price, tax, and credit instruments. The quota procurement system seemed no longer necessary in an era of surpluses, hence quotas were replaced by contracts between farmers and procurement agencies. Contract prices were fixed by the government; for grain and cotton at weighted averages of existing quota and above-quota prices. For these crops, this involved a reduction in the marginal producer price and in some areas a reduction in average price as well. For meat, fruit, and vegetables, official procurement prices were significantly increased. By the end of 1985, grain, meat, fish, fruit, and vegetables, as well as most other farm products, were all brought within the scope of products which could be freely marketed, provided that contractual obligations were first fulfilled. Urban free markets in these products were legitimized and encouraged to grow; and farmers took advantage of their new freedom to market individually or through private middlemen to the urban areas. At the same time, state retail prices of meat, fruit, and vegetables were increased to levels approaching urban free market levels, and state commercial organs generally reduced their role in distribution of all but a few key farm products.

TRANSITIONAL PROBLEMS

A number of problems emerged in 1985–1986, many transitional in nature. They are partly attributable to uncoordinated or poorly sequenced planning, uneven implementation, inexperience with market behavior, the contradictions implicit in a dualistic (administrative and market) distribution system, the extent of initial disequilibrium, lack of adequate commercial infrastructure, etc. In origin, they are similar to problems accompanying the industrial and urban reforms.

For example, the new grain procurement system has not yet been put into place; in 1985 sales obligations were distributed with as little regard for the principle of voluntarism as under the old quota system (Gao et al., 1986) and a dual price system reemerged as procurement organs sought extra grain to meet their targets. Grain production fell by 7% in 1985 and in 1986 will not match the 1984 peak level. About 40% of the decline was attributable mainly to poor weather in the northeast, and most of the remainder to reduced crop area nationwide (down 3.5%). Among the contributing factors were the reduced marginal price of grain, especially relative to other farm products, the declared intention of state procurement organs to cut procurements by about 10 million tons, and strong official encouragement for other uses of farmland. Actual procurement declined by about 17 million tons. The brunt of reductions in production and procurement fell on feedgrains such as corn, which was most affected by bad weather.

In May 1985, too late to influence the following year's feed supply, the procurement prices of livestock products were increased by an average of 24%, and retail prices of meat raised in comparable measure. Short-run supply and demand both proved substantially price-elastic, and, in 1986, as excess supplies accumulated in frozen storage, the demand for feed continued to rise. However, the feed ingredients weren't there: not only had 1985 production declined, but northern provinces were exporting all they could procure (while

banning sales to their neighbors) in response to their newly granted freedom
of action in foreign trade. Market prices of feed in 1986 rose by 35% or more
while prices of finished pigs and other livestock products were dropping and
official procurements all but ceased. By mid-1986, a full-fledged "hog cycle"
had begun its downturn, and the consequence will be a (probably severe)
decline in meat production in 1987 (*NMRB* June 3 and July 8, 1986; *ZGSYB*
May 15, 1986).

The developing "hog cycle" is only one manifestation of a more general
problem of market saturation. Before 1980, agricultural planning was dominated by a shortage mentality which reflected scarcity of virtually every significant product relative to potential consumer demand. However, in 1978–
1985 net income from farm sales has been growing at a rate (20.6%) much
higher than the growth of urban and industrial wage income (13.7%), a phenomenon which cannot last, in view of Engel's Law. Following the post-1979
expansion of acreage in cash crops, short-run market saturation has been
approached or reached in most major food and industrial crops. Following
the record 1984 grain harvest and the decrease in official grain procurements
beginning in 1985, farmers have found it necessary to reduce grain sown area
and shift into other crops. Because industrial crops occupy only a small percentage of total crop area and only a few of them have significant unsatisfied
demand, relatively small reductions of grain acreage are leveraged into huge
percentage changes in output of other crops: in 1985, a 7% reduction in grain
production resulted in increased production of oilseeds, sugar cane, bast fibers,
and tobacco of 33, 30, 128, and 35%, respectively. As a result, it is increasingly
difficult to identify primary agricultural products for which demand, at current
levels of income and industrial development, remains unsaturated; or for
which profitable export potential exists.

In an economic environment in which decentralized farm management
had led to high price elasticities of *relative* supply and excess demand is difficult
to identify, administrative pricing and procurement have become increasingly
cumbersome instruments. Price and procurement administration tends to be
paralyzed for long periods by its attempt to serve three masters—producer
and consumer interests, and the government budget—and then to overreact.
Although some may be tempted to conclude from the current instability of
agricultural markets in China that decontrol is a mistake, the lesson may be
that, on the contrary, the process should be speeded up. The most desirable
measure would be to further reduce the government's role in procurement
and distribution, which, for grain, cotton, oilseeds, and pigs, still overwhelms
the free market. Of course, in order to stabilize prices and procurement volumes, it is important to enlarge the flow of market information to producers,
and to thoroughly implement a genuine contract system, that is, one in which
official procurement quantities are set in advance by signed contracts, at prices
which afford little or no rent to contractees—i.e., are at par with (free) market

levels. It is also essential to eliminate the growing interference by local government with market mechanisms (*RMRB* Oct. 4, 1986).

EQUILIBRIUM OUTPUT AND PRICE STRUCTURE

If the issues discussed above are largely transitional problems, other unresolved long-term structural problems exist, i.e., questions of where to go rather than how to get there. In view of the lack of a general supply–demand gap for agricultural products in the cities and the extent of competition in the international market, further growth in Chinese agriculture must be sustained more by quality improvement than by increased quantity. Product standardization, quality improvement, product preservation, packaging and labeling, and advertising are virgin territories for Chinese agriculture, and will require significant investments. If improvements are made, then it would be possible to tap significant unfulfilled demand for high quality and/or specialty products in the cities, and enlarge China's share of international markets, which is now weak even in markets like Hong Kong where China has a comparative geographical advantage (Zhou, 1986).

Excess demand for foodstuffs and other agricultural products may still be found in the rural market, which has been neglected in the past because it was believed that on-farm consumption was usually self-supplied, and only the surplus over family requirements was marketed; and that rural demand for commercial commodities was limited by lack of cash income, as well as the poor commodity distribution system in the rural areas. However, the changing characteristics of the rural market deserve attention. Consumption of purchased goods and services by farmers has been rising at 23% per year since 1978. Cash food expenditures have risen at almost the same rate and, as a percentage of total food expenditures, increased from 24% in 1978 to 42% in 1985. Consumer demands for agricultural products in this market are now served mainly by local production; and there are likely to be large localized gaps between supply and demand which could be exploited if long distance trade were further developed. Aside from the farming population, the non-farm proportion of the rural (township and village) labor force has risen to 18%; not to mention the rapid growth of the population in market towns. In short, the search for markets for agricultural produce should not end with the international and urban markets.

Grain. Because the income elasticities of demand for food grains and edible oils tend to be lower than for other agricultural products, it is obvious that growth rates of production for these crops should be slower, but how much slower and from what base level are significant long-term policy questions. It had been assumed by planners that grain area would be roughly stable at slightly less than 80% of total sown area in the future, and that further adjustments in industrial crop areas would be marginal and have little impact on overall land use. However, grain area fell to 76% in 1985 and it was feared that relaxed administrative controls would result in a further decline. Most commentators at present argue for a long-term target of 400–440 kg/capita (unprocessed grain-equivalent), requiring an annual growth rate of 1.6–2.2% over a 1985 base of 379 million tons (World Bank, 1985).

Although the long-term target is reasonable, whether viewed from the supply or demand sides, most commentators in China fail to note the distinction between direct and indirect grain consumption, or (mainly) between food and feed grain (e.g., Wu, 1986). If one takes Government targets for population and per capita incomes in the year 2000 as a base for projections, and considers what the Chinese population is likely to demand in the way of direct grain consumption at that time, it emerges that the target per capita consumption of fine grain (rice and wheat) in the year 2000 should be slightly less than the amount produced per capita in 1980–1982 (146 kg of unprocessed grain); and total direct consumption should be close to the average of production in 1983–1984 (World Bank, 1985). Only with significantly slower growth of per capita incomes or higher growth of population would direct consumption of fine grains increase, and then by only about 8% over the 1984 level of production. In short, China's *food grain* production is not low by international levels, but its *feed grain* is, and only production of the latter needs to be further enlarged for domestic purposes.

Both the long- and short-term trends in China have been for the proportion of food grains (e.g., rice and wheat) to *increase,* rather than decline (from 53% in 1952, to 57% in 1957, 62% in 1979, and 65% in 1984) as they should; and, lately, for corn and soybean to be exported. Failure (until mid-1985) to properly adjust livestock product procurement prices (or abandon state control over livestock procurement) accounts for part of the problem; the concentration of state procurement organs on food grains another part. The present high free market prices for livestock feeds might help solve this problem, except for the fact that high procurement targets leave little surplus grain to flow into market channels.

Price distortions. These lie at the root of most economic problems in rural, not to mention urban China. In view of their pervasiveness throughout the economy, it is difficult to isolate prices for one or a few commodities and specify even the direction of change on the road to a market equilibrium. Matters are complicated by the existence of multiple prices for each commodity. The two most useful benchmarks—international market and domestic free market prices—are also problematic. For comparison with domestic prices, international prices must be converted to domestic currency through an exchange rate which itself is a disequilibrium rate. The results of comparisons can depend significantly on whether a commodity is viewed as a potential import or export (a switch may occur on the "road to equilibrium"). China's existing or potential role in the international markets for many agricultural commodities is too large to regard her as a price taker (e.g., rice or cotton). Finally, the domestic free market is small, fragmented, and highly influenced by distortions in administered prices as well as government procurement practices.

Taking into account these caveats, it nevertheless appears that contract (official procurement) prices for grain and probably oilseed crops are too low relative to other crops, and farm products on the whole are underpriced relative to industrial products; and this situation has deteriorated in the last few years. The evidence includes: (a) border prices[2] are presently higher than domestic farm gate prices (average of contract, negotiated, and free market prices) by about 60–70% for wheat or maize, 30–45% for rice and soybean, and 90% for groundnuts, but the relationship is narrower or the reverse for most other farm products. If the yuan remains overvalued at Y3.7:US$1, as seems likely, the difference net of distortions would be even wider. In contrast, fertilizer prices are now close to parity with border prices.

(b) A huge gap (80–85%) still remains between free market prices and official retail prices of grain and oilseeds, although the gap has narrowed slightly in the 1980s; the gap is much smaller (20–30%) for most other farm products.

(c) Farm surveys indicate little enthusiasm for farming, relative to non-farm or off-farm activities, and less for grain cropping; in areas where farmers have real alternatives, local governments are increasingly using taxes or profits from non-farm activities to subsidize grain production (e.g., added price subsidies). It is well-established that grain is less profitable than most other crops (Shi, 1986; Wu, 1986).

The fundamental obstacle to further price adjustment in the direction of a market equilibrium is that grain and edible oils are still sold under rationing at prices well below procurement cost; thus the burden of subsidizing urban consumers is still partly borne by the farmer, and further increases in procurement prices would shift it either to the state budget, urban consumers, or industrial profits—measures which are regarded by the government as financially or politically unacceptable. To indicate why, assume that, with no subsidies or forced procurements, a 55% increase in contract procurement prices of grains and oilseeds would be required: at present net procurement levels,[3] this would add about Y17 billion to present total direct price subsidies in China of Y37 billion (1984). This may be compared with total government expenditures of Y154 billion, and central government expenditures of Y73 billion (1984); or total non-farm consumption expenditure of Y151 billion (1985).

---

[2] International prices adjusted for costs of transport, processing, and quality differences to permit comparison with farm gate prices.
[3] Ignoring increased costs on grain resold in the rural areas, which presumably would be passed through to consumers.

Land tax. It has been recognized by some researchers in China that the needed price adjustment could only be politically acceptable if costs were largely borne by the farmers, through offsetting taxes or rents paid to government (Song, 1986). The level of direct taxation in Chinese agriculture is exceptionally low (about 3% of gross income, and 1.9% of government revenues). Moreover, even though the land is owned by collectives or the state, no rent or land use fees are directly collected on land cultivated to annual crops. At current crop prices, payment of a full economic land rent would leave too little net income to the farmer; yet in the absence of such rent, efficient land use practices and factor mobility are impeded (see below). Selective price increases coupled with increased taxes or land use fees (and elimination of various farm input subsidies) could boost marginal incentives without immediately increasing farm incomes, if the taxes or fees were to be fixed in value like the current agricultural tax. However, the program should be implemented so as to somewhat improve the incomes of farmers, and especially grain growers, relative to rural residents in non-farm or off-farm activities.

ALLOCATIVE EFFICIENCY

Specialization. The PRS has led to the resurrection of a "small-farm economy," one characteristic of which is diversified production oriented toward basic self-sufficiency. As specialized, market-oriented commercial farming is now regarded in China as both "modern" and "efficient," this characteristic of small-scale family farming has been treated as a serious drawback; and in China is usually blamed on the small economic size of the production unit. One of the main weaknesses of small-scale, family farming in the Chinese context is that a bureaucratic, state-run service and commercial sector is not efficient enough to serve (nor oriented toward) the needs of small-scale farming. Another drawback is that producers have little opportunity (or incentive) to develop high levels of managerial skill and technical efficiency, or to make other investments (e.g., in specialized equipment) which have scale economies.

However, there are social advantages as well as drawbacks to diversified, largely self-sufficient production. Diversification and self-sufficiency are efficient responses by farmers to lack of well-developed markets in inputs, outputs, credit, and other services (i.e., with high variability of supply and price); and also to environmental risks. Until these markets are better developed, and the financial system is in a position to supply much larger amounts of working capital, the "small-farm economy" should not be disparaged. Indeed, if absorption of labor in services and commerce is an objective, then small-scale, diversified (but not subsistence-oriented) farming has a greater need for such services than larger-scale, specialized farming.

The promotion of the *specialized household* (SH), a farm enterprise of above-average size deriving most income from one product, has been the major policy measure used to encourage specialization. As markets in inputs, outputs, credit, and other services develop in China, SHs would naturally tend to emerge. The creation and promotion of SHs in China as a "hothouse product" seems to have been based on the notion that Schumpeterian "entrepreneurs" could blaze a trail which would attract other "followers" (Schumpeter, 1936). However, the SHs in China, which are not quite the risk takers described by Schumpeter, have benefited from direct or indirect government subsidies and other connections with local government.

Promotion of SHs under current conditions involves some dangers. For one, the official agro-service sector is too readily lured into concentration on service to the SHs and neglect of the less commercial farmers. Also SHs, because of scale, specialization, and dependence on purchased inputs and credit, are exposed to much higher risks than other farmers, even when subsidized; they will much more frequently go under when faced with adverse market conditions. Bad debts or bankruptcies can be expected to become increasingly common as conditions pass from the stage in which a few "leaders" or entrepreneurs are involved, to one in which much larger numbers of "followers" enter the market and drive down prices. This was foreseen by Schumpeter, who built his theory of business cycles on this sequence.

Factor markets. Because it was recognized that the lack of factor markets prevented the transfer of surplus agricultural labor to non-farm activities, and hindered specialization and the exploitation of returns to scale, some market activity in the means of production (labor, land, and capital) is now officially tolerated in the rural areas. Farm labor can now migrate to market towns and hired labor use in farming or other rural occupations has been decontrolled; transfers of land use rights are permissible, although only with the permission of the collective; an informal credit market has emerged, and may already generate a higher lending volume than the Rural Credit Cooperatives.

However, all these activities exist in an extra-legal framework in which the permissible scope and terms of transactions are uncertain, and enforceability of contracts is always questionable. Land use rights are revocable in case of unsatisfactory management, are not heritable, and renewal possibilities are rarely specified in contracts. Land transfers with compensation occur, and indeed a market rent level of about Y900/ha on average rice-wheat double-cropped land has been established (Lin, 1986), equivalent to about 30% of gross value of product and byproduct, or nearly 50% of net value added, leaving the sublessee a residual compensation for labor and working capital averaging only Y1.38 per labor day. However, rents are disguised, e.g., as the supply of grain at subsidized list prices, and it is more common for use rights to be retained by putting some minimum effort into farming, often using the females, children, and old people as the only labor force except at the peak season (Shi, 1986). Market wage rates for labor have also been established, at approximate parity with average net farm and side-activity income per farm worker (i.e., the offer price is well above subsistence, let alone the marginal productivity of labor in farming). A zero rate of interest was reported in one survey of the informal capital market, where transactions are normally among relatives and friends; however, disguised interest may also be prevalent.

To facilitate increased factor mobility, legal recognition of rights and obligations associated with land use transfers, labor hiring, and money lending is necessary. On the other hand, legalization of private ownership of land (Li, 1986) would be unnecessary, if significant rents were collected to discourage idling or underutilization of land (crop price increases are a prerequisite) and subleasing for a fee is also recognized. This would be comparable to the relatively benevolent and productive system of "permanent tenancy," involving a recognition of separate "subsoil" and "topsoil" rights, which prevailed in parts of eastern China as early as the Ming dynasty.

Investment and rural industry. It is widely accepted that the last few years have seen a decline in the amount of China's investment in land improvement. This was not for want of savings; rather, investment in rural industry, private housing, and transport vehicles has absorbed most rural resources. There has been a declining commitment of resources from the government budget and failure to enforce "labor service" obligations, previously so important in water resource and road construction. However, the government is now poised to rectify this situation (Liang, 1986; Shi, 1986). Probably due to low crop prices and consequently low rates of return in crop cultivation, little private savings has been attracted into land improvement. The extent to which private credit or own-investment has been funneled in this direction is uncertain, but some local surveys suggest that no more than 10–15% of private lending goes into farm production, and that mainly for chemical fertilizer. The financial system (particularly the Rural Credit Cooperatives) has also failed, not to attract savings, but rather to relend a significant proportion for agricultural investment, particularly long-term investment (Zhou and Liu, 1986). Up until recently, the majority of RCC deposits have been directed out of the agricultural sector, rather than being relent locally; and 66% of increased lending in 1985 went into rural industry.

Rural industry and market town development. The development of rural factor markets is intended to allow up to one-third of the existing farm labor force, plus the entire annual increment in rural labor, to flow into rural industry and/or the commercial and service sectors centered on rural market towns. The Government expects that non-farm activities will employ as much as 44% of the rural labor force by the year 2000, compared to 12% in 1984 (World Bank, 1985). In other Asian developing countries, 20–30% is the norm, if part-time or seasonal work and medium-sized market towns (20,000–30,000 people) are excluded (Ho, 1984). To meet the government's target, a sustained 10% annual growth rate in non-farm rural labor is required.

It should be recognized that historically two main factors seem to account for successful development of rural industry—high levels of crop productivity and well-developed rural transport and power systems. For example, contrast South Korea, where real off-farm income has not increased beyond 12–13% of total farm household income since the early 1960s, with Japan, where it rose from 12% in 1921 to nearly 80% in 1980: in Japan development of rural railroads, highways and electric power has allowed medium- to large-scale urban-type enterprises to locate in the rural areas and draw on a rural workforce, whereas in South Korea, industrial development has been largely centralized in urban areas distant from most farms (Ho, 1984). Similar influences are at work in China. Some 84% of the variance among provinces in the (log of) net value added in township- and village-level enterprises, and 89% of the variance in labor employed, are accounted for by differences in the values of crop output and transport volume.[4] Agricultural surpluses generate important "forward linkages" to agroprocessing, rural transport, and commercial activities, and also provide a source of savings to support rural non-farm investments. Of course, the profits of rural non-farm activities also can provide the funds to support increased investment in agriculture.

The government's target for labor absorption is not necessarily infeasible; indeed, the cross-provincial multiple regression relationship implies that doubling crop output value and transport volume by the year 2000 would increase employment in rural industry at a rate equivalent to 11% annual growth. Yet improving farm productivity and transport or power infrastructure requires considerable investment, and at this stage these applications of financial resources need to be given greater priority relative to rural industry.

CONCLUSIONS

The interconnections among the structural adjustment problems discussed above can be summarized as follows: In the long run, because of Engel's Law, Chinese agriculture (excluding non-farm activities) should be targeted at nearly 5% real growth per year in order to induce rapid development of non-farm activities, which in turn can absorb surplus labor and generate new sources of rural income. This requires emphasis on quality improvement and a quest for new market opportunities to resolve demand limitations; quantitative growth also requires emphasis on the livestock sector and its growing demand for feed. However, without improved incentives, such a growth rate cannot be sustained for want of sufficient investment and managerial interest. Continuing administrative control, particularly over grain procurements, and of-

---

[4] All variables were expressed in logarithms, because the relationship is nonlinear, and on a per cultivated hectare basis, to control for size differences among provinces. The three province-level municipalities and Shansi Province were excluded from the 1984 data set as outliers (in Shansi, non-farm activities are based mainly on mineral resources, and have little connection with agriculture).

ficial underpricing of grain and oilseeds, due to the political difficulty of passing further price increases through to urban consumers, threatens agricultural incentives. If price increases were largely offset by increased rural taxes or land use fees, the revenues could be used to compensate urban consumers for retail price increases. While average rural incomes would not benefit immediately, marginal incentives in farming could be greatly increased and the procurement price structure could approach that of a market equilibrium, permitting the completion of the transition to a market system.

REFERENCES

Gao, Xiaomeng, Gao Shan, and He Jianzheng, "Giving the New Mechanism More Room to Expand." Beijing *Renmin Ribao,* Sept. 20, 1986; *Trans.* Joint Publications Research Service. *China: Agric.* **86,** 37:4, Oct. 17, 1986.

Ho, Samuel, "Rural Nonagricultural Development: The Asian Experience and Prospects for China." Unpublished, February 1984.

Li, Qingzeng, "A Discussion on Reforming the Structure of Rural Land Ownership in China." Beijing *Nongye Jingji Wenti* **4,** 23:26–28, April 1986; *Trans.* Joint Publications Research Service. *China: Agric.* **86,** 35:13–17, Oct. 15, 1986.

Liang, Buting, "Developing the Commodity Economy is the Focus of Rural Work." Jinan *Dazhong Ribao,* Sept. 23, 1986; *Trans.* Joint Publications Research Service. *China: Agric.* **86,** 39:42–55, Nov. 18, 1986.

Lin, Justin Yifu, "Rural Factor Markets in China After the Household Responsibility System Reform." Unpublished, August 1986.

NMRB, Beijing *Nongmin Ribao (Farmer's Daily).*

RMRB, Beijing *Renmin Ribao (People's Daily).*

Schumpeter, Joseph, *The Theory of Economic Development.* Cambridge, MA: Harvard Univ. Press, 1936.

Shi, Fu, "Immediate Agricultural Problems and CPC Foresight." Hong Kong *Zhongguo Tongxun She,* Sept 26, 1986; *Trans.* Joint Publications Research Service. *China: Agric.* **86,** 38:5–6, Nov. 6, 1986.

Song, Guoqing, and Meng Xiaopeng, *Jingji Jiegou yu Jingji Gaige (Economic Structure and Economic Reform).* Beijing: China Rural Development Problems Research Group, 1986.

State Statistical Bureau, *Chongguo Nongcun Tongji Nianjian (China Rural Statistics Yearbook, 1985).* Beijing: China Statistics Press, 1986.

State Statistical Bureau, *Chongguo Tongji Nianjian (China Statistics Yearbook, 1986).* Beijing: China Statistics Press, 1986.

World Bank, *China: Long-Term Development Issues and Options. Annex 2: China: Agriculture to the Year 2000.* Washington, D.C., 1985.

Wu, Xiang, "Rural Reforms and the Agricultural Problems." Hong Kong *Liaowang* **33,** Aug. 18, 1986; *Trans.* Joint Publications Research Service. *China: Agric.* **86,** 38:7–12, Nov. 6, 1986.

ZGSYB, Beijing *Zhonguo Shangye Bao (China's Commerce).*

Zhou, Shulin, and Liu Ningjun, "Roundup of Studies in Recent Years of Rural Funding Problems." Beijing *Jingjixue Zhoubao* Apr. 27, 1986; *Trans.* Joint Publications Research Service. *China: Agric.* **86,** 36:8–10, Oct. 20, 1986.

Zhou, Yichang, "Construct Bases to Produce Agricultural Goods that will Earn Foreign Exchange." Beijing *Liaowang* **21,** May 26, 1986; *Trans.* Joint Publications Research Service. *China: Agric.* **86,** 36:16–18, Oct. 20, 1986.

JOURNAL OF COMPARATIVE ECONOMICS **11**, 385–398 (1987)

Between Plan and Market: The Role of the Local Sector in Post-Mao China[1]

CHRISTINE P. W. WONG

University of California, Santa Cruz, California 95064

Wong, Christine P. W.—Between Plan and Market: The Role of the Local Sector in Post-Mao China

The Chinese economy has long been characterized by multilevel planning, with local governments controlling nearly half of total industrial output and allocating substantial resources. Because of the important role played by local governments, market reforms have not brought a straight-forward transfer of decision-making authority from the central government to economic agents. Instead, there has been a good deal of "leakage" in the reform process, with local governments retaining and even expanding control over enterprises through a variety of informal mechanisms, as well as through their control over geographically immobile factor resources. This paper looks at the local sector and how market reforms have affected it. *J. Comp. Econ.,* December, 1987, **11**(3), pp. 385–398. University of California, Santa Cruz, California 95064. © 1987 Academic Press, Inc.

Journal of Economic Literature Classification Numbers: 124, 513, 941.

One of the most notable features of the Chinese economy is its strong regional character, where local governments allocate substantial resources. Planning is done not only at the central government level, but also at various local levels including province, city, county, and even townships.[2] Given the multiple levels of decision-making, decentralization is a complex process that can generate a number of possible outcomes, and a reduction in the scope of central planning does not necessarily mean a shift to market allocation.

Defining decentralization as a shift of decision-making power from the top toward the bottom, with "+" indicating gains and "−" indicating losses, we can enumerate five different outcomes in a three-level economy as follows:[3]

---

[1] I am indebted to David Granick, Gail Hershatter, Emily Honig, and participants of the Arden House Conference on Economic Reform in China for helpful comments and criticisms.

[2] The multilevel planning system is discussed in a number of recent studies. See Wong (1985, 1986b), Granick (1986), and Tidrick and Chen, forthcoming.

[3] This enumeration draws from Neuberger (1985), pp. 18–26.

CHINESE ECONOMIC REFORM

95

	1	2	3	4	5
Central units	−	−	−	−	−
Intermediate units (local governments)	−		+	+	+
Primary units (enterprises)	+	+	+		−

These outcomes are arranged in an order of declining "thoroughness," which is defined according to Chinese reformers' stated objective of transferring decision-making power to enterprises. In the best case (type 1), decision-making power is transferred from both the central and local governments to the enterprises. In the worst case (type 5), "positive intermediation" occurs, where the intermediate units of local governments gain at the expense of both the central government and the enterprises. Between the best and worst cases are scenarios where "leakage" occurs, with local governments usurping some or all of the decision-making power passed down by the central government (types 3 and 4). The success of market reforms in China obviously depends on the type of outcome that is obtained in the decentralization process, as well as on the behavior of local governments.

Previous decentralizations of the Chinese economy (especially during 1958 and 1970) were of type 4 ("administrative decentralization"). While post-Mao reforms have broken decisively from that tradition by transferring much greater decision-making power to enterprises, there has also been a good deal of "leakage" to the intermediate units. In fact, it will be argued that decentralization through 1983 was closer to type 5 than to type 1. In the more recent period, market pressures have eroded local control in some respects, but much remains to be done to ensure that reforms continue to make progress toward the objective of increasing enterprise autonomy.

This paper looks at the local sector and its role in the reform process. In this paper, "local" will refer to administrative levels below the central government: province, municipality, prefecture, county, township, and village. Two sets of interrelated questions are explored. The first set concerns the nature of decentralization and the size of the local sector in the reform period. The second set concerns the behavior of the local sector: how is the local sector managed? What is the relationship between local governments and enterprises? And what are the implications of local control of resource allocation?

THE LOCAL SECTOR AND THE STRUCTURE OF CHINESE PLANNING

During the 1960s and 1970s, the local sector was a "catch-all" category that absorbed the spillovers from the state (central) sector, when the market sector was virtually nonexistent. Through the successive rounds of decentralization and rapid local industrialization, it grew to rival the state sector in size. By the mid-1970s, it had developed substantial growth momentum based on resources generated within the sector itself. To understand the key role played by the local sector, it is necessary to look at the structure of Chinese planning.

A number of features distinguish the Chinese economy from other socialist planned economies. The first is the extremely large number of industrial enterprises. The *Chinese Statistical Yearbook* counts a total of 437,200 enterprises at the end of 1984; with 84,100 in the state sector (SSB[4] 1985, p. 305). Even though this number excludes most enterprises in the rural sector, it is extremely large compared to socialist economies in Eastern Europe. Moreover, the number has increased by over 25% in the reform period, with the addition of nearly 90,000 enterprises since 1978, almost entirely in the collective sector.

The second feature is the preponderance of small-scale enterprises. By World Bank estimates, only 0.6% of Chinese enterprises have more than 243 workers, compared to 65.1% in Hungary and 33.5% in Yugoslavia.[5] It is difficult to convert Chinese enterprise size categories for cross-country comparisons since they are based on annual output, productive capacity, or fixed assets. However, even if the World Bank numbers underestimate the portion of large-scale Chinese enterprises by as much as 5- to 10-fold, it remains true that the size structure of Chinese industry is very unusual for a socialist planned economy, though not for a developing country. In addition, while the trend has been toward merging enterprises into ever-larger units in other socialist countries, in China the share of output from small plants has grown steadily from 45% of gross value of industrial output in 1970 to about 55% today.

Given the large number and small scale of industrial enterprises, the Chinese planning system has by necessity evolved differently from those in Eastern Europe. Through the mid-1960s and 1970s, when rapid industrialization at the local level was adding large numbers of small enterprises, the impossibility of incorporating them into the planning structure led to the creation of a multitiered, regionally based system where much of the responsibility for planning and coordination devolved to local governments. In this system, enterprises were divided by their importance and by ownership. Large-scale, key enterprises remained in the central plan, while non-key enterprises were left to planning and coordination at the provincial, prefectural, and county levels.[6]

---

[4] List of abbreviations: CASS, Chinese Academy of Social Science; CESRI, Chinese Economic System Reform Institute; CMJJ, *Caimao Jingji (Finance and Trade Econ.)*; CZ, *Caizheng (Finance)*; JJGL, *Jingji Guanli (Econ. Manage.)*; JJNJ, *Zhongguo Jingji Nianjian (Econ. Yearbook of China)*; JJYJ, *Jingji Yanjiu (Econ. Res.)*; MTNJ, *Meitan Nianjian (Coal Yearbook)*; RMRB, *Renmin Ribao (People's Daily)*; SSB, State Statistical Bureau.

[5] World Bank (1985) p. 28.

[6] For a history of the evolution of this multitiered system, see Wong (1985).

CHRISTINE P. W. WONG

TABLE 1

ESTIMATED DISTRIBUTION OF INDUSTRIAL ENTERPRISES BY OWNERSHIP
AND ADMINISTRATIVE LEVEL, 1983[a]

State	Collective	
(1) 2500 Large enterprises controlled by central government (30–35%)		Urban (75%)
(2a) 30,000–40,000 Small–medium enterprises controlled by province and city governments (25–30%)	(2b) 100,000+ "Large" and "small" urban collectives (10–12%)	
(3a) 40,000–50,000 County and prefectural enterprises (13–15%)	(3b) 20,000–25,000 "Large" and "small" collectives (3–5%)	Rural (25%)
	(4) 186,100 Enterprises owned by townships and villages (7%)	
(78%)	(22%)	

[a] Figures in parentheses denote shares of gross value of industrial output.
Sources: Breakdown of collective sector output by urban and rural: SSB (1985), pp. 306, 315. Estimated breakdown of urban–rural GVIO: Liu Suinian, "The Issue of Concentration and Dispersal in China's Economic Development." In Liu Guoguang, Ed., *Zhongguo Jingji Fazhan Zhanlue Wenti Yanjiu (Research on the Issues of China's Strategy for Economic Development).* Beijing: p. 502, 1984.

The approximate distribution of enterprises by administrative level is presented in Table 1. At the top are some 2500 enterprises controlled by the central government and its ministries, which produce 30–40% of total industrial output. In addition to key enterprises in the defense industry, this group comprises the largest producers in important industries. In 1980, for example, they included 84 coal mining administrations (with 553 mines), 20-odd iron and steel enterprises, 53 large and medium cement plants, 50-odd producers of sulfuric acid, 5 producers of soda ash, and 10-plus key forestry regions (Ma, 1981, pp. 312–313).

In the second tier are enterprises run by provinces and cities. These include 30,000–40,000 mostly small and medium enterprises in the state-owned sector, as well as over 100,000 collective enterprises. Collective enterprises in this group range from very small (with a few employees) to very large (with over 1000 employees). Even though the bulk of these collective enterprises belong to vertically oriented light industrial systems, they are also subject to a high degree of local control.[7]

[7] For a detailed description of the collective sector, see Wong (1986b), pp. 582–584.

In the third tier are enterprises in the prefectural and county systems. These include perhaps 40,000–50,000 state-owned enterprises and some 20,000–25,000 collective enterprises. These enterprises are mostly small-scale, and they operate largely free of state plan control. At the bottom are rural collective enterprises run by townships and villages (formerly communes and brigades). In 1983 the State Statistic Bureau included 186,100 township enterprises in its industrial statistics (1985, p. 313). In addition, there were several hundred thousand enterprises at the village level and below.[8] The shares of industrial output by enterprise categories are derived from reported breakdowns of output by sector and urban–rural division.

In this hierarchical ordering of enterprises, a rough correspondence exists between enterprise size and the degree of incorporation into the central plan. In general, the share of enterprise output included in the central plan declines as we move down the enterprise hierarchy. In 1977–1978, for example, when the central plan included some 50–55% of gross value of industrial output, it accounted for close to 100% of output in centrally administered enterprises, but less than 20% of output in rural collective enterprises.[9] Interpolating from these two extremes, we estimate that the central plan accounted for perhaps one-half to two-thirds of the production in provincial and city enterprises, and one-fourth to one-third that in county and prefectural enterprises during the late 1970s.[10] By 1984, with the share of gross industrial output included in the central plan declining to 30–40%, there has been a corresponding decline in planned shares of output in all categories, though not necessarily proportionally. With most enterprises and so much of the industrial output outside of direct control by the central government, the success of market reform in the post-Mao period depends critically on whether local governments introduce appropriate changes, *pari passu,* at the lower levels.

In the post-Mao period, there is some uncertainty about the size and behavior of the local sector. On the positive side, the rapid response of local production to market stimuli has greatly improved the supply of many consumer goods as well as producers' goods such as coal and building materials.[11] The more rapid growth of the non-state sectors during the reform period is generally attributed to the greater dynamism of the local economies. On the

[8] For 1983, the *Agricultural Yearbook* listed 744,000 rural collective enterprises engaging in industrial production. 43.5 billion yuan of output from village and team enterprises was counted as agricultural output (1984, pp. 71, 79).

[9] Estimates for the central plan's share of gross value of industrial output and for tier one enterprises are from Wong (1986b), pp. 586–588; rural collective share is from RMRB August 21, 1980.

[10] These estimates are supported by anecdotal accounts. The portion of industrial output under state plans was 70% for Wuxi Municipality, 30% for Wuxi County (Zuo, 1980, p. 32), and one-third for Guangdong's Nanhai County (Chinese Association of Material Economics, 1984, Vol. 2, pp. 343–344).

[11] For example, during the 1978–1984 period, local mines accounted for nearly 80% of the increase in coal production (MTNJ 1982, pp. 9, 16; 1983, p. 61, 1985, p. 50).

other hand, a good deal of anecdotal evidence indicates that in at least some spheres, local growth has come at the expense of the state sector and to the detriment of overall economic efficiency. Because of competition from local producers, for example, state procurement plans for a variety of agricultural products are substantially underfulfilled, including tobacco, wool, raw silk, animal skins, and high grades of cotton. As a result, production in large-scale, modern processing plants is being displaced by less efficient production in local small plants (Wu, 1986, and CASS, 1985). More importantly, the rapid growth in local investment in the 1980s has been squeezing out state investment projects, even in the bottleneck sectors of transportation and energy production.

While there is little question of the continuing significance of the local sector, its true size is difficult to ascertain. In 1984, Chinese planners estimated that about 30–40% of total industrial output was included in the central plan. Another 20% was said to be produced "primarily according to market principles."[12] This latter figure was also the estimated portion of industrial output traded at market prices.[13] The 40–50% of industrial output that falls outside of both the central plan and the market constituted the upper limit for the size of the local sector, though the actual size of the sector was probably somewhat smaller.[14]

A major source of difficulty in estimating the size of the local sector is the paucity of information on the relationship between local governments and their enterprises. During the prereform era, when enterprises had virtually no autonomous decision-making authority, whatever was outside of the central government sphere of control could safely be treated as within the local sphere. This applied, for example, to the disposal of funds that were nominally retained by enterprises, such as depreciation and technical renovation funds. Through the Cultural Revolution period, these funds were frequently pooled by local governments for use in local investment projects. With the reforms strengthening enterprise autonomy, however, the use of these funds may have slipped out from under local government control. Since over 70% of all extrabudgetary funds are retained by enterprises, the nature of local government–enterprise relations is an important determinant of local sector behavior. Unfortunately, this relationship appears to be a rapidly changing area for which data is difficult to obtain. Moreover, there is undoubtedly a great deal of regional variation in the nature of these relationships. In the absence of definitive information, the charges that local governments are continuing to wield primary control

[12] Briefing given to the American Economists Study Team, December 1984, reported by Naughton (1986), p. 625.

[13] Estimate made by Zhang Zhuoyuan in a seminar at the University of California, Berkeley, October 1984.

[14] If the local sector approached this limit, however, the 20% market portion came entirely out of the central plan's share, since the local sector included 45–50% of industrial output on the eve of reform in the late 1970s.

over local resources, use "commandist workstyles" in managing local economies, etc., have to be viewed against reform efforts to reduce their influence.[15]

MECHANISMS OF LOCAL CONTROL IN
THE REFORM PERIOD

In the prereform period, local governments could directly control production, supply, and sales in local enterprises through the allocation of material supplies. The pooling of enterprise profits and depreciation allowances also enabled them to allocate investment funds. In the reform period, while compulsory and guidance plans are still formulated by local governments, these direct control mechanisms have declined in importance, since the development of goods markets have allowed enterprises to be less dependent on administrative allocations. A 1984 survey of 429 enterprises found, for example, that although local levels accounted for nearly half of the compulsory plans assigned to enterprises, compulsory planning accounted for an average of only 24% of total production in these enterprises (CESRI, 1986, p. 53). Instead, with the decline in the use of direct mechanisms, there has been a shift to informal mechanisms of control, which have been left largely untouched by market reforms.

The most important informal mechanisms available to local governments are their control over factor resources. The allocation of workers and appointment of managers gives local officials substantial leverage for influencing enterprise behavior. In the absence of national capital markets, there is widespread consensus that local governments continue to exercise significant control over the allocation of investment finance. In spite of the near-universal introduction of enterprise profit-retention schemes, a good deal of evidence indicates that local enterprises, especially at lower administrative levels, enjoy less financial autonomy than enterprises at higher administrative levels. The 1984 survey mentioned above found a profit-retention rate of only 21.6% among small-scale enterprises, compared with an average of 57% for large- and medium-sized enterprises in the sample. Given that these small enterprises had an average of only 100,000 yuan for production development funds from retained profits, they were left highly dependent on external finance (CESRI, 1986, p. 171).

Aside from the growing funds collected from enterprise profits and taxes which fiscal decentralization has transferred to local coffers (see below), local officials continue to exert substantial influence over bank lending, since the regional structure of the banking system places bank officials at the mercy of local officials for a variety of supporting facilities including housing for the bank staff (Zhou and Zhi, 1987). In addition, other studies found that profit-retention contracts are often violated, with local officials arbitrarily requisi-

---

[15] For examples of these charges, see Ding (1985), Zhao (1986), and Zhu (1985).

tioning enterprise funds for investment in local infrastructural facilities, development of new products, or to support local welfare expenditures (Zhao, 1986; Ding, 1985). In a report reminiscent of complaints of the Cultural Revolution period, one writer told of officials in Sichuan province issuing quotas for local development projects in imitation of "advanced experiences" elsewhere. In order to fulfill these quotas, local units were forced to "blindly" start projects that were inappropriate to local conditions, and banks were coerced into granting loans in support of these investments (Zhu, 1985).

With local governments continuing to exercise control through these informal mechanisms, market reforms in the post-Mao period have left enterprises with a "dual dependence."[16] Not only are enterprises forced to be more responsive to market pressures, they also remain highly dependent on the administrative bureaucracy to provide vital support. With the economy moving away from the use of physical allocations to an emphasis on financial indicators, enterprise dependence on the bureaucracy has similarly shifted from plan bargaining to the financial sphere, in bargaining over profit quotas, subsidies, investment funds, etc.

THE IMPACT OF REFORMS ON LOCAL PLANNING

During the first phase of reform, through their formal and informal control over the three principal sources of extrabudgetary funds (enterprise funds, bank loans, and local government revenues), local governments greatly expanded their allocative powers, as reforms spurred the growth of extrabudgetary funds from 36.1 billion yuan to 89.1 billion yuan from 1978 to 1983 (JJNJ, 1983, p. III–90; 1984, p. IV–43). In this section it is argued that decentralization during this first phase of reform resulted in an outcome that was somewhere between type 4 and type 5, not only with local governments gaining substantial resources, but also with some "positive intermediation," since enterprises became even more dependent on local officials.

Under the profit-based bonus schemes in use during 1979–1984, profit-retention rates were set at low levels of the bureaucracy, and the rates were subject to negotiation between enterprises and their supervisory agencies.[17] Under this system, the welfare of workers and managers became very much dependent on the goodwill of local officials, who held the authority to set profit-retention rates for the enterprises. Beyond setting the retention rates, local officials had a good deal of control over the *level* of after-tax profits through their price and tax-setting authority. For any given level of output and X-efficiency, the level of after-tax profits is directly related to the level of prices and taxes.

---

[16] This is a term used by Kornai (1986) to describe the condition of firms in the reformed Hungarian economy.

[17] For discussions of the problems of these profit-sharing schemes, see Naughton (1985) and Wong (1986a).

The ability of local governments to set prices is a legacy of Cultural Revolution policies. In order to allow small-scale, local enterprises to cover costs, local governments were allowed to set higher "temporary" prices for local products. In the reform period, this price-setting authority has been formalized under the principle of *gaojin gaochu,* whereby enterprises can charge high (market) prices for their output if inputs were procured at high (market) prices. Since much of local production is based on market-allocated inputs, local outputs are not constrained to state prices.

For any local administrative unit, this price-setting authority is dependent upon (1) the amount of resources available for allocation at below-market prices; (2) its ability to procure output at below-market prices, which is linked to the first; and (3) the gap between state and market prices. For both inputs and outputs, as long as a divergence exists between the market price and the state allocation price, local governments can set the average price level in one of two ways. They can set the mix of the two prices, by stipulating the portions to be sold at each price for outputs, and by setting the portions allocated at each price for inputs. Or more commonly, they can set *local* prices at some intermediate level.

Market liberalization during the first phase of reform greatly increased the price-setting authority of local governments, since the growing gap between market and state prices provided them with a growing margin for changing prices. Obviously, this price-setting authority varies with the administrative level. At the provincial level, where the pool of materials that can be allocated is large relative to total demand, officials have substantial price-setting authority. At the township level, this authority may well be negligible. In 1982, allocations accounted for 70–80% of total materials supplied at the provincial level, 60–70% at the prefectural and municipal level, and less than 50% at the county levels (Li, 1983, p. 1).

While the rates for both income and industrial–commercial taxes were standardized nationwide, local governments in fact had substantial power to change them. When an enterprise ran into financial difficulties, it could turn to tax authorities for help, by asking for temporary tax reductions or exemptions. In spite of numerous attempts to recentralize this tax-relief granting authority, it rested at levels as low as the county. Efforts to make tax offices independent of local governments appeared to have been quite unsuccessful, with tax officials frequently taking the view that it was their duty to aid development of the local economy.[18] Interestingly, the "harder" prices faced by enterprises at the lower levels (where officials have less price-setting authority) were often partially offset by the "softer" taxes, with closer working relationships between the tax bureau and the economic planning agencies at the lower levels.

---

[18] Fieldwork information, June 1982. Also, numerous articles in CZ and CMJJ corroborate the pervasiveness of these attitudes.

Through this period of reform, all the changes transferred more resources to local control, without any countervailing pressures to force local governments to behave in more economically efficient ways. Indeed, with fiscal reforms transferring the bulk of local enterprise profits and taxes to local revenue incomes, local governments had improved incentives to expand the local economic base. Not surprisingly, these changes brought an explosive growth in investment in revenue-generating activities, accompanied by an outburst of local protectionism. Protectionistic tactics ranged from excluding outside products from local markets to threatening local enterprises with cutoffs of funds and bank loans, supplies of fuel, etc., should they dare to buy the products of competitors (Li, 1982, p. 12).

Even though fiscal reforms that made local governments more revenue-oriented should have reduced their willingness to subsidize loss-making enterprises, several factors militate against the beneficial impact this was intended to have in forcing enterprises to adjust to market pressure. One was the fact that local governments try to maximize net revenues, which consist of profits and taxes paid by the firm. They would be willing to allow the survival of money-losing firms as long as sufficient tax revenues were generated to offset the losses. Since taxes were wholly unrelated to enterprise efficiency, this thwarted the reform's intent. In addition, local governments were often under heavy pressure to preserve or create local jobs and to respond to social and political concerns, and cost-cutting seemed less pressing in an era of growing revenues. Through the first phase of reform, some local governments took extraordinary measures to protect high-cost enterprises from bankruptcy, in clear violation of the attempt to shut down inefficient enterprises.

In recognition of the problematic role played by local governments, the second phase of reform, beginning in 1984, introduced two measures to reduce local government control and break down administrative barriers to resource flows. The first was the measure to promote the "economic role" of cities. The other was the reform to "substitute taxes for profits." Neither has succeeded to date in fundamentally altering the administrative setup.

The movement to promote the economic role of cities was intended to utilize the natural coordinating functions of cities to break down the rigidities and irrationalities of the hierarchical system. Under this measure, some central and provincial enterprises have been transferred to city management. In some provinces the administrative level of prefecture has been abolished, and counties have been reassigned to supervision by cities. Some improvements have been reported under this measure, most notably in eliminating some of the circuitous shipment of goods caused by routing shipments along administrative lines. (State Materials Bureau, 1984, passim.) In other areas, transferring enterprises to city management has improved the horizontal coordination of enterprises formerly belonging to different planning systems. However, progress toward reducing regionalism and "departmentalism" has not been universal, since cities are themselves "local" units, and the change has sometimes merely substituted one administrative unit for another, with little change in workstyle.

A more concerted assault on local control came in the tax-for-profit reform that was introduced in 1983–1984. The main part of the reform shifted state-owned enterprises at all administrative levels from the system of remitting profits to paying a series of taxes. The objective was to formalize the financial interaction between enterprises and their supervisory agencies and end the era of profit negotiation under previous enterprise incentive schemes. Aside from "hardening" enterprise budget constraints, this measure would have the effect of stripping local governments of an important source of control.

The reform would also reduce the financial incentives for local expansion. By pooling all enterprise income tax revenues and apportioning them along the different levels of government regardless of enterprise ownership, it would separate local government revenues from the ownership and profitability of enterprises.

Finally, the reform was to reduce the scope of local government intervention in enterprise operations by mandating that many small-scale enterprises be contracted out to private or collective management. Accompanying the tax-for-profit reform was the announcement that over a 3-year period beginning in 1985, all small-scale, state-owned enterprises with fixed assets of less than 1.5 million yuan and annual profits of 200,000 yuan or less would be contracted out to individuals or groups (Zhao, 1984). If fully implemented, this measure would turn over to private or collective management as much as half of the 81,000 state-owned enterprises classified as "small-scale."

Not surprisingly, due to its potentially significant impact in redistributing income and resources across administrative units, the tax-for-profit program has run into much opposition. Through 1985, implementation was slow, and its objectives remained largely unfulfilled.

CONCLUSION

The existence of local governments with substantial allocative power has been detrimental to economic efficiency for three reasons. First, the fragmentation of control under local governments continues to impede resource flows. The slowness of the development of capital markets may be partly attributable to local opposition. Despite a promising start, investment trust companies have not developed into serious competitors to state-owned banks as financial intermediaries, perhaps because of their inability to cross over administrative barriers in their investment activities. Reports of interregional investments seem to be confined to "interregional cooperation" projects undertaken by local governments to secure raw material and energy supplies.

Second, when local governments are making the bulk of investment decisions, resource allocation is not following "market regulation," since local government maximands are net revenues rather than profits. Even with market reforms incrementally improving the information carried by prices, tax signals continue to be problematic guides for investment. In addition, local governments make investment choices based on administrative considerations rather than purely economic ones. In many areas the pressure to create jobs remains strong. And as the earlier example from Sichuan demonstrated, local officials are often susceptible to "emulation drives" and model-building practices that run counter to economic rationality.

Third, local governments reduce competition by shielding enterprises from market pressure and by intervening in interregional trade. In addition, they slow down market adjustments by helping to perpetuate sellers' markets in a variety of producer and investment goods through their vigorous investment activities. These investment projects may in the long run make prices downwardly sticky: the development of buyers' markets may spur new attempts at regional protectionism rather than price-cutting, as local governments try to protect their newly created productive assets. They may even reach oligopolistic compromises that divide markets geographically to avoid competition. For all of these reasons, it is necessary to curb local control in order to achieve reform objectives.

To date, attempts at curbing local control through administrative restructuring have been largely ineffective. It is probably in the realm of price-setting authority that market forces have had the greatest impact in eroding local control, by reducing the amount of resources that local governments can allocate administratively, at below-market prices, and by reducing the gap between plan and market prices for many goods. Since local governments derive substantial leverage through their ability to set prices, these changes have reduced their maneuverability. However, market forces alone cannot close the price gaps, which can be closed only through a combination of raising state prices to realistic levels (where average costs are covered), and eliminating sellers' markets. Numerous adjustments in state prices since 1982–1983 have helped to close the gap for many products, especially consumer goods, where buyers' markets had developed.

Furthermore, market forces cannot always be expected to turn sellers' markets into buyers' markets even with improved resource mobility. Too many factors persist in the economy to fuel excessive investment, including soft budget constraints at the enterprise and local government levels. In the reform period, sellers' markets have persisted for many producer and investment goods, where price gaps remain large. For rolled steel, for example, the market price continues to be two to three times the state price.

Price reform is, therefore, necessary to realign prices to cover average production costs and to eliminate the gaps between state and market prices. A price reform that reunifies the price structure will substantially limit the bargaining power of local governments over their enterprises and go a long way toward "hardening" the enterprise budget constraint.

Given the importance of taxes in conferring bargaining power on local governments, tax reform is also necessary. The "softness" of the present system must be eliminated by introducing standardized taxes. The authority to grant tax relief must also be recentralized to higher levels to reduce the incidence of abuse. Under the present revenue-sharing system, local officials can often afford to be generous in granting tax reductions or exemptions because the loss of revenue is shared with higher levels. This system is particularly subject to abuse at the lower levels, where local officials see this as an opportunity to "rob" the state treasury by reducing total tax payments. To really wrest control of tax rates from local control, then, a new system must be set up to separate local taxes from state taxes, with separate agencies for collection.

Even though these changes are necessary to reduce local influence, they will not be sufficient. The greatest mechanisms of control available to local governments are their control over factor resources, whose geographical immobility confers tremendous power on local governments. Until market reforms extend into the development of factor markets, local governments will continue to wield substantial control in the Chinese economy.

REFERENCES

Agricultural Yearbook of China (*Zhongguo Nongye Nianjian*). Beijing: Agricultural Press, 1984.

Chinese Academy of Social Science, Institute of Industrial Economics, "An Investigation: Reform of the System of Monopoly Sales of Tobacco and Liquor," JJYJ 11:1985.

Chinese Association of Material Economics, *Wuzi Jingji yu Guanli Wenji* (*Compendium of Essays on Material Economics and Management*), Vol. 2. Beijing: Materials Press, 1984.

Chinese Economic System Reform Institute Comprehensive Investigation Group. Eds, *Gaige: Women Mianlin de Tiaozhan yu Suanzhe* (*Reform: The Challenges and Choices We Face*). Beijing: Chinese Economics Press, 1986.

Ding Jiatiao, "The Separation of Government and Enterprise Factors is the Key to the Reforms of the Urban and Rural Collective Economies," JJGL 5:1985.

Economic Yearbook of China (*Zhongguo Jingji Nianjian*). Beijing: Economic Management Press, 1983, 1984.

Granick, David, "Prices and the Behavior of Chinese State Industrial Enterprises: Focus on the Multi-Price System," unpublished, 1986.

Kornai, Janos, "The Hungarian Reform Process: Visions, Hopes and Reality." *J. Econ. Lit.* 24: 1687–1733, Dec. 1986.

Li Kaixin, *Wuzi Guanli* (*Materials Manage.*) 4:1983.

Li Yue, "(We Must) Build a Mass Production Structure by Unifying Vertical and Horizontal Systems." *Kexue Jingji* 4:19–23, 1982; reprinted in *Gongye Jingji* 23:1982.

Ma Hong, Ed., *Xiandai Zhongguo Jingji Shidian* (*Contemporary Handbook of Chinese Economic Affairs*). Beijing: Chinese Academy of Social Science Press, 1981.

Naughton, Barry, "False Starts and Second Wind: Financial Reforms in the Chinese Industrial System." In Elizabeth J. Perry and Christine Wong, Eds., *The Political Economy of Reform in Post-Mao China*. Cambridge: Harvard Univ. Press, 1985.

Naughton, Barry, "Finance and Planning Reforms in Industry." In U.S. Congress, Joint Economic Committee, *China's Economy Looks toward the Year 2000*, Vol. 1, *The Four Modernizations*. Washington D.C.: U.S. Govt. Printing Office, 1986.

Neuberger, Egon, "Classifying Economic Systems." In Morris Bornstein, Ed., *Comparative Economic Systems*. Homewood, IL: Richard D. Irwin, Inc., 1985.

Shashi Materials Bureau, "Use Cities as the Basis for Reforming the System of Material Circulation."
    In State Materials Bureau, *Kaichuang Wuzigongzuo Xinjumian Jingyanxuanbian* (*The
    Collected Experience in Opening up New Situations in Materials Work*), pp. 166–182.
    Beijing: Materials Press, 1984.
State Statistical Bureau, *Zhongguo Tongji Nianjian* (*Chinese Statistical Yearbook*). 1984, 1985.
Tidrick, Gene, and Chen Jiyuan, Eds., *China's Industrial Reform*. London: Oxford Univ. Press,
    forthcoming.
Wong, Christine P. W., "The Economics of Shortage and Problems of Reform in Chinese Industry."
    J. Comp. Econ. **10**, 4:363–387, 1986a.
Wong, Christine P. W., "Material Allocations and Decentralization: Impact of the Local Sector
    on Industrial Reform." In Elizabeth J. Perry and Christine Wong, Eds., *The Political
    Economy of Reform in Post-Mao China*. Cambridge, MA: Harvard Univ. Press, 1985.
Wong, Christine P. W., "Ownership and Control in Chinese Industry: the Maoist Legacy and
    Prospects for the 1980s." In U.S. Congress, Joint Economic Committee, *China's Economy
    Looks toward the Year 2000*, Vol. 1, *The Four Modernizations*. Washington D.C.: U.S.
    Govt. Printing Office, 1986b.
The World Bank, *China: Longterm Development Issues and Options*, 1985.
Wu Jinglian, "Economic Instability and the Dual System" CMJJ **6**:1–8, 1986.
Zhao Yujiang, "The Present Problem of Controlling Extrabudgetary Funds." In Chinese Economic
    System Reform Institute Comprehensive Investigation Group, Eds, *Gaige: Women Mianlin
    de Tiaozhan yu Suanzhe* (*Reform: The Challenges and Choices We Face*). Beijing: Chinese
    Economics Press, 1986.
Zhao Ziyang, "Report on the Work of the Government at the Second Session of the 5th National
    People's Congress." *Remin Ribao* (*People's Daily*), June 2, 1984.
Zhou Xiaochuan and Zhu Li, "China's Banking System: Current Status and Perspective on
    Reform." *J. Comp. Econ.* **11**, 399–409, 1987.
Zhu Xiaowen, "Two Problems to Which We Must Attach Importance in Developing Rural
    Enterprises." *Sichuan Ribao,* June 5, 1985.
Zuo Mu, "On the Role of Local Planning and the Relations between Plans and Markets." *Jingji
    Yanjiu* 7:1980; translated in JPRS *Econ. Affairs* **86**, 28–35.

JOURNAL OF COMPARATIVE ECONOMICS 11, 399–409 (1987)

China's Banking System: Current Status, Perspective on Reform[1]

ZHOU XIAOCHUAN

China Economic System Reform Research Institute, Beijing, China

AND

ZHU LI

The Commission on Economic System Reform, Beijing, China

Zhou Xiaochuan and Zhu Li—China's Banking System: Current Status, Perspective on Reform

The paper describes the structure of the Chinese banking system at the end of 1985, including interest-rate determination. A simulation model is used to explore system performance. The model features excessive decentralization to loan agents by branch staff; excessive local government intervention; excessively frequent monetary adjustments; and quantity adjustment with inflexible interest rate. The model predicts a destabilizing cycle between easy and tight money policies. *J. Comp. Econ.,* September, 1987, **11**(3), pp. 399–409. China Economic System Reform Research Institute, Beijing, China; The Commission on Economic System Reform, Beijing, China. © 1987 Academic Press, Inc.

Journal of Economic Literature Classification Numbers: 124, 134, 310.

1. EVOLUTION AND STATUS OF THE BANKING SYSTEM IN CHINA

China long ago instituted a system of central planning and unified management, under which everything was decided by the planning authorities and the market mechanism was neglected. Banks in China were not banks as the term is used in developed economies, but rather a cashier's counter of the State Ministry of Finance and the State Planning Commission. It was hard for them to play their financing role. This system has changed since the

[1] The views and interpretations in this paper are those of the authors and should not be attributed to the Research Institute of Economic System Reform and the Commission of Economic System Reform of China.

109

onset of China's economic reform in 1979. In particular, in 1983, with the setting up of the People's Bank of China (PBC) as the nation's central bank, China's banking system entered a new historical period. Figure 1 illustrates the structure of China's banking system at the end of 1985, after 7 years of reform.

There is a high degree of monopolistic specialization among China's subsidiary banks. Overlapping is rarely allowed, as the following descriptions show. The Industrial and Commercial Bank of China handles urban industrial and commercial credit and deposits of urban households. The Agricultural Bank of China handles credit and deposits in the countryside and small towns. The People's Construction Bank of China is the specialized bank for financing the State's investment projects from the state budget and household savings. The Investment Bank of China is the bank designated by the Chinese government for financing construction projects from abroad and handling foreign exchange investment credits. The People's Insurance Company of China (PICC) is responsible for various insurance operations. Its branches, the Insurance Company of China and the Pacific Insurance Company, are specialized in insuring foreigner's business and trade transportation. The China International Investment and Trust Company (CITIC) introduces foreign in-

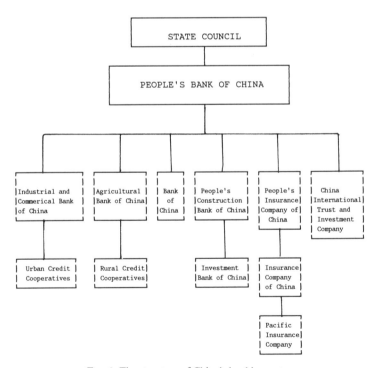

FIG. 1. The structure of China's banking system.

vestment, engages in trust investment for foreigners, and handles the ordinary banking business of foreign currency within China. Urban Credit Cooperatives and Rural Credit Cooperative are collectively owned financial organizations. Their operations are directed separately by the Industrial and Commercial Bank of China and the Agricultural Bank of China.

As a central bank, the People's Bank of China uses four main instruments to implement monetary policy. First, it formulates and ratifies, in accordance with the credit plan approved by the State Council, the individual plans for credit rationing of each specialized bank, and in this way controls the aggregate money supply and the issue of currency. Second, it concentrates a part of the funds from fiscal deposits and currency issue, to supplement and regulate credit expansion. Third, it stipulates the reserve requirement rate for all specialized commercial banks (at present, 10% for all banks except 30% for the People's Construction Bank of China). Fourth, it sets differential PBC interest rates for deposits with and borrowing from each specialized bank (currently, 0.36% monthly interest for deposits of commercial banks in PBC, 0.39% monthly interest for planned borrowing, 0.42% monthly interest for temporary borrowing).

In the 2 most recent years, the regulatory instruments used by the PBC over each specialized bank are mainly to formulate and ratify separately its loan quota and refinancing quota (or rediscount rate) for PBC, within the overall plan for money issue approved by the State Council and the general scope of credit (M1). In addition, PBC also gives guidance plans for capital investment loans to the specialized banks.

Interest rates in the Chinese banking system have long been relatively low. Since 1979, the PBC has raised the interest rate five times. Now the previous low-interest rate situation has been changed somewhat (see Table 1). Before 1979, China set the interest rate centrally. Branches at the grass-roots level had no authority to change the rate. Since 1979, floating rates (in a narrow range) have been put into effect, in order to bring the regulatory function of interest rates into play. The head office of the PBC stipulated that specialized banks and branches at the grass-roots level may, based on the rate standards provided by PBC, float the interest rate within a 20% range. So banks could

TABLE 1

AVERAGE ANNUAL INTEREST RATE

	1971–1978 (%)	After August 1985
Total deposits	1.09	3.0
Interest-bearing deposits	2.10	4.5
Savings deposits	3.06	7.2
Loans	6.48	7.0

set individual rates for loans with different economic efficiency and risk. But generally speaking, the interest rate still diverges from an equilibrium level.

There are four significant differences between commercial banks in China and those in developed economies. First, just as the overall political and economic management system of China is decomposed into geographic and sectoral management systems, so in banking as well, local governments at various levels and the concerned departments under the State Council are able to intervene in the credit business operations of commercial banks to a great extent. At a minimum, they have strong bargaining power. Second, central and local governments lay out a number of mandatory loans with different priorities, which commercial banks and their branches have to obey. These interventions seriously compromise the independent operations of commercial banks.

Third, because of the way in which public ownership unbalances the bargaining relationship between labor and management, there is a critical shortage of bank supervision over the financial affairs of enterprises. People in enterprises (both manager and employees) are biased toward more bonus funds and less capital accumulation. For this reason China stipulated all along that the commercial banks should supervise the finances and the wage bill of enterprises. Every enterprise can open its accounts in only one of the local bank branches. Net earnings must be divided into an award fund, a fund for welfare and for labor protection, and a fund for production, with no transfers permitted. As consumers were not allowed to use checks in China in the past, cash in circulation was closely related to consumer demand. Therefore, close supervision over cash withdrawals of firms was crucial in order to control the abuse of firms' profit. (Of course, assigning this supervisory function to a single bank branch had a negative effect on competition among commercial banks.) In recent years, commercial banks took no interest in this function and relaxed their supervision, which led to the inflation of consumer goods prices in 1984–1985.

Fourth, for the various reasons mentioned above, the various big specialized banks in China are not enterprises with independent management and responsible for their own loss and profit. Grass-roots branches experience intervention by both their head offices and local governments. There is not a clear link between branch operational profits and staff earnings. Therefore, despite experiments with all kinds of "responsibility mechanisms," none have gained much success. Banks at various levels show no strong concern about operational efficiency of credit. A large number of bad debts emerge and are cancelled from the bank's asset column periodically by the State's orders.

2. PROBLEMS IN BANKING-SYSTEM PERFORMANCE

Figure 2 shows the relations among China's banking institutions: the information flows and the control instruments. The upper feedback lines indicate proper market-information feedback, while the lower feedback lines indicate

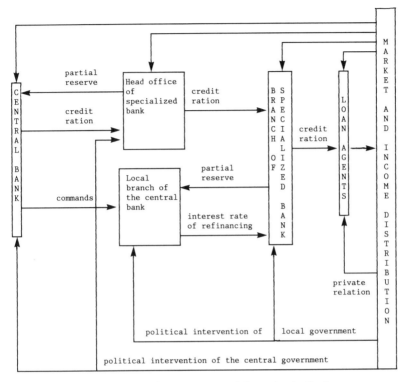

FIG. 2. The regulation structure and information feedback.

improper feedback control. Quantity rationing and quotas are still the major control instruments among banks and their branches. Within this framework, we may identify the following six problems of system performance.

First, given the planning tradition and administrative character of commercial banks, it is not possible to exercise effective control over the aggregate money supply through the partial reserve rates, rediscount rates, open market operations, and other instruments of the market mechanism. Therefore PBC has to rely heavily on quantity rationing to regulate aggregate demand. Except for loans for mandatory projects, the various big specialized banks disaggregate the greater part of their loan rations to their branches. A manager of a grassroots branch thinks that loan efficiency and profit are not related to the interests of himself and the branch staff. So he usually assigns a large part of the loan quotas to several loan agents in his branch. For this reason, the economic efficiency of the banking system in the whole country relies, to a great extent, on the behavior of the loan agents.

Second, because of the absence of a comprehensive set of effective instruments for parametric macroeconomic regulation, the loan agents are unlikely to implement a loan structure or investment structure which is consistent with the national social welfare. Instead, they are directed by the existing distorted prices, taxes, and other parameters of income distribution, not to mention their own subjective ideas. Within the limitation of the loan quotas of each loan agent, personal relationships play a role to varying degrees. Some of the loan agents violate the law and take unambiguous bribes, while others move in the gray area between illegal activities and bad-risk lending. It becomes difficult to recognize and penalize such activity.

Third, local government at each level often intervenes seriously in the business of commercial bank branches, investment bank branches, and even the local branches of the central bank. At present, local governments in China have financial power and materials allocation power sufficient to directly engage in profitable investment activities. As they seek to increase revenues of local governments, they too are influenced by the distorted prices and taxes. Some projects which they put investment in are often in great conflict with macroeconomic interests. For example, every province and large city wants to set up color TV factories and automobile plants, or to build a "Silicon Valley" whose products now have high selling prices and considerable profits. The central government has to call frequent meetings to give local leading cadres warnings to correct their behavior. All local branches of various banks rely excessively on local governments for infrastructural inputs, and even for appointment and removal of personnel. Therefore the intervention of local government always gets results. A person in charge of a local bank branch has to mediate between the commands from higher levels within the bank and from local government authority.

Fourth, the central government is not prepared to make the central bank an aggregate demand controlling body which is independent of government, so it often intervenes in the policies of the central bank. The financial relations between the State Treasury (the Ministry of Finance) and the central bank have not been normalized yet. Mandatory loans still account for a quite large portion of the total. As a result, the central bank has to frequently adjust its short-term monetary policy.

Fifth, financial institutions in China run their business based on the principle of operational specialization and monopolistic division. The Industrial and Commercial Bank of China accounts for 70% of the total volume of banking business in the whole country. Though PBC has been considering weakening the monopoly for 2 or 3 years, the competition in the system is still very weak. It is quite difficult for the central bank to regulate the nationwide banking business. The head offices of the relatively small number of the specialized banks stand in strong monopolistic positions, making readjustment by the central bank more difficult.

Sixth, the interest rate is still not rational, nor flexible enough. It does not properly reflect the cost of capital. On the one hand, it does not stimulate the specialized banks to attract deposits, but on the contrary, leads them to refinance from the central bank. On the other hand, profit as it is presently calculated does not represent properly the operating efficiency of specialized banks.

A simulation model (described in the Appendix) reveals that under the conditions of the above-mentioned regulations and the price distortion in China, the banking system will characteristically generate a monetary policy cycle—cycling between tight and easy money policies. In 1983 when the banking system preliminarily came into being as shown in Fig. 1 and Fig. 2, there were already some economists who pointed out the possibility of oscillations. That is, when an easy money policy is carried out, the behavior of loan agents causes damage to the sectoral structure due to the distorted price signals. With the intention of improving the sectoral structure and giving play to enterprise initiative, the bank is urged by governmental intervention to extend its easy money policy further. Once aggregate demand becomes seriously excessive, the Central Bank has to use a comprehensive shrinking policy through credit rationing and loan quotas without appropriately differentiating among individual transactions, which causes a slump and many depressed enterprises. As a result, the sectoral structure of loans and control of the aggregate money supply are always in contradiction.

We may say that from the end of 1983 to the fall of 1984, the preliminary liberalization of the banking system and relatively easy money policy did enhance economic efficiency and stimulate enterprise initiative with an accompanying high growth rate. From the end of 1984 to the summer of 1985 excessive aggregate demand gradually arose. It became serious in the middle of 1985; therefore, the very tight quantity rationing of the banking business was again adopted and the excessive growth rate slowed down step by step within a half year. But at the beginning of 1986, while the aggregate money supply had not yet been tightened enough, the irrational sectoral structure of loans emerged. The big coastal cities and large-scale industry were seriously short or working capital. Some local growth rates became zero or negative, while the impact on small industries and industry in the countryside, which are more dependent on private relations with loan agents and the protection of grass-roots government officials, was relatively small. With a view to improving this sectoral structure and supporting the scale of the economy, another round of easy money policy came along.

To be sure, periodic fluctuations in monetary policy can be broadly attributed to the government's haphazard investment before 1980, and its recent eagerness to promote reform at the expense of sectoral balance and rational sequencing. At the least, one could conclude that the current banking system in China, unable to bring shocks of this sort under effective control, to some degree simply lets the shocks trigger periodic fluctuations.

The periodic fluctuations discussed here are not necessarily chronic, but may be peculiar to the transition period. Some parameters and behavioral assumptions used in our model are already verified statistically; but others, emerging only recently in the midst of reform, need further testing. Having drawn a useful lesson from the episode of 1984–1985, the Chinese government, along with academic economists, is actively searching for summary macro-economic indicators which could serve as a guide to overcome these periodic fluctuations. However, indicators such as these are unlikely to be trusted and adopted by policy makers until they have proved their usefulness over a period of years. Furthermore, constructing summary indicators raises controversial theoretical issues over how to measure aggregate demand when the economy is in microeconomic disequilibrium. Until such indicators are available and effective regulations have been fashioned, periodic fluctuations will be the price of drastic reform.

Both experience and model exercises show that until the price distortion and indirect-tax distortion are cured and as long as banks in China are assigned the dual responsibility of controlling aggregate demand and sectoral structure, a series of problems such as business cycles and inefficiency are produced. Further reform is urgently needed. However, some people consider that the cooling of the hot growth in the second half of 1985 is evidence that the quantity rationing performed by the central bank is an effective measure, which can continue to be used so that reform of the banking system should be postponed.

3. THE OBJECTIVES OF BANKING SYSTEM REFORM

What should banking reform aim for? To develop bank institutions as real enterprises, each of them should be an enterprise with independent manage-ment and accounting, paying taxes by law, getting rid of excessive political intervention, and raising operating efficiency. To strengthen the authority of the Central Bank in macroeconomic monetary policy, we should mainly use guidance regulation instruments and use direct quantity controls as auxiliary supplements to regulate aggregate demand, control inflation, and promote harmonious economic development. Credit rationing should be retained where necessary, but greater attention should be paid to indirect control in general, and to partial reserve ratio and rediscount rate control in particular. China should set up a financial system with bank credit as its core and with varied channels, varied approaches, and varied credit tools, invigorated financing activities, guided movement of liquidity, and raised operating efficiency, and thus gradually form a financial market compatible with China's conditions of economic reform. We should constitute several general-purpose banks in order to develop overlapping operations of financing business, strengthen competition among banks, and raise efficiency. In order to modernize oper-ations of the financial institutions, we must enhance the quality of our per-sonnel. A lack of trained staff is a major problem facing the banking system.

Furthermore, we should prohibit political intervention and free the com-mercial banks at every level from a subordinate connection to local govern-ment. Let grass-roots branches and other supervisory bodies rationally divide up their supervisory responsibilities over firms. Bank branches should continue to undertake strict bookkeeping and monitor the legality of internal income distribution of firms. If a successful reform in enterprise ownership could be fashioned, the supervisory function of the grass-roots banks could be further relaxed. Last, the banking system in due course should be freed from the responsibility for improving the sectoral structure. This should be the job of tax and other fiscal policies. The Central Bank should concentrate on control of aggregate demand.

The central task of banking reform is to solidify macroeconomic control of the central bank over aggregate demand, and to guarantee a relatively independent position for the central bank. The monetary policy instruments of the market mechanism will gradually become its major tools. Grass-roots branches behave like profit-maximizing enterprises are a prerequisite for these tools to be effective. The Central Bank should rationalize the interest rate, grasp the whole power of determining its own interest rates, and take control over aggregate demand as its main task, but not be assigned the duty of adjustment of sectoral structure.

What sorts of changes elsewhere in the economy will banking system reform require? First, we must gradually liberalize prices and rationalize the indirect tax system. This will give enterprise banks correct market signals. Second, we must reshape the functions of local governments, eliminating their direct role in management production and investment and their intervention in banking business. Third, we must harden the financial constraint on production units, improve decision making procedures and the responsibility system in enterprise investments, and reform enterprise ownership, so as to ensure that bank credit will be utilized properly and repaid. Ideally, banking system reform will proceed in step with progress in these areas.

Some economists hold that we should make a breakthrough by trying experiments in specific areas as a way of pushing forward overall banking system reform. But very often, these experiments relax constraints only in one area. For example, suppose that the monetary policy is tight, but the interest rate set by the State Council is still low in the whole country (coupled with credit rationing); meanwhile, an experimental area is given the power to raise the interest rate, consequently drawing in large amounts of deposits from other areas. One can imagine the problematic outcome of this experiment. We are now trying some different experiments in several regions in China. The government and academic circles are waiting to analyze the outcome of these experiments. Meanwhile the overall comprehensive design for banking system reform is also under preparation and continual reassessment.

APPENDIX: A BRIEF DESCRIPTION OF THE MODEL

The author is of the opinion that control of aggregate demand in China is closely related to sectoral structure. Therefore a multisector general purpose policy model, built a couple of years ago, was pressed into service, expanded to include the banking system. This model was used to simulate the performance of the banking system studied in this paper. Space limits make it impossible to describe this model in detail. Only its main features will be mentioned here.

Technically speaking, Block I is a recursive nonlinear programming model, which is used to maximize welfare in the light of socialist planning objectives, subject to constraints such as the requirements of balance in various accounts, and of supply–demand equilibrium in product and factor markets. Some markets clear solely by means of price, wage, interest rate or exchange rate adjustment. In other sectors, where prices are rigid, or their flexibility is limited, or where quantity rationing is imposed, supply–demand equilibrium must come through some other process, such as regulation of imports and exports (which can in turn be effected by tariffs and export subsidies). There are still other sectors where supply–demand disequilibrium may ultimately prevail. The dual form of this nonlinear optimization model is a model of non-Walrasian computable general equilibrium, similar to a CGE model in form, but differing from the latter in that some inequality constraints, representing quantity rationing and price rigidity, are imposed. This difference will also change the solution strategy of the model.

In view of the presence in Block I of production functions, consumption demand functions, import demand functions, and export functions, etc., and the fact that historical base data represent a period when the economy was in disequilibrium, we have used disequilibrium estimation methods, characterized by sample separation over different sectors, to estimate some of the

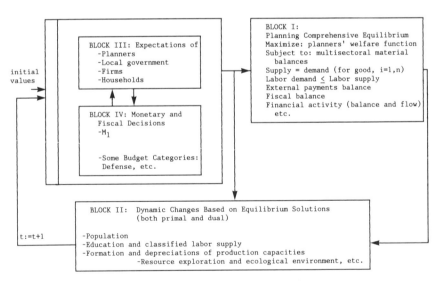

FIGURE 3

functions. For all the lack in robustness of the estimators, this method turns out to be better than the routine method, as is shown by the analysis of errors.

In addition, we also try to represent forced substitution and forced saving in the demand system. Shadow price vectors are used to endogenously generate, under microeconomic disequilibrium, an indicator of the aggregate excess demand, which reflects the extent to which the economic structure has deteriorated.

In order to analyze the performance of the banking system, we posit the following three behavioral assumptions, based on updated data and casual empiricism.

1. The State Council and the Central Bank (in Block IV) responds to indications of aggregate excess demand with a time lag, due to an unsophisticated information system, a weak theoretical basis, and conflicting views among advisers. They tend to use instruments of indirect control when money is easy, but fall back on quantity rationing and command control when tight money policy is adopted.

2. Local governments (in Block I) intervene less when money is easy than when money is tight.

3. Bank branches and loan agents (in Block I) make decisions autonomously, in an easy money period, so as to maximize their profits subject to the constraint and distortions imposed by prices and taxes. On the other hand, when money is tight, they implement instructions regarding mandatory project loans which are passed down by the State Planning Commission through the Central Bank, and become more vulnerable to intervention by local governments. This behavior can be explained by their eagerness to avoid committing any serious mistakes.

JOURNAL OF COMPARATIVE ECONOMICS 11, 410–426 (1987)

China's Economic Reforms in a Comparative Perspective[1]

BELA BALASSA

The Johns Hopkins University, Baltimore, Maryland 21218 and World Bank, Washington, D.C. 20433

Balassa, Bela—China's Economic Reforms in a Comparative Perspective

The paper makes recommendations for extending the reform effort while establishing macroeconomic equilibrium in China. The recommendations concern increasing the decision-making power of enterprises, which are to respond to profit incentives; creating the conditions for effective competition in Chinese industry; reforming prices; linking bonuses to work performance; establishing an effective monetary policy; rationalizing the banking system; and setting realistic interest rates. The paper indicates the need for taking simultaneous action in all these areas. *J. Comp. Econ.,* September, 1987, **11**(3), pp. 410–426. The Johns Hopkins University, Baltimore, Maryland 21218 and World Bank, Washington, D.C. 20433. © 1987 Academic Press, Inc.

Journal of Economic Literature Classification Numbers: 052, 123, 124.

This paper will briefly review the economic reforms introduced in China after 1978, analyze the performance of Chinese agriculture and industry following the reforms, and examine prospective changes in the future. In the discussion, planning and markets, competition and profit incentives, price reform, as well as wages and bonuses will receive attention. Consideration will further be given to the macroeconomic preconditions of the reform effort. In regard to the individual topics, the experience of European socialist countries and, in particular, that of Hungary will be noted, based largely on the writings of the author (Balassa, 1983a, 1983b, and 1985).

[1] The author prepared this paper following a visit to China on November 11–21, 1985. He is grateful for helpful discussions he had at the Institute of Economics and the Institute of World Economics and Politics in Beijing, at the University of Nankai in Tianjin, and at the Economic Research Center and the Institute of World Economy in Shanghai. The author further acknowledges the valuable comments made on the first draft of the paper by A. Doak Barnett, William Byrd, Dong Fureng, Nicholas Lardy, Dwight Perkins, Thomas Rawski, Bruce Reynolds, and Edward Schuh, as well as comments received at the Arden House Conference on Chinese Economic Reform on October 9–12, 1986. He alone is responsible for the contents of the paper, however, and they should not be interpreted to reflect the views of the World Bank.

CHINESE ECONOMIC REFORM

AGRICULTURAL REFORMS AND PERFORMANCE

As in the case of Hungary, the first major reforms in China were introduced in agriculture. After 1978, agricultural prices were substantially raised, resulting in improvements in agriculture's terms of trade. Also, mandatory quotas for sown area and output were eliminated and purchase (compulsory procurement) quotas were reduced, with the sale of above-quota output on free markets, and increased possibilities were provided for undertaking so-called sideline activities. Finally, the commune system gave place to family responsibility systems, among which the bao gan dao hu[2] has come to dominate, accounting for 94% of peasant households in 1984.

There are similarities as well as differences in the agricultural reforms introduced in China and in Hungary. Agricultural prices were raised in both cases; however, Hungary abolished the system of compulsory delivery as early as 1957. But, it retained the cooperatives as basic farming units while giving greater scope to household plots, with production on these plots accounting for one-third of agricultural output. Finally, similar to China, Hungary encouraged the expansion of sideline activities.

There are several reasons for the observed differences in institutional structure. The Hungarian farming cooperatives are relatively small, possess considerable flexibility, and provide performance incentives to their members whereas the Chinese communes were huge, unwieldy units. Also, the high degree of mechanization in Hungarian agriculture has necessitated the maintenance of large production units that has not been the case in China.

In response to the reforms, per capita grain production in China rose by one-sixth between 1978 and 1985, although the acreage devoted to the cultivation of grains declined. As grains accounted for a large proportion of total acreage, land under other crops increased considerably, notwithstanding some decline in the total sown area.[3] With rising yields, the per capita output of cotton rose by two-thirds, that of oilseeds, sugar, and tobacco approximately doubled, and substantial increases were observed also in the case of minor crops. Assisted further by the expansion of livestock raising and sideline activities, per capita gross agricultural output grew by two-thirds, with crop output per head rising by two-fifths during the 1978–1985 period (Ma, 1983, Table 1; "Communique," 1986). According to one estimate, about one-half

---

[2] Under this system, land (adjusted for quality) is divided equally among households in per capita terms, or on the basis of the number of able-bodied workers per household. The obligations of individual households are limited to the payment of taxes, the fulfillment of purchase quotas, and contributions to social welfare funds. These obligations have been defined in absolute terms, rather than as a proportion of output, thereby providing incentives for increasing production.

[3] In the 1979–1983 period, for which data are available, the area devoted to grains was reduced by 4%, that under other crops increased by 20% while the total sown area declined by 3% (Lim et al., 1985, Annex 2, p. 11).

of the increase in farm output (crops and livestock) between 1978 and 1984 can be attributed to increases in inputs and one-half to the growth of total factor productivity, which had fallen in the preceding 26 years (Johnson, 1986, Table 2).

The rapid rise of agricultural output was achieved, even though the share of agriculture in budget allocation for new investment and for current expenditures fell during the period and the agricultural credit system restrained investment, with increases in rural deposits substantially exceeding the rise in lending to agriculture (Lardy, 1986). Also, due to uncertainty about land tenure, private investments concentrated in housing.

It has been suggested that increases in prices might have led to the rise in output even in the absence of organizational changes (Khan and Lee, 1983, p. 52). But, in Soviet Central Asia, cited as evidence in support of this proposition, increases in agricultural production were much smaller than in China. And, the observed rise in yields could not have been accomplished under the commune system, where the link between performance and rewards was lacking. This conclusion is supported by the findings of a cross-section investigation, which show that the growth of agricultural production was positively correlated with the extent to which the family responsibility system was applied in individual provinces in the early 1980s (Lin, 1986).

The reduction in the number of agricultural commodities under compulsory procurement from 29 to 10 in 1984, followed by the replacement of compulsory procurement quotas by purchases under contract for grains and cotton, represents a further easing of controls although the state will continue to set the purchase price under the contracts. Zhao Ziyang, the Premier of the State Council, announced that agricultural prices and purchase quotas will be further liberalized in the future, with a view to developing exports (*Beijing Review*, No. 7–8, February 18, 1985, p. 16). In this connection, comparisons of domestic agricultural prices with world market prices are of interest.

According to a study by the Research Institute of Prices, in 1984 the average purchase prices for 18 major agricultural products were, on the average, 26% lower than world market prices, with large disparities shown among commodities. Thus, average prices paid for wheat were 22% and for oil and fat 17% higher than prices on the world market, while cotton and jute prices were 28% and average prices for animal products 48% lower than world market prices (Dong, 1985b, p. 26).

In 1985, prices for pig meat were raised to a considerable extent, so as to encourage production through improved profitability that was compromised as a result of earlier increases in the prices of feed grains. This change conforms to the price relationships found on the world market. Further changes in this direction would be desirable to permit the exploitation of China's comparative advantage in agricultural products, with account taken of the possible effects of Chinese exports and imports on world market prices.

Thus, China would export rice if its quality improved, although large exports would depress the world market price. Rapid expansion of Chinese exports of cotton, jute, and tea may also lower world market prices somewhat. However, for all remaining products, in particular for potential new exports, world market prices will provide an appropriate guide.

In the statement referred to above, the Premier of the State Council noted the possibility that in the coastal areas, where considerable potential exists for exports, as well as in areas suitable for forestry and animal husbandry, peasants may in the future pay a tax instead of delivering grain to the state. This alternative may be generalized by freeing markets for all agricultural products and replacing sales to the state at below-market prices, which represent an implicit tax, by a land tax.[4]

Such changes would contribute to the growth of agricultural output and incomes through increased intraregional and interregional specialization, complemented by international trade. This is of a particular importance since the large gains in yields, obtained chiefly through increased work effort, better organization, and improved marketing, could not be duplicated in the future. At the same time, the introduction of a land tax would also permit reducing interregional income inequalities that result from differences in the quality of land both within and among regions (Balassa, 1982, p. 329).

The development of Chinese agriculture would further require the increased availability of modern inputs, such as fertilizer, agricultural machinery, and improved seeds, as well as credit and support services. While higher agricultural prices would permit peasants to pay for modern inputs without the granting of input subsidies that tend to encourage their excessive use, improvements in infrastructure and the provision of extension services and research have to be a governmental responsibility as the social benefits exceed the benefits to the individual peasants.

Finally, there is need to encourage investments by the peasants themselves. This would require changing existing land tenure arrangements. Short of the privatization of land, granting for its use for a period of, say, 30–40 years and permitting the transfer of the contract would provide inducements to investment.

INDUSTRIAL REFORMS AND PERFORMANCE

The expression "responsibility system," originally applied to agriculture, has come to be employed in reference to state-owned industry as well. It is

---

[4] There is today a rudimentary land tax in the form of an output tax that has changed little over the years, but the revenue it provides is rather small, considerably below 2% of value added in agriculture (Lardy, 1986). At the same time, the experience of other countries indicates that the difficulties of establishing a land tax can be overcome. Such a tax has long been used in Hungary, where the elimination of compulsory procurement in 1957 has led to higher output through increased specialization and exports.

used to refer to the increased role of material incentives, including profit retention schemes and productivity-based bonuses, the increased power of managers vis-à-vis party officials in the affairs of the firm, and the greater latitude given to the firm for making its own production and investment decisions, with above-quota output sold to consumers either directly or indirectly through commercial channels.

But, whereas under the family responsibility system there is a direct link between performance and reward, in state-owned industry the link is indirect through profit allocation and bonus schemes, in which profits are affected by factors extraneous to the firm, in particular prices, and profit retention by the firm depends on the norm established by the supervisory authorities. Also, with reductions in the scope of compulsory deliveries, together with the encouragement of sideline activities, the scope of market-oriented activities has been greater in agriculture than in industry, and the share of these activities in industry has varied considerably among firms. By contrast, Hungary abolished plan targets on January 1, 1968.

Following an initial slowdown, the growth of industrial output accelerated in China ("Communique," 1985, 1986). At the same time, while greater reliance on markets has encouraged production for the needs of the population, the pursuit of profits has often led to changes in the product mix that did not conform to demand. Also, there is conflicting evidence in regard to changes in the efficiency of industry in China.

According to one study, the ratio of value added net of depreciation to output value increased by 6% between 1978 and 1981 (Byrd, 1982, Table 2). However, other researchers found a decline rather than an increase in the share of value added in industrial output for the same period, with value added rising by 19.4% and output volume by 22.9%, both expressed in 1970 prices (Ma, 1983, Table 1; Rawski, 1984, Table 1). Also, available estimates show that total factor productivity in state-owned industry declined between 1978 and 1983 as the 28.4% growth in net output involved a 49.3% increase in capital and a 16.7% rise in employment (Tidrick, 1986, Table 2).

PLANNING AND MARKETS

In contradistinction to Hungary, after 1978 China maintained plan targets for its state-owned firms. While planning has subsequently been liberalized, the products remaining subject to mandatory plans continue to represent a substantial segment of industry, with estimates ranging from 20% upward. The products in question include coal, crude oil, petroleum products, rolled steel, nonferrous metals, timber, cement, electricity, chemical materials and fertilizer, synthetic fibers, cigarettes, newsprint, imported machinery and equipment, as well as munitions. For these products, the state continues to set production quotas and prices, although above-quota sales are permitted at so-called floating prices.

The October 20, 1984 Decision of the Central Committee stated that "other products and economic activities [i.e., those not subject to mandatory quotas] . . . should either come under guidance planning or be left entirely to the operation of the market, as the case may require" ("Decision," 1985, p. VIII). However, the meaning of guidance planning has not been clarified, and a large number of products, which do not come under mandatory planning, are subject to quota allocation for part of their output, with the rest marketed outside the plan at floating prices.

The two-tier system of sales and prices increases the freedom of decision-making for the firm, but may have adverse effects on the national economy. Since raising the quota allocation of inputs and reducing that of output may affect the firm's profits to a much greater extent than any improvements in production, bargaining and influence-peddling are at a premium. Nor should it be assumed that profitability at the prices of above-quotas sales represents social profitability, in part because these prices differ from equilibrium prices that would be obtained in the absence of quotas, and in part because the prices of capital and labor do not reflect scarcity relationships.

In order for China to reap the benefits of a market-oriented economy, it would have to reduce the number of commodities subject to mandatory planning, and to phase out quotas on all other products, relying on indirect policy instruments, such as taxes and monetary policy, to guide enterprises. Furthermore, one should reaffirm the freedom of decision-making for the enterprise vis-à-vis the various surrogates for the central planning authorities, including the industrial bureaus and corporations as well as the "guiding" role assigned to localities, which have assumed importance in recent years. As one observer noted:

In the early stages of reform implementation the position of enterprises was enhanced and the "excessive" control previously exercised by their immediate supervisors criticized. . . . Starting in 1980 and especially with the campaign to promote ERSs [economic responsibility systems] of 1981, the orientation of reforms shifted to the next higher level in the industrial management—the bureaus and corporations. Under the ERS these organizations commonly determine all of the key financial provisions of incentive schemes affecting their subordinate enterprises. (Byrd, 1982, p. 14)

According to the same author,

there are good economic reasons why in many cases decentralization should not proceed all the way down to the enterprise level. In particular, decentralization of investment decisions and control over investment funds to enterprises is likely to generate an inefficient and duplicative pattern of investment, in the absence of effective financial intermediation of the banking system. (Byrd, 1982, p. 15)

Decision-making on investment should not be divorced, however, from responsibility for profits and losses since otherwise profitability considerations will not appropriately enter into investment decisions. In this connection, the experience of Hungary is of interest.

At the time of the introduction of the economic reform, it was decided to decentralize investment decisions in manufacturing industries, except for large investments that substantially added to capacity in a particular industry and for the establishment of new enterprises. In subsequent years, however, there were increased government interventions in investment decisions in linking the provision of budget support to state preferences.

Eventually, it came to be understood that the sharing of responsibility for the investment decision was not conducive to efficiency, and firms were provided with the opportunity to request government aid in the event that the investment proved to be unprofitable. Correspondingly, steps have been taken to restore decision-making authority on investment to the enterprise.

China is well-advised to follow Hungary's example in linking investment decisions to responsibility for profits and losses at the firm level, with government organizations retaining decision-making authority only over large investments in basic industries and the establishment of enterprises of nationwide importance. Thus, the recent inclusion of investments by collective and individual enterprises in the overall state plan (*Beijing Review,* No. 13, March 31, 1986, p. 26) represents a backward step. Rather than relying on central interventions, duplication in investment may be avoided through competition and rational pricing.

At the same time, to the extent that the industrial bureaus and corporations combine firms manufacturing particular products, as in the case of shipbuilding and the automotive industry, competition will be reduced. In any case, the industrial bureaus and corporations, established through the transformation of government offices, have remained administrative organizations imposed on the enterprises. In order to free enterprise decision-making from undue interference, similar organizations have been eliminated in Hungary.

Nor does the regional decentralization of administrative organizations represent an appropriate solution. Localities have played an important role in recent years in setting profit conditions for the enterprise and, under a recent State Council decision, the Ministry of Machine Building Industry will delegate its management power to the major cities where subordinate enterprises are located. Apart from the division of decision-making authority, the problem associated with this arrangement is that local interests may predominate over the national interest.[5]

In any event, there have been repeated reports of the localities setting barriers to incoming products and to the sale of raw materials in other regions. As in the Soviet Union at the time of the regionalization of decision-making, such actions aim at increasing regional self-sufficiency. This objective has also been served by investments undertaken by localities, which have assumed increasing importance notwithstanding exhortations to the contrary by the central government.

---

[5] This was noted in the October 1984 Decision of the Central Committee that exhorted "city governments to separate their functions from those of enterprises . . . and not repeat the past practice of mainly depending on administrative means to control enterprises so as to avoid creating new barriers between departments and regions" ("Decision," 1984, p. x).

In presenting the Sixth Five Year Plan, the Premier of the State Council underlined the need that "no locality or department shall make investment in fixed assets outside the plan without prior approval by the appropriate higher authorities" ("Report," 1982, p. 25). As unplanned investments nevertheless increased rapidly, the need for checking their growth was repeatedly stated. Yet, in the first 7 months of 1985, unplanned investments were 95% higher than in the corresponding period in 1984, bringing the average increase of new fixed investments (in Chinese parlance, investments in capital construction) to 45%, although planned investments rose by only 9% (*Beijing Review*, No. 37, September 16, 1985, p. 2).

Investments by localities, undertaken to the neglect of national economic considerations, have led to considerable duplication of capacity. The financing of these investments has been accomplished in part by withdrawing funds from enterprises and in part by borrowing from the local branches of banks. Increasing the freedom of action of the enterprises would limit the availability of the first of these sources of funds while the second may be dealt with through the reform of the banking system, discussed below.

COMPETITION AND PROFIT INCENTIVES

Freeing enterprises from the dominance of the central and local authorities is a necessary step toward assuring that they bear "complete responsibility for profits and losses" and that "all enterprises compete on an equal footing"—the stated objectives of the Seventh Five Year Plan ("Proposal," 1985, pp. XVIII and XIX). This is because instructions and interventions by supervisory organizations cannot fail to affect the economic performance of the firm and the conditions under which it operates.

In this connection, it should be emphasized that the firm's profits and the conditions of competition depend to a considerable extent on its relationships with the supervising organizations and on its bargaining power in obtaining favorable treatment in the allocation of materials, the extent of above-quota sales, and the setting of profit targets (compensating taxes). Hierarchical differences among the supervising organizations have been further sources of differentiation among enterprises.[6]

Competition has also been limited by the desire of industrial bureaus and corporations to safeguard all firms under their jurisdiction. Protection at the provincial and local levels, referred to earlier, has represented another limitation to competition. According to one observer "barriers to interregional trade erected by local and provincial governments may be the most serious

---

[6] According to an informed observer, there is a distinction between enterprises directly under the central government and local enterprises (including provincial enterprises, county enterprises, etc.), a distinction between key enterprises and non-key enterprises, and even distinctions between ministerial, departmental, and board categories. All these different enterprises were treated differently in terms of funds, materials, labor (including technical personnel), product marketing, foreign-directed economic activities, raw materials prices, and so on" (Dong, 1985a, p. 25).

obstacle to the development of competition and to such resulting benefits as improved efficiency and increased regional specialization" (Byrd, 1987, p. 259).

Apart from removing obstacles to competition, the pursuit of the stated objectives would require that the director of the enterprise be given full power to manage the firm's affairs. Thus far, directors have been freed from the tutelage of party committees in about one-third of the industrial firms; the rest should follow under the decision of the Central Committee, which calls for establishing "a system of the director or manager assuming full responsibility" for the firm ("Decision," 1984, p. XI). This objective was reconfirmed by Premier Zhao Ziyang in his report on the Seventh Five Year Plan ("Report," 1986, p. xii) and a new directive to this effect was promulgated on October 1, 1986 (Beijing Review, No. 44, November 1, 1986, p. 4).

Responsibility for the firm's operations means making the manager financially interested in the profits and losses of the enterprise. In addition to decision-making power over the distribution of enterprise funds, the director, and management in general, should share in the profits of the firm in the form of bonuses and in the losses through reductions in compensation. At the same time, unless they can be rehabilitated, enterprises which experience continuing losses would have to be eventually closed down.

The need for closing down enterprises that could not meet the test of the market has been recognized in the Decision of the Central Committee, according to which "our enterprises are put to the test of direct judgment by consumers in the market place so that only the best survive" (1984, p. X). But while a considerable number of collective enterprises have closed their doors in recent years, this has reportedly been the case for only one state-owned firm. At the same time, there would be a need to introduce bankruptcy legislation regulating the conditions and the modalities of closing down firms as has already been done in Hungary. However, for profits and losses to reflect enterprise performance in the context of the national economy, prices need to express resource scarcities. This, in turn, leads to the question of the rationality of prices and the need for price reform in China.

PRICE REFORM

Official prices in China are the result of governmental decisions taken at different points of time and for different purposes. They correspond neither to production costs nor to market conditions, and the few adjustments made since 1978 have changed the situation but little. Yet, price distortions favor some enterprises and penalize others; provide the wrong signals for production and investment; and entail a cost for the national economy.

To begin with, price distortions exist in input–output relationships. For example, the revenue derived from exporting one ton of granular active charcoal is $800 while exporting the fuel necessary for its production would bring $1680 (Chang and Lin, 1985, p. 4). More generally, prices are low for energy and raw materials and high for finished products, compared with world market prices. On the average, the domestic prices of petroleum and petroleum products are 78%, and the prices of metallurgical products 47%, below world market prices. In turn, the prices for 21 chemical products are, on the average, 80% higher than world market prices and the prices of steel-based products also tend to be higher (Dong, 1985b, p. 26).

Distortions in the relative prices of inputs and outputs encourage the excessive use of energy and raw materials and discourage increasing their production. Furthermore, distortions in the prices of substitute products raise the economic cost of providing for domestic consumption. For example, despite the adjustments made in 1982, the domestic prices of cotton yarn and raw silk are 35 to 74% lower, and the prices of polyester and polyamide filaments 97 to 113% higher, than world market prices (Dong, 1985b, p. 26).

Furthermore, artificial differences in the prices of the enterprise's products have an adverse impact on the users, and hence on the national economy, in reducing product variety and compelling users to buy products that do not fully conform to their needs. This is of particular importance in the case of intermediate products, where the unavailability of the requisite variety adds to costs and reduces product quality.

It has been reported, for example, that a zinc smelter has abandoned the production of Grade 2 electrolytic zinc that had a similar cost but a lower price than Grade 1 zinc. For the same reason, a cement factory has ceased to produce lower grades of cement (Byrd, 1987, p. 260). Also, steel products do not conform to requirements because of artificial differences in their prices. Thus, it has been reported that the profit margin is 10 times as high on hot rolled steel than on cold rolled steel (*The Economist,* October 27, 1984), thereby favoring the production of the former over the latter.

Finally, high-quality product varieties are in excess demand, and low-quality varieties in excess supply, leading to shortages in the first case and to the accumulation of unsold inventories in the second. Prices do not perform their equilibrating function as the maximum price differential for consumer goods of different qualities has been set at 15%.[7]

These considerations indicate the need for price reform. Such reform is necessary, first of all, to ensure that profits and losses reflect the enterprise's performance rather than the vagaries of the price system. The setting of profit quotas and, more recently, the imposition of differential taxes on profits, designed to compensate for profit differentials that are unrelated to performance, cannot adequately cope with the situation.

---

[7] The adverse economic effects of the regulations applied have been well-expressed by Tian Jiyun, the Vice-Premier of the State Council, "fine-quality products cannot have their prices raised and poor-quality goods cannot have their prices reduced. Therefore, the supply of fine-quality products falls short of demand, but production cannot be developed because of the low price. Poor-quality products do not sell well and they get stock-piled, but their production cannot be reduced" (1985, p. 17).

To begin with, compensating taxes are levied on existing profits that may result from favorable prices but may also reflect superior performance. Also, the setting of these taxes is subject to bargaining and may depend on the favoritism shown by the supervising organizations in regard to particular enterprises. And while periodical price adjustments are made for unfavorable changes in the underlying conditions of the enterprise, e.g., increases in the prices of inputs, an asymmetry is introduced by the fact that enterprises tend to conceal favorable changes in these conditions (Byrd, 1982, pp. 19–20).

Apart from eliminating the effects of price distortions on profits, the price reform would channel the energies of the enterprise from trying to obtain better treatment by the supervisory organizations to improving performance. It would further contribute to the objective of having enterprises compete on an equal footing. In turn, the appropriate valuation of fixed capital, with realistic charges made for their use, would permit eliminating differences in profits due to the age and the technical level of machinery in the enterprise.

Establishing realistic prices would also avoid having enterprises choose to manufacture products on the basis of their favorable prices. At the same time, greater price differentiation is necessary to establish equilibrium in product markets by providing appropriate signals for consumers as well as for producers.

Greater price differentiation would bring about an increase in demand for low-quality varieties, and a decrease in demand for high-quality varieties, of a particular product. This is of especial importance in regard to imports that have been encouraged by relatively low prices of high-quality products.[8] Appropriate pricing provides a better way to limit the imports of consumer goods than controls, which invite evasion through smuggling and bribery.

Greater price differentiation would also encourage the manufacture of high-quality products and discourage that of low-quality products. Apart from contributing to product upgrading, this would permit avoiding a situation in which new capacity is created by existing firms, as well as by firms entering the industry, to manufacture outdated products for which there is little demand, in response to misleading price signals.

Market-clearing prices would thus permit demand to guide production decisions. Furthermore, apart from providing incentives for energy and material savings, establishing appropriate price relationships as between inputs and outputs would encourage low-cost transformation activities while discouraging high-cost activities. More generally, rational prices would contribute

---

[8] In the first half of 1985, China imported more consumer goods than it did in all of 1984 when these commodities already reached one-fifth of total imports (*Beijing Review*, No. 29, July 29, 1985, p. 2). Compared with the same period of the previous year, imports of television sets from Japan increased four times, reaching an annual rate of $1.0 billion in the first half of 1985 (*The Economist*, August 10, 1985). Further increases occurred in subsequent months, leading to the subsequent introduction of restrictions.

to efficient resource allocation through changes in consumption, production, and trade.

The existing two-tier system of prices provides a basis for establishing market-clearing prices in China. In this connection, the interdependence of pricing and competition should be emphasized, when the possibilities for effective competition depend on the size of the domestic market. Comparisons with Hungary are of interest in this regard.

At the time of the introduction of the reform, Hungarian industry was greatly concentrated, with monopoly positions existing in some industries and oligopolistic market structures in others. In order to increase the scope of market prices, efforts were made to establish competition by breaking up trusts and large enterprises. Still, in a number of industries, the extent of competition is limited by the smallness of Hungary's domestic market, necessitating import competition.

While population is not an appropriate measure of market size, China's gross domestic product is 15 times that of Hungary and its manufacturing sector is about 12 times larger. Furthermore, China has much more state-owned enterprises than Hungary and individual enterprises are also assuming a greater role. Correspondingly, China has important advantages over Hungary in its possibilities to establish domestic competition in manufacturing industries, which is a precondition for the market determination of prices. At the same time, competition should also extend to commercial activities, including the establishment of multiple channels in wholesale and retail trade and the creation of trading companies operating across provincial boundaries.

In some basic industries shortages cannot be eliminated overnight, due to the lack of sufficient capacity. In these cases, mandatory targets and price fixing would need to be maintained on a temporary basis. But, the number of such products should be kept to a minimum, lest difficulties are created for the expansion of market relations in the rest of the economy. At the same time, world market prices would provide an appropriate standard for setting the prices of these commodities. Placing increased reliance on world market prices, in turn, necessitates establishing a realistic exchange rate.

The proposals made here would entail the establishment of a mixed price system in Chinese industry, with the market determination of prices in industries where planning targets are abolished and central price fixing retained in industries under mandatory planning, with links established to world market prices in the latter case. Apart from standardized products, world market prices could not be readily utilized in China because the varieties produced there generally differ in quality and specifications from those available abroad. At any rate, as the author earlier noted, given its large market and relatively low level of industrial development, it would seem appropriate for China to have domestic prices reflect domestic scarcities rather than world market relationships for such products (Balassa, 1982). This contrasts with Hungary, where small domestic market competition needs to be complemented with import competition, involving reliance on world market price relationships.

WAGES AND BONUSES

The long-standing custom of providing practically equal wages to every worker, regardless of productivity, expressed by the saying, "everybody eating from the same big pot" gave place to a bonus system after 1978. Bonuses were supposed to reward performance and be paid from increases in profits. In fact, however, bonuses were often provided indiscriminately to all workers, even in the absence of profits, thereby contributing to general wage increases.

In order to combat these tendencies, in May 1984 the government introduced a tax on enterprises whose yearly bonus awards exceeded a certain level. The tax was set at 30% in cases when bonuses equalled 2.5 to 4 months' wages; 100% on bonuses between 4 and 6 months' wages; and 300% above this limit (*Beijing Review*, No. 26, June 25, 1984, p. 4).

The imposition of the tax on bonuses encountered practical difficulties of collection, however. Also, enterprises increased basic wages, in the place of providing bonuses, in order to escape the tax. Increases were undertaken, in part in response to worker demands and in part to establish a high base for the newly announced system of taxing increments in wages and bonuses from their 1984 level.

In any event, the growth of labor compensation accelerated, with the total wage bill of enterprises rising by 19% in 1984 over the previous years' level ("Current," 1985, p. XI). The government's exhortations notwithstanding, a further increase of 22% occurred between 1984 and 1985 (*Beijing Review*, No. 51, December 23, 1985, p. 23). These figures do not include increases in compensation in kind, such as clothing and free lunches, which have assumed considerable importance (*Beijing Review*, No. 16, April 22, 1985, pp. 4–5).

Apart from the need to soak up the resulting excess purchasing power, to be discussed below, questions arise about the appropriateness of the wage regulations actually applied in China. It is evident that the combination of hourly wages and bonuses has contributed to wage inflation. Nor do exhortations suffice to deal with the situation in the framework at the present wage system. Thus, the cited increases occurred notwithstanding the fact that, in his report to the Fifth National People's Congress on November 20, 1981, Premier Zhao Ziyang demanded that "the present practice of handing out bonuses indiscriminately snould be strictly checked and bonuses payable in 1982 limited to the 1981 level (*Beijing Review*, No. 51, December 21, 1981, p. 21).

Furthermore, one may object to linking labor compensation to profits, which depend on managerial decisions rather than on the performance of individual workers. It would be more appropriate to generalize the use of the piece-wage system that links wages directly to the worker's performance as is increasingly done in Hungary. The use of such a system was proposed by Ma

Hong, one of China's leading economists.[9] Although piece wages are utilized today in less than one-tenth of Chinese industry, Ma's conclusions continue to be valid.

Following the example of Hungary, it would further be desirable to tax wage increments above a certain level. One such alternative would involve taking increases in the wage bill in excess of the rate of increase in profit taxes paid to the state ("Current," 1985, p. X); another would entail taxing wage increments in excess of a predetermined rate. The former of the two alternatives has the disadvantage that, under the present irrational price system, increases in profits do not necessarily reflect improved performance; in turn, the latter alternative does not take account of changes in the firm's productive activity. A possible compromise would be to tax increments in the wage bill in excess of increases in the firm's value added.

But the latter method, too, has the shortcoming that it takes the previous year's wages and output as the basis, although these may not represent an appropriate ratio of wages to output. And while enterprises have been told that "they must see to it that all irrational factors in their total payrolls of last year are eliminated" ("Current," 1985, p. X), the practical application of these instructions may encounter difficulties.

The ultimate objective should be to consider wages as a cost element as is done under the new wage regulations a number of Hungarian firms introduced in 1985. This, in turn, would necessitate progressive taxation for income recipients, for which the taxes on wage incomes above a certain level, introduced recently in China, provide a basis.

Further, there will be need to promote the movement of labor, permitting workers to leave their jobs and reducing the work force if conditions warrant. Steps in this direction were taken in September 1986 through the introduction of the contract system for newly hired employees, regulations concerning the dismissal of workers who violate labor discipline, and a system of unemployment compensation (*Beijing Review,* No. 37, September 15, 1986, pp. 37–38).

MACROECONOMIC PRECONDITIONS

We have seen that China experienced rapid increases in investment activity and in wage and bonus payments in 1984 and in 1985. These increases were supported by the expansion of bank loans. The loans financed a substantial proportion of unplanned investment undertaken by the localities. Also, the easy availability of financing allowed enterprises to increase wages and bonuses as they could finance investment from bank borrowing and may even have used borrowed funds directly to raise labor compensation.

[9] "When the system of time wages plus bonuses was carried out in the past, bonuses were often divided equally among workers and staff members. The principle of distribution according to work was not followed. Only by implementing the general piece-rate wage system, or alternatively, piece-rate wages for output which exceeds the quota can we really adhere to the principle of more income for more work, less income for less work and no income for no work" (Ma, 1983, pp. 107–108).

The observed developments reflected the lack of ability of the People's Bank, newly becoming the central bank of China, to control the money supply. Thus, the local branches of the specialized banks (the Agricultural Bank, the People's Construction Bank, and the newly established Industrial and Commercial Bank), and of the People's Bank itself, reportedly did the bidding of the localities rather than following instructions from the People's Bank. Furthermore, it has been reported that, in response to the suggestion that "the amount of credit funds at the disposal of the specialized banks be determined with the amount of loans granted in 1984 as a base figure for 1985, . . . some monetary units . . . vied in granting loans so as to increase the base figures of credit" ("Current," 1985, p. VII).

In order to remedy the situation, the State Council decided to "introduce a unified credit and monetary policy, strengthen the regulatory functions of the People's Bank of China over macroeconomic activities, and firmly control the amount of credit and cash in circulation. . . . The People's Bank of China will fix in a unified manner currency issue ceiling for its branches . . ." ("Current," 1985, p. XI). The practical implementation of these measures is an urgent priority, so as to provide the macroeconomic conditions for the successful application of the reforms.

In fact, the interdependence of macroeconomic policies and economic reform has come to be emphasized in China. Attention has further been given on the need to improve the financial structure. Thus, in his report on the Seventh Five Year Plan, Premier Zhao Ziyang speaks of the need "to give full play to the role of the banking system in raising funds, guiding the flow of funds, making better use of them, and regulating social demand" ("Report," 1986, p. xiii).

In the meantime, it would be necessary to raise interest rates for loans as well as for deposits. While China has made progress in raising interest rates in recent years, the 4.8% interest rate on investment loans provides inducement for using borrowed funds in preference to profits to finance new investments and it permits undertaking investment projects that have low economic rates of return. Also, deposit rates are negative in real terms, thereby discouraging savings.

Higher deposit rates, then, would syphon off some of the excess purchasing power created by rapid increases in wages and bonuses. The increased use of financial instruments sold to individuals by enterprises would have similar effects. It would further be desirable to encourage the movement of funds among enterprises, to ensure the better allocation of savings.

CONCLUDING REMARKS

The economic reforms introduced since 1978 have led to considerable increases in production and in living standards in China. The growth in agricultural output permitted raising food consumption and upgrading its pattern, with substantial increases in the consumption of meat, dairy products, fruits, and vegetables; the growth of industrial output made it possible to ease shortages and to expand the consumption of high-quality products; while average floor space per person rose by about two-fifths in both urban and rural areas. Also, national income per head rose by 6.6% a year between 1978 and 1984, compared with an increase of 3.9% in the 1953–1978 period (*Beijing Review,* No. 10, March 10, 1986, p. 14).

At the same time, the greater use of prices and markets should not carry the blame for excessive investments and increases in labor compensation or for profiteering and corruption. For one thing, excessive money creation has importantly contributed to rapid increases in investments and in wages and bonuses, with the delegation of decision-making power to the localities adding to the former and inadequate financial restraint on enterprises to the latter. For another thing, profiteering and corruption flourishes in a situation in which controls on prices and markets continue.

These considerations, then, call for adopting appropriate macroeconomic policies and simultaneously extending the reform effort. In fact, the former is a precondition for the latter; in particular, the application of price and wage reforms is hindered by the existence of a excess demand in China.

To establish macroeconomic equilibrium, China would have to utilize the tools of fiscal and monetary policy. While recent developments show success in eliminating the budget deficit, much remains to be done to establish an effective monetary policy that would aim at avoiding the excessive credit expansion. Also, there is need to modernize the financial system and to set realistic interest rates.

In extending the reform effort, one should reduce the decision-making power of the localities and increase that of enterprises while freeing prices and markets. Also, measures should be taken to establish the conditions for effective competition, to give full responsibility to the manager for the firm's operations, to reform the system of prices, and to improve the wage and bonus system.

Although it has often been argued that social and political considerations advise caution in the implementation of the reforms, the example of Hungary indicates the potential benefits of simultaneous actions on a broad front. This is because reforms in various areas are interdependent and only their simultaneous introduction can assure full success.

REFERENCES

Balassa, Bela, "Economic Reform in China." *Banca Naz. Lavoro Quart. Rev.* 35:307–333, Sept. 1982; republished as Essay 14. In Bela Balassa, *Change and Challenge in the World Economy*, pp. 310–336. London: Macmillan, 1986.

Balassa, Bela, "The Hungarian Economic Reform, 1968–81." *Banca Naz. Lavoro Quart. Rev.* 34:163–184, June 1983; republished as Essay 12. In Bela Balassa, *Change and Challenge in the World Economy*, pp. 216–281, London: Macmillan, 1985 (1983a).

Balassa, Bela, "Reforming the New Economic Mechanism in Hungary." *J. Comp. Econ.* 7:253–266, Sept. 1987; republished as Essay 13. In Bela Balassa *Change and Challenge in the World Economy*, pp. 282–309. London: Macmillan, 1985 (1983b).

Balassa, Bela, (1985), "The 'New Growth Path' in Hungary." *Banca Naz. Lavoro Quart. Rev.* 38:347–372, Dec. 1985.

Byrd, William, "Economic Reform and Efficiency in Chinese State-Owned Industry." Washington, D.C., World Bank, Dec. 1982 (mimeo).

Byrd, William, "The Role and Impact of Markets." In Gene Tidrick and Chen Jiyuan, Eds., *China's Industrial Reform.* New York/London: Oxford Univ. Press, 1987.

Chang Pei-Kang and Lin Shao-Kung, "China's Modernization: Stability, Efficiency, and the Price Mechanism." Paper prepared for the Meetings of the Pacific Area Association held in New York on Sept. 30–Oct. 2, 1985.

"Communique on the Fulfillment of China's 1984 National Economic Plan." State Statistical Bureau, March 3, 1985.

"Communique on the Statistics of 1985 Economic and Social Development." State Statistical Bureau, Feb. 28, 1986.

"The Current Economic Situation and the Reform of the Economic Structure." Report on the Work of the government delivered by Zhao Ziyang, the Premier of the State Council, at the Third Session of the Sixth National People's Congress on March 27, 1985.

"Decision of the Central Committee of the Communist Party of China on the Reform of the Economic Structures." Beijing, October 20, 1984.

Dong Fureng, "Questions on Increasing the Vitality of Enterprises under the System of Ownership by the Whole People." Beijing, Institute of Economics, Chinese Academy of Social Sciences, March, 1985 (mimeo) (1985a).

Dong Fureng, "The Reform of Economic Structure in China." Paper prepared for the Seminar on Economic Reforms, held in Paris on July 29–Aug. 2, 1985 and organized by the Economic Development Institute of the World Bank (mimeo) (1985b).

Johnson, D. Gale, "Economic Reforms in the People's Republic of China." Paper prepared for the 30th Anniversary Conference of the Graduate Program in Economic Development, Vanderbilt University, Oct. 17–19, 1986.

Khan, Azizur Rahman, and Lee, Eddy, *Agrarian Policies and Institutions in China after Mao.* Bangkok: International Labour Organization, Asian Employment Programme (ARTEP), 1983.

Lardy, Nicholas R., "Prospects and Some Policy Problems of Agricultural Development in China," *Amer. J. Agr. Econ.* May 1986.

Lim, Edwin et al., *China: Long-Term Development Issues and Options, A World Bank Country Economic Report.* Baltimore: Johns Hopkins Univ. Press, 1985.

Lin, Justin Y., "The Household Responsibility System in China's Agricultural Reform: A Theoretical and Empirical Study." Paper prepared for the 20th Anniversary Conference of the Graduate Program in Economic Development, Vanderbilt University, Oct. 17–19, 1986.

Ma Hong, *New Strategy for China's Economy.* Beijing: New World Press, 1983.

"Proposal of the Central Committee of the Chinese Communist Party for the Seventh Five-Year Plan for National Economic and Social Development." Adopted at the National Conference of the Communist Party of China on September 23, 1985.

Rawski, Thomas G., "Productivity, Incentives, and Reform in China's Industrial Sector." Paper prepared for the Annual Meetings of the Association for Asian Studies, held in Washington, D.C. on March 23, 1984.

"Report on the Sixth Five Year Plan." Delivered by Zhao Ziyang, Premier of the State Council at the Fifth Session of the Fifth National People's Congress on November 30, 1982.

"Report on the Seventh Five Year Plan." Delivered by Zhao Ziyang, Premier of the State Council at the Fourth Session of Sixth National People's Congress on March 25, 1986.

"The 6th Five-Year Plan (1981–85) of the People's Republic of China for Economic and Social Development." Adopted by the Fifth Session of the Fifth National People's Congress on December 10, 1982.

Tian Jiyun, "Price System Due for Reform." *Beijing Review,* No. 4, January 29, 1985.

Tidrick, Gene, "Productivity Growth and Technological Change in Chinese Industry." World Bank Staff Working Paper No. 761, Washington, D.C. 1986.

JOURNAL OF COMPARATIVE ECONOMICS 11, 427–443 (1987)

Economic Liberalization in China and India: Issues and an Analytical Framework

T. N. SRINIVASAN

Yale University, New Haven, Connecticut 06520

Srinivasan, T. N.—Economic Liberalization in China and India: Issues and an Analytical Framework

A simple analytical framework is proposed for assessing the credibility and prospects for success of economic liberalization policies of China and India. It is argued that liberalization of *external transactions* is likely to yield only limited benefits unless it is accompanied by elimination of controls on *domestic transactions.* Further, in China economic liberalization is likely to generate demands for political liberalization which in turn may result in a retreat from economic reforms. In India, on the other hand, interest groups enjoying "rents" from economic controls may try to prevent their elimination. *J. Comp. Econ.*, September, 1987, **11**(3), pp. 427–443. Yale University, New Haven, Connecticut 06520. © 1987 Academic Press, Inc.

Journal of Economic Literature Classification Numbers: 112, 123, 422.

1. INTRODUCTION

China and India had comparable levels of real per capita income in 1950, with both economies being overwhelmingly rural and around 70% of the labor force employed in agriculture. China had been traumatized by the Second World War and the Civil War. The Second World War and the violent partition of colonial India into India and Pakistan at independence left deep scars on India. China had smaller arable land per capita but its productivity (crop yield per hectare) was higher than that of India. The transportation (particularly railways) and communication networks were more extensive in India. Both regimes adopted comprehensive planning as the organizational mode for articulating and implementing their development strategy. India's democratic polity and commitment to individual liberties severely constrained the policy instruments for implementing plans. Even more important, India's leaders, particularly Prime Minister Nehru, firmly believed that a mixed economy with a significant private sector was crucial to the maintenance of a democratic polity. Chinese leaders were not burdened with excessive concerns with liberal democracy and individual freedoms.

CHINESE ECONOMIC REFORM

137

Interestingly, both countries assigned a minor role to foreign trade and aid. After its rift with the Soviet Union in the fifties, China did not receive any foreign aid until the eighties. Although India has continued to receive foreign aid since the early fifties, it rarely exceeded 20% of her investment and 5% of gross domestic product. Self-reliance, in general, and technological independence, in particular, were important goals in both countries, though the strategies to achieve them were different. While China abolished private ownership of means of production, in India the private sector was excluded from the development of crucial industries and infrastructure. Indeed, in successive 5 year plans, additional industries were brought under the public sector through nationalization (e.g., life insurance, banking, coal mining, road transport), so that public sector accounted for the dominant and increasing share of total investment. China achieved a substantial reduction of economic inequalities among households with the onset of the revolution. Achieving social justice and reduction of economic disparities have been enshrined as directive principles of state policy in the Indian Constitution, and each 5 year plan has continued to pay obeisance to this objective.

The rate of growth of real GDP during the period since 1950 has been similar and unspectacular in both economies, with the Chinese economy growing slightly faster. Chinese industrial growth, particularly of heavy industry, has been considerably more rapid than India's. Although regional as well as rural–urban disparities remain, China has succeeded in eliminating abject poverty, and achieved impressive gains in life expectancy and other indicators of health and nutrition. A substantial proportion of India's population continue to be poor, illiterate, and malnourished. Yet, while India managed to avoid any major famine in over 3 decades, under the Chinese political system and its periodic shake-ups under Mao Zedung there was a catastrophic famine in the late fifties in which more than 20 million people have been estimated to have died. Neither economy has succeeded in reducing the proportion of the labor force employed in agriculture significantly.

The costs of an inward-oriented development strategy have been substantial in both economies. Several studies have documented the economic cost and corruption induced by the system of administrative controls on the Indian economy. The relatively low shares of foreign trade and aid in India's GDP are misleading as indicators of the importance of external resources to Indian development. In fact, foreign exchange has been a perennially scarce resource. An exchange crisis in the wake of the ambitious second 5 year plan in 1956 spawned the labyrinthian bureaucracy to allocate foreign exchange and license investment and initiated the involvement of aid donors in the Indian economy. Another foreign exchange crisis in 1966, following a war with Pakistan and a drought that reduced food output by 20%, led to the devaluation of the rupee in June 1966 and the introduction of hesitant steps toward economic liberalization. Still, the hold of the inward-oriented development strategy was sufficiently strong to prevent liberalization from proceeding very far in the subsequent decade and a half. Rajiv Gandhi, who became the Prime Minister in 1984, is less committed to the earlier strategy although the old guard in his party continue to oppose liberalization.

Economic liberalization in China came more abruptly after the death of Mao Zedung, the disgrace of the gang of four, and the ascendance of Deng Xiaoping. The abolition of the communes, the introduction of the responsibility system in agriculture, the entry into the World Bank, and the courting of foreign aid, technology, and investment, have brought a sea of change to the Chinese economy. With World Bank and other institutions sending economic missions to China, more detailed statistical data are becoming available.

A study of economic liberalization in the two radically different institutional settings of India and China will be valuable and timely. If liberalization substantially raises their rate of growth, and if the benefits of such growth are widely shared, there will be far fewer poor people in the two countries and in the world. Successful liberalization and outward orientation by the two giants can have a significant impact on the global trading and monetary system. Equally, a liberal global environment and a moderation of the increasing protectionist tendencies in industrialized countries is essential for their success.

A comparative study has to encompass social, political, and economic factors that can make or break the liberalization attempt. It is an open question whether economic liberalization in China can go far enough without generating forces clamoring for political liberalization.[1] Further, given the likely *initial* "unequalizing" effects of liberalization (those who are better endowed may be quicker at capturing the gains), social tensions may increase. The political economy of India's development strategies has been analyzed by several scholars. Perhaps by drawing on their approaches, one may attempt a similar analysis of China. Equally, the Chinese experience may provide a fresh perspective on Indian analyses. On the one hand, in India's mixed economy an institutional framework (particularly a functioning set of markets) for taking advantage of liberalization already exists, while building political support for liberalization is more difficult. On the other hand, in China many new institutions have to be created, but the existing political framework can carry forward its economic liberalization with less fear of opposition.

The present paper has a modest aim of analyzing the Indian experience with economic controls and their hesitant relaxation in the expectation of their relevance to China. It begins with a brief discussion of the traditional arguments for a liberal external trade regime in Section 2. Then the set of economic controls that were used from time to time in India in the last 4 decades is described in Section 3. In Section 4 a very simple analytical frame-

---

[1] The recent (December 1986) demonstrations by students in Shanghai and Beijing are indications of this.

work is developed for sorting out the issues involved in assessing the potential benefits of economic liberalization. It suggests that liberalization of the external sector is likely to bring limited benefits, certainly in the short run, but possibly even in the long run, unless it is accompanied by internal liberalization. This conclusion emerges from looking at the Indian experience in light of the framework of Section 3. It has some relevance for Chinese reforms. Section 5 offers some concluding remarks.

2. FOREIGN TRADE REGIME AND ECONOMIC DEVELOPMENT[2]

The role of foreign trade in the development process has been stressed by economists since Adam Smith, some characterizing it as an "engine" that spearheaded growth, and others viewing it more as concomitant or "hand-maiden" of successful development. By participating in the world markets, an economy can augment its domestic availability of goods and services through a more efficient allocation of its resources. Thus, exchanging some home produced goods and services for those produced abroad is just another "technique" of transforming one set of goods into another analogous to domestic production techniques. Efficient use of the foreign trade "technique" in conjunction with domestic production technology will lead to a better use of available resources than following an autarkic development strategy. By also participating in world capital markets an economy can achieve efficiency in capital accumulation and growth. Thus, through an outward-oriented development strategy a society can attain an equilibrium growth path along which patterns of production, investment, and capacity creation follow static and dynamic comparative advantage, thereby minimizing resource costs (in terms of present value) of meeting final demands (domestic demand plus net export demand). The role of imports (actual or potential) in increasing competition in domestic markets, thereby acting as a stimulus for improving product quality and efficiency of production of import substitutes, etc., cannot be underestimated. Equally, the need to retain one's competitive edge in export markets imparts the same stimuli on producers of exportables. And trade in goods (particularly capital and intermediate goods) could transmit technical change and improvement across countries. In the real world, where random shocks to supply (for instance, due to weather) and demand are present, participation in a global trading system enables an economy to adjust to these shocks better, particularly if it exploits the opportunities provided by world insurance markets as well as forward and future markets. And the efficiency of operation of these markets can be expected to increase with improvement in the technology of transport, communications, information transfer, and processing.

[2] This section draws on Srinivasan (1986).

Although the above arguments are as old as economics as a field of intellectual inquiry, yet a more or less autarkic development strategy with import-substituting industrialization as its core was adopted with little dissent by many developing countries. It was in part due to the then widespread pessimism about future foreign trade prospects based on the disastrous inter-War experience. An erroneous belief that a more open trade strategy would relegate the developing countries to be the "drawers of water and hewers of wood" for the world also played a part. In particular, it was asserted that the income elasticity of demand for the primary product exports of developing countries was low and, as such, any expansion of primary product exports could only reinforce the secular decline in terms of trade. This led to the prescription of import-substituting industrialization as a strategy of development. While not all the investment choices made under the import substitution strategy were necessarily bad, it was still the case that the strategy was pushed too far and too long. Further, many countries established an elaborate administrative machinery for implementing their chosen strategy. Quantitative restrictions on imports and exports of goods, services, and technology, licensing of investment in capacity creation and expansion, and controls on foreign investment, collaboration, etc., were used as primary instruments of resource allocation with tariffs, taxes, subsidies, and other price incentives as secondary instruments.

3. ECONOMIC CONTROLS IN INDIA

Controls on economic activities, including in particular on exports and imports, date back to the years of the second world war under the colonial administration. These control measures and the administrative machinery to implement them came in handy after independence when the government sought to channel the allocation of scarce resources (capital and foreign exchange) to conform to the social priorities laid down in the successive 5 year national development plans.

A system of comprehensive capacity licensing was instituted under which prior government approval was required for any investment in capacity creation. Capacity licensing was operated alongside a foreign exchange allocation system under which exporters surrendered their foreign exchange earnings to the Reserve Bank of India, and received rupees in return at the (overvalued) official exchange rate. Importers of raw materials, capital goods, and a very restricted set of consumer goods received foreign exchange to the extent allocated by the authorities. These quantitative restrictions (QRs) on imports were in addition to and indeed far more constraining than the import duties (at different rates) to which most imports were also subject.

The licensing system was also used to serve other social and political objectives such as reduction in the concentration of economic power, removal of regional disparities, and promoting self-reliance in mobilizing resources for development and in technology. The importation of any commodity for which a domestically produced substitute was available was prohibited with little attention paid to the cost, quality, or delivery schedule of the substitute. The capacity to be created in any 5 year plan in an industry was divided into a number of small-sized plants to be located in different states so as to promote regional balance, although economies of scale would have dictated the establishment of fewer plants of a larger size. Generally, just enough capacity was licensed to conform to targeted capacity in each 5 year plan. This limited domestic competition, and the prohibition of imports when domestic substitutes were available eliminated foreign competition. With competitive pressures for efficiency blunted, a high cost industry of uneconomically sized plants, often based on not so up-to-date, if not altogether obsolete, indigenous technological designs was built up.

Exclusive but inefficient operation by the public sector of major infrastructural industries, such as energy, transport, and communications had economy-wide repercussions. For instance, thermal power stations often could not operate at rated capacity because coal was not available; and coal was not available because railways often could not transport them from pit heads because of wagon shortages. Capacity utilization in power plants has rarely exceeded 50%. Without an uninterrupted and reliable power supply, underutilization of installed industrial capacity became widespread. Industries sought and obtained licenses to install their own captive power plants, by necessity of uneconomic size and using relatively more expensive fuel oil.

Inappropriate pricing of public sector output combined with operational inefficiency led to massive and increasing losses. With general revenues available for financing such losses, there were no financial or budget constraints to force such enterprises to improve their functioning or else go out of operation altogether. Civil servants (bureaucrats) rather than professional managers were in charge of most public enterprises. Over staffing and provision of subsidized benefits of various kinds, including housing to employees, were rampant, not to mention political influence and corruption in recruitment, purchases, and sales.

In India's political system organized labor in manufacturing industries enjoys some political power. Apart from ensuring that the wage structure in such industries was way above that of the mass of unorganized rural workers in agriculture, organized labor put pressure on the public sector to acquire the so-called "sick" *private* enterprises, (i.e., any *enterprise* threatened with closure because of mounting losses) in order to save jobs. With few exceptions, such enterprises rather than regain good health made even greater losses in the public sector! It has been alleged that some private entrepreneurs deliberately siphoned off funds from their enterprises in the confident expectation of unloading them on the public sector once they were sufficiently sick!

Capacity and import licensing were by no means the only controls on industrial development. For example, an investment involving the issue of shares in the local capital market, foreign collaboration, capital goods, and technology imports, and to be undertaken by a private industrialist belonging to one of the so-called "monopoly houses" would need several clearances. The Monopolies and Restrictive Trade Practices Commission had to certify that the investment will not increase market concentration significantly. The controller of capital issues must approve the floating of shares. Approval of foreign collaboration and technology imports and a license for equipment imports were also needed. In many instances public sector investment went through even more hoops within the bureaucracy.

Although the economic control apparatus came down heavily on the industrial sector, agriculture was not left alone. A major concern of the government was to ensure that the urban population had access to a certain minimum quantity of basic staples, particularly food grains at "reasonable prices." This was achieved through sales of limited rations of wheat, rice, sugar, sometimes edible oils, and kerosene at subsidized prices. The supplies needed were purchased from domestic producers at below market prices and supplemented by imports. While the more or less compulsory purchase at below market "procurement price" was in effect a tax on producers, a number of subsidies were offered in the expectation that they will raise output and in part compensate for the implicit procurement tax. Agricultural income was largely tax free and land tax was negligible. Charges for irrigation water from reservoirs built with public funds were set ridiculously low and they did not even cover the costs of maintaining the reservoirs and irrigation channels. Fertilizers were subsidized and so were diesel and electricity to run tube-well irrigation. Credit was also subsidized.

The successful and extensive adoption of the cultivation of the high yielding varieties of wheat introduced in the mid-sixties led to a rapid growth in the output of wheat. With a lag, a similar technical change and growth of output of rice followed. The growth in the output of food grains has almost eliminated the gap between the procurement price and open market price. The rationale for government purchases of food grains gradually changed from supplying the urban rationing system adequately to a price support operation. The government in effect buys whatever quantity is offered at the announced procurement price rather than limit the purchases to the quantity needed for the urban rationing system. A powerful farm lobby has also emerged to agitate for ever-increasing procurement prices and input subsidies. The net result is that public stock of food grains at the end of the 1985–1986 agricultural season is nearly 30 million tons. The storage and wastage costs of this stock are substantial and not much of it can be exported without large losses. A tenth of the final expenditures of the central government is on subsidies to agriculture and urban consumers of rationed food. Self-sufficiency in food in the sense of producing enough to meet the effective demand at *the prevailing distribution of incomes and prices* has been achieved. Yet, while millions of people still lack enough income to buy nutritionally adequate amounts of food, some of the problems of *developed* country agriculture, i.e., mounting subsidizes and surplus stocks are emerging in India!

The plethora of controls on economic activity made those in charge of these controls very powerful. It also generated a premium on the success in making these authorities decide in one's favor. Consequently corruption of bureaucracy and politics became inevitable. Those who managed to obtain the economic rents generated by the controls naturally developed a vested interest in their continuation. A part of the rents is also alleged to have financed the campaign expenses of major political parties in successive elections. Resources got diverted from producing goods and services to lobbying, evasion, and avoidance of irksome controls. A recent careful estimate (Acharya et al., 1985) of the extent of evasion (and avoidance) as exemplified by the transactions in the so-called "black" economy puts it at about a fifth of measured national income.

It became increasingly clear over time that attempting to steer the economy through quantitative rather than price-based controls was strangulating the economy, and that import controls did not alleviate the foreign exchange problem. This led to selective export subsidization measures. Motivated by a desire to rationalize the plethora of foreign exchange controls, the rupee was devalued in June 1966 and a short-lived attempt was made to liberalize the economy.[3] The attempt was short-lived because the announced policy of liberalization was not credible. We will return to the credibility issue below.

Even though the June 1966 liberalization measures were short-lived, ever since there have been several relaxations of the severity of controls. With Rajiv Gandhi's assumption of power, a systematic attempt at liberalizing and rationalizing the economic system and giving it a sense of stability is being made. A number of reports based on studies initiated earlier[4] have been published. A number of liberalizing steps have been taken, including a drastic reduction in the number of companies subject to controls under the Monop-

---

[3] See J. Bhagwati and T. N. Srinivasan (1975) for a detailed analysis of this episode.

[4] "Report of the Committee on Trade Policies," Ministry of Commerce, December 1984. Public release August 1985. "Report to the Committee to Examine Principles of a Possible Shift from Physical to Financial Controls," January 1985 (industrial licensing and MRTP) and April 1985 (capital goods imports, foreign collaboration, capital issues control, exchange control). Public release December 1985. "Aspects of the Black Economy in India," National Institute of Public Finance and Policy, March 1985. "Report of the Committee to Review the Working of the Monetary System," Reserve Bank of India, April 1985. Public Release January 1986. "Long Term Fiscal Policy," Ministry of Finance, December 1985.

olies Act (from 1500 to 230), a major increase in the number of industries in which no capacity license is required, reduction in the bureaucratic hoops through which investment and import licensing applications have to pass, a considerable freeing up of capital goods imports, and increases in export incentives. The success or failure of these liberalization attempts will depend at least in the short and medium run on the structure of the economy as determined by its evolution during the long period of economic controls. In the next section, a simple analytic framework is developed to sort out the issues involved.

4. EXTERNAL AND INTERNAL LIBERALIZATION: AN ANALYTICAL FRAMEWORK

The optimality of free trade for a (small) open economy, i.e., an economy that cannot influence its terms of trade through its own actions, is illustrated in Fig. 1. By allocating its resources *efficiently,* the economy can *produce* any combination of two goods that is on the production possibility frontier (*PPF*) *AB.* Under autarky its consumption possibilities are also represented by *AB.* For simplicity, if we represent consumer preferences by a set of social indifference curves, under autarky the economy will maximize welfare by producing and consuming at the point C^A. Suppose now an opportunity opens up to trade with the rest of the world at a relative price of good 2 (in terms of good 1) represented by the slope of the straight line *PQ.* Then, even if

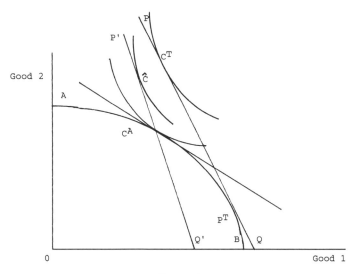

FIGURE 1

production of the two goods remains unchanged at C^A, the economy can now trade with the rest of the world along the straight line $P'Q'$ parallel to PQ through C^A, consume at $\hat{C}$, and achieve a higher level of welfare compared to the welfare at C^A. This is the consumption gain from trade. The economy can do even better by reallocating resources to shift production to the point P^T and trading with the rest of the world along PQ and consuming at C^T. Thus, the total gain to the economy by trading freely and reallocating resources optimally is the increase in welfare associated with the indifference curve through C^T compared to the welfare associated with the indifference curve through C^A. *To be able to reap these gains fully the institutions and public policies that govern the allocation of resources in the economy should allow enough flexibility for production to shift to P^T from C^A and consumption to shift to C^T also from C^A.* Even more important, whether or not the economy allocates its resources efficiently (in autarky or in a trading environment), i.e., produces at some point on the production possibility frontier AB, depends on the institutions and public policies.

A necessary condition for efficiency of resource allocation is that the marginal return to a resource is the same in all its uses. In a competitive market economy in which all economic agents are too small to influence market prices, the private profit maximization (and the associated cost minimization) by producers and utility maximization by consumers ensure that marginal returns are equalized across all uses. However, in economies such as India's or China's with many quantitative restrictions on resource allocation, marginal returns to a resource are unlikely to be equalized in all its uses except by accident. Administrative allocation of imports through licensing is unlikely to bring about their efficient use if for no other reason than it is almost impossible for the allocating authority to acquire the detailed information on the marginal returns to imports in alternative uses. A black market in India reallocated the licensed imports, thereby reducing the efficiency loss at the cost of distributing the scarcity premium on imports as illegal income to the licensee and others whom he had to bribe or compensate in obtaining his license.

Investment licensing was meant to allocate investible resources according to the social priorities laid out in 5 year plans. In a moderately complex economy a socially and intertemporally optimal investment allocation among sectors and enterprises within sectors is hard to devise. In any case, the operation of the licensing system in practice could not have ensured adherence to the plan, even an optimal plan. There were built-in incentives for producers to apply for a license for larger capacity than they intended to operate: producers who succeeded in effect reduced potential competition for themselves, since the licensing authority granted licenses only for a specified *total* capacity. Besides, the license for raw material imports was linked to installed capacity.

Thus, the system encouraged creation of excess capacity and not necessarily efficient allocation of investment.

Segmentation of markets is a feature of most less developed economies including Indian and Chinese economies. In China the prereform commune system and the restrictions on rural–urban labor migration segmented the labor market. In India, even though there are no legal restrictions on labor migration, linguistic, cultural, and ethnic diversity acts as a natural barrier to interstate migration, though not high enough to preclude poor landless laborers from eastern India to move temporarily to the agriculturally dynamic and prosperous state of Punjab in response to higher wages. Still wage rates for narrowly defined tasks have been found to differ substantially among nearby villages. Obviously if markets are segmented and the rewards to the same type of labor differ among regions by more than what could be rationalized by cost of living differences and movement costs, the efficiency of allocation of labor is impaired.

Segmentation in the market for savings, investment, and credit is even more serious. In India a large proportion of domestic savings is done by households and unincorporated enterprises and directly invested by them in the form of physical assets, such as housing and productive assets of their enterprises, indicating the limited extent of financial intermediation. Since it is extremely unlikely that the returns to one's saving are greater in one's own enterprise beyond a point or that returns to investment in one's own enterprise are the same across households, the limited financial intermediation implies serious inefficiencies in the allocation of savings and investment. Even though the penetration of commercial banks and other financial institutions into the rural areas where the majority of the population live has increased enormously over the years, particularly since the nationalization of commercial banks in 1968, the regulated interest rates on deposits are low. Only a small proportion of the rural population has access to the credit provided by the banks. Although credit rationing may exist for reasons of moral hazard and adverse selection even in a competitive market, the allocation of often subsidized credit by the financial institutions is influenced more by political clout and wealth of borrowers than by consideration of risk of default. Indeed, the default rate in agricultural loans is much higher among wealthier farmers than small peasants.

It is clear that even in the absence of any diversion of resources to lobbying the controls on economic activity would prevent the economy from operating on the *PPF* and in fact push it to a point inside the frontier. But there are reasons to suggest that in addition the flexibility for reallocating resources will be considerably reduced as well. For example, consider an economy producing two goods, an urban good and a rural good, and in which workers are free to move between rural and urban sectors, except that urban wages have to be twice as much as rural wages. Then there will be some unemployment and

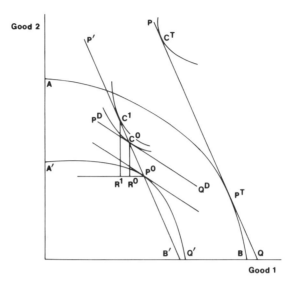

FIGURE 2

the *PP* frontier given this constraint will be inside the unrestricted curve AB of Fig. 1 except at the two end points. The economy can operate anywhere on the restricted *PP* curve in response to the prevailing commodity price ratio. Suppose now that in addition to the wage differential there were also labor movement restrictions as in China. Then the production of the urban good above a certain level becomes impossible because it would require more workers to move from the rural areas than the movement restrictions would permit. Thus, the production possibility curve with *both* constraints factored in is only a part of the curve already restricted by the wage differential.

External sector liberalization programs often start from an initial situation of extensive controls on economic activity and an incipient balance of payments deficit that has been suppressed by foreign trade and exchange controls to a level that can be absorbed by the available capital inflow from abroad. Such an initial situation is depicted in Fig. 2, by production at P^0 on the restricted production possibility curve $A'B'$ and consumption at C^0 assuming for simplicity that no external capital inflow is available.[5] The curve $A'B'$, as drawn, shows very limited flexibility in resource allocation under the preli-

---

[5] In general, there is no presumption that with the domestic distortions present the domestic price line will be tangential to the restricted *PPF*. The possibility of nontangency is ignored here for simplicity.

beralization regime. The world price ratio is represented by the slope of the line PQ, while the domestic price line is $P^D Q^D$ assuming again for simplicity that the only external restriction is a tariff on the imports of good 2 and that the government returns the tariff revenue to consumers in a lump sum fashion. Thus, producers and consumers face the same tariff-inclusive price and the consumer budget line is $P^D Q^D$.

Suppose the government announces an external liberalization program which in this example means abolition of the tariff. If, at the same time, all internal restrictions were abolished, and if the internal and external reforms were *credible* to consumers and producers in the economy in the sense that the resources available to the government were seen to be adequate to absorb any adjustment problems, then the economy would produce in the long run equilibrium at P^T and consume at C^T as in Fig. 1. Suppose no reform measures other than the abolition of the tariff are undertaken. In the very short run production is unlikely to shift from P^0. However, consumers can respond faster and their demands move to the point C^1 corresponding to the tangency of the indifference curve to the world price line through P^0, a demand that can be met with no capital inflows if only the economy can increase its exports of good 1 from $P^0 R^0$ to $P^0 R^1$. If the exporters are unable to sell the entire domestic excess supplies of $P^0 R^1$ in the world markets and sell only $P^0 R^0$ as before while the consumers succeed in importing $C^1 R^1$ of good 2, there will be a drain on foreign exchange reserves. Given that external liberalizations are attempted in situations which have developed to crisis proportions with incipient payment deficits that are substantial but suppressed and reserves are low, external liberalization will not be credible unless the very short-run reserve drain can be financed with external reserve flows as in IMF stabilization programs. A situation of lack of credibility means that the government will either refrain from liberalization or abandon it after it can no longer sustain the reserve loss.

Even though the above credibility story is rather simplistic, it is not without parallels in the real world. The Indian devaluation of June 1966 and the associated liberalization measures were undertaken in part in response to pressures from the World Bank and the IMF. A measure of credibility was given to the program with the promise by the World Bank of a significant amount of non-project assistance (balance of payment support) that was to be disbursed in the period following the devaluation. It so happened the World Bank reneged on the promise just as the short-run pressures on the balance of payments due to liberalization were emerging. The consequence was that not only were many of the liberalization measures reversed and/or diluted but Mrs. Gandhi, who had assumed office as the Prime Minister only 6 months before devaluation, had to face the political cost of what was widely viewed as failure of liberalization. Her party fared badly in the general elections of

1967 and she became wary of liberalization from then on. That external liberalization of a severely restricted economy can give rise to serious pressures on the balance of payments in the short run is also seen in the Chinese experience.

In the absence of internal liberalization, *credible* external liberalization simply means that the economy will respond by moving to a point on the curve $A'B'$ where its slope is the world market relative price. Consumption will shift to a point on the world price line (through the production point) at which a social indifference curve is tangent to it. However, the gains from these production and consumption shifts are likely to be modest as long as the internal controls continue to limit the flexibility of resource reallocation.

The above analysis is equally relevant to internal liberalization in the form of market integration. One could view the grains-first policy in China as segmenting markets by promoting regional self-sufficiency and drastically reducing if not completely eliminating trade based on regional comparative advantages. The fact that the introduction of the responsibility system in agriculture has been spectacularly successful can be explained by three mutually reinforcing features: first the abolition of the commune as a production organization and replacing it with the household-based system enormously enhanced the flexibility of resource (land and labor) reallocation. Second, it augmented the effective resource supply by reducing work shirking because of better incentives. Third, the weakening of market segmentation allowed the new production units to take advantage of producing for the market. It is not surprising that in the nonagricultural sectors large gains from reform have not been reported. It is much more likely that the resources used in these sectors are more specific and less easily shifted among production activities.

It was argued earlier that the inefficient operation of India's major infrastructural industries in the public sector significantly affected the performance of the rest of the economy. It is clear that it can also severely restrict the gains from trade liberalization. Riedel et al. (1984) found a statistically significant negative correlation in India between growth of manufactured exports and their dependence on railways and electricity. With a less extensive transport and communications system compared to India's, China will be even more severely restricted in gaining from liberalization in the short and medium run.

Resource specificity, that is the relative inflexibility of movement of resources from the sectors in which they are being employed in the prereform equilibrium mainly because of internal controls, has significant implications. Resources specific to the sectors whose relative price goes up (down) after liberalization will gain (lose) from liberalization. Further in an administratively controlled economy some groups are likely to take greater advantage of the opportunities opened up by reforms than others, either because they are quicker in perceiving the potential gains and are willing to take the risks involved or, more likely, their political connections enable them to do so. There are anecdotes from China of some individuals becoming immensely rich and of corruption of officials (Dernberger, 1986) after the recent reforms. Thus the impact of liberalization among socioeconomic groups can be varied and can create political opposition from losing groups.

It is obvious that even a very inefficient economy, i.e., an economy that operates way inside its production possibility frontier, can nevertheless grow rapidly as long as it can mobilize sufficient resources for growth and, as such, growth rates are poor indicators of efficiency. High rates of growth were achieved in the Chinese industrial sector primarily through high rates of growth of inputs. Yet Swamy (1986) reports that total factor productivity *declined* in China. In India, while gross fixed investment rate as a proportion of gross domestic product GDP doubled from about 10% in 1950–1951 to 21% in 1984–1985, the trend rate of growth of GDP remained at 3.5% per year. Even allowing for understatement of income generated in the black economy and for shifting industrial composition of GDP toward more capital intensive industries, it would appear that the efficiency of capital use declined over time. A more comprehensive total factor productivity estimate for manufacturing also confirms the increasing inefficiency of resource use in India (Ahluwalia, 1985; Lucas, 1986).

Liberalization, particularly comprehensive liberalization covering domestic and external sectors, eliminates allocative inefficiencies. Sectors in which resource use is particularly inefficient in the preliberalization era and in which flexible resource reallocation is possible can achieve impressive rates of growth as resource use efficiency improves with liberalization. However, *generally* the boost to growth that comes from efficiency improvement is a "once-and-for-all" gain limited to the period in which the economy moves from a point inside the production possibility frontier to a point on it. It cannot be sustained indefinitely. Once such efficiency gains are exhausted, further growth will depend on rates of factor accumulation and more importantly on technical progress. In contemporary developed countries, the contribution of the growth of factor inputs to the observed growth in total output has been far less than the growth brought about by technical change. Although the role of factor accumulation is likely to be somewhat greater in the early stages of growth and development, the importance of technical change and productivity improvements cannot be emphasized enough.

The determinants of technical progress are, however, not as well understood as those of factor accumulation. Competition, in particular the need to maintain one's competitive edge over others, stimulates it; liberalization, by increasing internal and external competition, can augment technical progress.

On the other hand, from Schumpeter to modern industrial organization theorists have made a case for noncompetitive market structure as a spur to innovation. However, given the technological gap between China and India on the one hand and the advanced industrial economics on the other, the former can look toward a long period of "catch-up" technical progress even if they do not themselves add to the stock of technical knowledge in a major way. During this period, a vigorous and competitive environment is far more important.

A brief reference to the political implications of liberalization is in order. In any political system, those in power, if they wish to remain in power, have to take into account the impact of any economic reform on the balance between their supporters and opponents. In an electoral system, such as India's, the party in power will weigh the consequences of reform on its future electoral prospects. Presumably, in China Deng Xiaoping has to keep a wary eye on the factions in the Central Committee. Recent theories attempt to integrate the political lobbying and log-rolling for the adoption of particular policies, the lobbying for the rents and revenues generated by them, and the ultimate effects of resource diversion to these activities on general economic welfare (Bhagwati, 1982; Colander, 1984; Krueger, 1974). Resources diverted to directly unproductive (socially) but privately gainful activities in a controlled system can be substantial. I have analyzed elsewhere (Srinivasan, 1985) the implications of these theories to economic development in general and Indian experience in particular. It suffices to say here that whether a credible reform is adopted or not, and once adopted whether it will succeed or will be reversed, will depend on the impact of reforms on the alignment of political forces. It is inevitable that some of the high cost industries that managed to operate profitably in a protected and sheltered environment will not be able to survive under a liberalized competitive environment. Unless there is political will strong enough to resist pressures for their continuing to operate with state subsidies, reforms will flounder. Equally important is a more open attitude toward technology imports and foreign collaboration.

5. CONCLUSIONS

Successful economic liberalization in China and India, the two giant economies of Asia, can have far-reaching implications for the choice of development strategies by other developing countries and for the international trading and financial system. The inflexibilities in the resource allocation process inherited from a long era of internal economic controls may restrict the gains from liberalization of external trade in the short run. They may even precipitate a balance of payments problem that can assume crisis proportions and blunt, if not reverse, the thrust of reforms by threatening their credibility. Provided credibility of reforms is somehow assured, as the economy reallocates its resources efficiently and moves toward operating on its production possibility frontier, spectacular growth rates may be achieved in some sectors (and even in the aggregate) in the short and medium run. However, these growth rates cannot be sustained indefinitely. Once the economy begins operating on its efficiency frontier, the process of factor accumulation and above all the rate of technical advance will determine its rate of growth. Since India and China have long ways to go relative to the state of technology in the contemporary developed world, the two can grow relatively fast even after reaching their efficiency frontiers by trying to catch up technologically with the advanced countries. The political implications of reforms can hardly be underestimated. Indeed, the success or failure of the reforms will depend very much on their impact on the political system and whether it will strengthen the reformist faction in the political system.

REFERENCES

Acharya, S. N., and associates, "Aspects of the Black Economy in India." Report of a study by National Institute of Public Finance and Policy, New Delhi, Ministry of Finance, Government of India, 1985.

Ahluwalia, I. J., *Industrial Growth in India.* New Delhi: Oxford Univ. Press, 1985.

Bhagwati, J., "Directly-Unproductive Profit-Seeking (DUP) Activities." *J. Polit. Econ.* **90,** 5:988–1002, 1982.

Bhagwati, J., and Srinivasan, T. N., *Foreign Trade Regimes and Economic Development: India.* New York: Columbia Univ. Press, 1975.

Colander, D., Ed., *Neo-Classical Political Economy.* Cambridge: Ballinger Publishing, 1984.

Dernberger, R., "Financing China's Development: Needs, Resources and Prospects." Asia Society, New York (mimeo), 1986.

Krueger, A., "The Political Economy of the Rent-Seeking Society." *Amer. Econ. Rev.* **69,** 3:291–303, 1974.

Lucas, R., "Liberalization of Trade and Industrial Controls." Department of Economics, Boston University (mimeo), 1986.

Reidel, J., Hall, C., and Grawe, R., "Determinants of Indian Export Performance in the 1970's." *Weltwirtsch. Arch.* **120,** 1:40–63, 1984.

Srinivasan, T. N., "Development Strategy: The Success of Outward Orientation at an End?" In Guhan, S. and M. R. Schroff, Eds., *Essays on Economic Progress and Welfare in Honour of I. G. Patal.* New Delhi: Oxford Univ. Press, 1986.

Srinivasan, T. N., "Neo-Classical Political Economy, the State and Economic Development." *Asian Devel. Rev.* 3:2, 1985.

Swamy, S., "Efficiency, Productivity and Income Distribution in China and India, 1952–84: A Comparative Appraisal." Paper presented at the annual meetings of the Eastern Economic Association, Philadelphia, April 10–12, 1986.

JOURNAL OF COMPARATIVE ECONOMICS 11, 444–461 (1987)

Economic Policy and Income Distribution in China

IRMA ADELMAN AND DAVID SUNDING

University of California, Berkeley, California 94720

Adelman, I., and Sunding, D.—Economic Policy and Income Distribution in China

Using the Kakwani interpolation method to reconstruct rural and urban size distributions, the authors present Lorenz curve estimates for Chinese income distribution by period, 1952–1986. The level of inequality is one of the lowest in the world. The change in inequality over time conforms to the experience of other less-developed countries. Although rural inequality increased after 1978, national inequality fell, due to a reduction in the rural–urban income gap. *J. Comp. Econ.,* September, 1987, pp. 444–461. University of California, Berkeley, California 94720. © 1987 Academic Press, Inc.

Journal of Economic Literature Classification Numbers: 124, 225, 921.

INTRODUCTION

China's economic policy since 1952 may be usefully divided into six policy regimes (Adelman, 1977; Chang, 1986, p. 4; Shen, 1985, p. 10; and Eckstein, 1977). One way of systematically differentiating among the six regimes, focusing on the incentive system, the choice of technique, and the sectoral emphasis of each period, is presented in Table 1. First, the years from 1952 to 1958 saw the socialist transformation of agriculture through land reform initially and then through the establishment of producer and consumer cooperatives. This period was characterized by sectoral economic imbalances as nearly 90% of all state investment went into capital goods. Second, the Great Leap Forward, which began in 1958 and ended in 1961, successfully collectivized Chinese agriculture. The concurrent withdrawal of Soviet aid led to a temporary virtual collapse of many sectors of the economy. Third, the period 1961–1966 was characterized by the adjustments and reforms designed by Liu Shao Qui. The state's role in planning was increasingly decentralized in the hope of achieving a more widespread use of production incentives. For example, in agriculture, peasants were permitted to own private plots. The relative economic normalcy of this reform period was upset by the massive social unrest of the fourth period, the Cultural Revolution, which ran from 1966 to 1968, and had major effects up to 1978. Finally, the historic

CHINESE ECONOMIC REFORM

TABLE 1

ECONOMIC POLICY REGIMES

Regime	Incentive system	Choice of technique	Sectoral priority
1952–1958	Material	Capital intensive	Heavy industry
1958–1961	Nonmaterial	Labor intensive	Heavy industry
1961–1966	Material	Capital and labor intensive	Agriculture
1966–1968	Nonmaterial	Labor intensive	Heavy industry
1968–1978	Nonmaterial	Labor intensive	Heavy industry
1978–1986	Material	Technology intensive	Balanced

Source. Adapted from Chang (1986, p. 4) and Eckstein (1977, pp. 31–65).

reforms announced at the Third Plenum marked the beginning of the current policy regime. This sixth period is significant primarily because of the restructuring of agriculture and the introduction of market incentives.

What have been the effects of these often radical changes in Chinese economic structure? In this study, we trace the effects on the national size distributions of income for the period 1952–1983, an important criterion for evaluating the success of Chinese policies.

THE BASE DISTRIBUTIONS

The basic data are rural size distributions of income for the years 1952, 1978, and 1983 and urban size distributions for the years 1981 and 1983. These distributions are derived from recently released information compiled by the Chinese State Statistical Bureau. This section will discuss the method by which these distributions are, when possible, represented by continuous Lorenz curves and how the sectoral distributions are combined to give national distributions for 1952, 1978, and 1983.

The 1984 edition of the *Statistical Yearbook of China* (henceforth, *SYC*) reports the distribution of peasant households by per capita total income for 1978 and 1983. Total income in this case is defined as the sum of income distributed from the collective, net income from sideline production, and other nonborrowing income, e.g., remittances from persons working outside the collective, subsidies for working on public projects, and disability income (State Statistical Bureau, 1984, p. 473). The size distribution of peasant income in 1952 is taken directly from Roll (1974)—as reported in Perkins and Yusuf (1984, p. 108)—whose definition of total income corresponds to that employed in the various editions of the *SYC*. As discussed in Perkins and Yusuf (1984, p. 108), the 1952 distribution is based on sample surveys of the period.

The distribution of urban staff and worker households by per capita income for 1983 and 1981 is given in the 1984 and 1981 editions, respectively, of the *SYC* (State Statistical Bureau, 1984, p. 462; and State Statistical Bureau, 1982, p. 438). Income is defined here as "income available" or "total household income minus supporting expenses, gifts, and subsidies for diary-keeping of respondent households" (State Statistical Bureau, 1984, p. 462).

There are no urban size distributions for 1952 and 1978. For these years, we assume that the distribution of urban income had the same shape as in 1981, but each income class had proportionally less income and population than in 1981. Average urban income in 1978 and 1952 is found by multiplying average annual worker wage by the number of workers and dividing by the urban population.

The conversion from household to population size distributions of income in the rural sector is made using World Bank estimates of the relationship between household size and per capita income (see below). These estimates reflect the fact that poorer households tend to be larger and richer households tend to be smaller than average.

Per capita income as ratio to sectoral average	Persons per household as ratio to sectoral average
1.5	0.8742
1.3	0.9199
1.0	0.9921
0.7	1.0924
0.5	1.1240

Source. World Bank (1983, p. 278).

To compute the average income in each class, we fit a log-normal density for 1978 and 1983 and compute mean incomes for all but the top (unbounded) class using the sample location and scale parameters. The mean income in the top class is then chosen to give the sectoral mean income per capita given in the *SYC*. The resulting distributions are given in Table 2 along with the rural size distribution for 1952 taken from Perkins and Yusuf (1984).

We are fortunate to have more information for the urban distributions. The *SYC* gives average household sizes and mean incomes for each income class. Thus, the transition from household to population size distributions can be made directly (Table 3). There has been some discussion recently concerning the adequacy of the average per capita urban income figures. Lardy (1984) has pointed out that urban residents receive huge subsidies for transportation, medical care, pensions, vacations, energy, and food and that these subsidies are not available to peasants. Further, the average subsidy per worker increased enormously between 1978 and 1983. The influential economist Ma

TABLE 2

SIZE DISTRIBUTIONS OF RURAL INCOME

1952		1978		1983	
Population 1 (10,000)	Average income 2 (Rmb)[a]	Population 3 (10,000)	Average income 4 (Rmb)[a]	Population 5 (10,000)	Average income 6 (Rmb)[a]
5,031.9	115	—[b]	—	7,735.9	683
5,031.9	71	—	—	8,039.4	442
10,063.8	56	1,185.9	419	17,229.3	342
10,063.8	46	9,334.3	229	27,127.4	247
10,063.8	40	12,733.4	169	11,429.1	176
5,031.9	34	25,324.5	122	5,532.7	131
5,031.9	27	30,435.9	88	1,275.2	89

[a] Mean rural income in 1952 is inferred from Lardy's assertion that average urban income in 1952 was 1.8 times that of the average rural income (Schran, 976, p. 9 in Lardy, 1983, p. 179).

[b] The top three income classes were combined into one in 1978.

Sources. Columns 1 and 2: Perkins and Yusuf (1984, p. 114). Columns 3–6: State Statistical Bureau (1984, pp. 81, 472, and 473) and World Bank (1983, p. 278).

Hong reported that for state employees the value of these subsidies equaled 82% of the wage received in 1978 or Rmb526 (Ma, 1983, p. 16). This implies an average per capita income of Rmb646. In 1983, however, these subsidies had increased to nearly Rmb1000 per worker, implying an average per capita income of Rmb1159 (Lardy, 1984). The effects of these subsidies will be considered below when inequality indices are calculated.

The data in Tables 2 and 3 are not detailed enough to permit accurate construction of Lorenz curves. The most common method for estimating such indices from grouped data has traditionally been linear interpolation which assumes perfect equality within each income range. More recently, Kakwani (1976 and 1980) has proposed a general interpolation device which we use here. Kakwani's method involves connecting the points of the empirical Lorenz curve, constructed directly from the grouped data, with a piece-wise continuous differentiable function within each income range. For the first and last income ranges, the Pareto function is fitted as a refinement (Kakwani, 1976, p. 483).

Kakwani's interpolation method starts from grouped observations defined by N income units grouped into $(T + 1)$ income classes (x_{t-1} to x_t). The proportion of persons receiving an income less than or equal to x_t is p_t; the cumulative proportion of income received is q_t; the relative frequency is f_t; the mean income in range t is μ_t; and μ is the overall mean income. To fit a

TABLE 3

Size Distributions of Urban Income

1981		1983	
Population 1 (10,000)[a]	Average income 2 (Rmb)[b]	Population 3 (10,000)[a]	Average income 4 (Rmb)[b]
992.3	875	2,779.3	895
2,103.7	704	3,672.0	706
8,082.3	537	11,083.5	548
7,082.5	399	5,479.0	408
1,361.8	299	909.6	305[c]
548.5	227	200.2	242[c]

[a] Computed from household distributions by multiplying the number of households in each income class by the household size in that class.

[b] Defined as "total household income minus supporting expenses, gifts, and subsidies for diary-keeping of respondent households" (State Statistical Bureau, 1984, p. 462).

[c] The *Statistical Yearbook* provides no explanation for the fact that these incomes lie outside the income class boundaries.

Source. Columns 1 and 3: State Statistical Bureau (1982, p. 438). Columns 2 and 4: State Statistical Bureau (1984, pp. 81 and 466).

third-degree polynomial for the Lorenz curve within each income class, four data points are needed: the estimated curve must pass through the two end-points of the income class (p_{t-1}, q_{t-1}) and (p_t, q_t); and, to be continuously differentiable, the slope at these points must be equal to x_{t-1}/μ and x_t/μ, respectively, since $dq/dp = x/\mu$. Thus, if we write the Lorenz curve for tth income class as

$$q = q_{t-1} + \alpha_{1t}(p - p_{t-1}) + \alpha_{2t}(p - p_{t-1})^2 + \alpha_{3t}(p - p_{t-1})^3,$$

then the parameters α_1, α_2, and α_3 are

$$\alpha_{1t} = \frac{x_{t-1}}{\mu},$$

$$\alpha_{2t} = \frac{(3\delta_t - 1)(\Delta x_t)}{\mu f_t},$$

and

$$\alpha_{3t} = \frac{(1 - 2\delta_t)(\Delta x_t)}{\mu f_t^2},$$

where $\delta_t = (\mu_t - x_{t-1})/\Delta x_t$ and $\Delta x_t = x_t - x_{t-1}$ (Kakwani, 1976 and 1980).

The Pareto distribution function for the lowest and highest income ranges is (Kakwani, 1976, p. 484):

$$\text{lowest:} \quad p = A_1 q^{\alpha_1}$$

and

$$\text{highest:} \quad (1 - p) = A_{T+1}(1 - q)^{\alpha_{T+1}}.$$

The parameters obtained using the condition $dq/dp = x/\mu$ are

$$A_1 = f_1 \left[\frac{\mu}{\mu_1 f_1} \right]^{\alpha_1},$$

$$\alpha_1 = \frac{\mu_1}{x_1}, \qquad A_{T+1} = f_{T+1} \left[\frac{\mu}{\mu_{T+1}} f_{T+1} \right]^{\alpha_{T+1}}$$

and

$$\alpha_{T+1} = \frac{\mu_{T+1}}{x_T}.$$

The Kakwani interpolation method is used to reconstruct each of the rural and urban size distributions for 1952, 1978, and 1983 and reform them into vintiles (Table 4). National size distributions (Table 5) are then formed by combining the sectoral size distributions empirically and using linear interpolation to form vintiles. Because the total distributions are based on 42 data points (21 from each sectoral distribution), the implicit assumption of equal incomes within each income class does not impart a significant downward bias to the overall inequality measures.

There were two exceptions to this general method. A condition guaranteeing the convexity of the interpolated Lorenz curve is not fulfilled for the 1983 urban distribution given in the *SYC;* consequently, the original distribution in Table 3 is used. The second exception concerns the 1952 rural size distribution. As reported in Perkins and Yusuf (1984), this distribution contained no information about income class boundaries. For 1952, we used the midpoints between class average incomes as boundaries.

Kakwani's general interpolation device may be extended to the construction of Gini coefficients to account for within-group inequality by adding the sum of the Gini coefficients within each class to the lower bound of the Gini index derived by assuming perfect equality within each class. This method is employed where one could construct a continuous Lorenz curve. The national inequality indices were computed with the lower bound formula (see Table 6) since national Gini coefficients are estimated with data for 42 income classes and the resulting income ranges are quite narrow.

Based on the data in Tables 4–6, one can draw some tentative conclusions. First, rural inequality was almost identical in 1952 and 1978, an assertion supported by both the vintiles and the Gini coefficients, and consistent with the analysis of Perkins and Yusuf (1984, p. 109).

TABLE 4

LORENZ CURVES

Rural income

	1952				1978				1983		
Cumulative percentage of		Average income (Rmb)	Ratio of class income to average income	Cumulative percentage of		Averge income (Rmb)	Ratio of class income to average income	Cumulative percentage of		Average income (Rmb)	Ratio of class income to average income
Population	Income			Population	Income			Population	Income		
0.05	0.02	25	0.48	0.05	0.03	67	0.50	0.05	0.02	108	0.35
0.10	0.05	29	0.54	0.10	0.06	80	0.60	0.10	0.04	145	0.47
0.15	0.08	31	0.59	0.15	0.09	86	0.64	0.15	0.07	165	0.53
0.20	0.11	35	0.65	0.20	0.12	90	0.67	0.20	0.10	182	0.59
0.25	0.15	38	0.71	0.25	0.16	93	0.70	0.25	0.13	198	0.64
0.30	0.19	39	0.74	0.30	0.19	95	0.71	0.30	0.16	210	0.68
0.35	0.22	41	0.77	0.35	0.23	98	0.73	0.35	0.20	223	0.72
0.40	0.26	42	0.78	0.40	0.27	100	0.75	0.40	0.24	237	0.76
0.45	0.30	43	0.81	0.45	0.30	105	0.78	0.45	0.28	252	0.81
0.50	0.35	45	0.84	0.50	0.35	110	0.83	0.50	0.32	266	0.86
0.55	0.39	47	0.89	0.55	0.39	118	0.88	0.55	0.37	283	0.91
0.60	0.44	50	0.94	0.60	0.44	125	0.94	0.60	0.41	298	0.96
0.65	0.49	53	0.99	0.65	0.49	134	1.00	0.65	0.47	314	1.01
0.70	0.54	55	1.03	0.70	0.54	144	1.08	0.70	0.52	332	1.07
0.75	0.59	58	1.09	0.75	0.60	153	1.14	0.75	0.58	355	1.15
0.80	0.65	61	1.16	0.80	0.66	163	1.22	0.80	0.64	385	1.24
0.85	0.71	64	1.20	0.85	0.73	180	1.35	0.85	0.71	418	1.35
0.90	0.78	78	1.48	0.90	0.80	198	1.48	0.90	0.78	466	1.50
0.95	0.88	98	1.86	0.95	0.88	220	1.64	0.95	0.88	542	1.75
0.99	0.97	119	2.25	0.99	0.97	276	2.07	0.99	0.96	709	2.29
1.00	1.00	177	3.34	1.00	1.00	470	3.52	1.00	1.00	1,261	4.07

Urban income

1981				1983[a]			
Cumulative percentage of		Average income (Rmb)	Ratio of class income to average income	Cumulative percentage of		Average income (Rmb)	Ratio of class income to average income
Population	Income			Population	Income		
0.05	0.03	249	0.50	0.008	0.004	242	0.42
0.10	0.06	312	0.63	0.046	0.024	305	0.53
0.15	0.09	340	0.68	0.273	0.186	408	0.72
0.20	0.13	362	0.73	0.732	0.629	548	0.96
0.25	0.17	387	0.78	0.885	0.819	706	1.23
0.30	0.21	406	0.82	1.000	1.000	895	1.56
0.35	0.25	423	0.85				
0.40	0.29	437	0.88				
0.45	0.34	447	0.90				
0.50	0.38	460	0.93				
0.55	0.43	477	0.96				
0.60	0.48	498	1.00				
0.65	0.54	519	1.04				
0.70	0.59	544	1.09				
0.75	0.65	571	1.15				
0.80	0.71	599	1.21				
0.85	0.77	631	1.27				
0.90	0.84	673	1.35				
0.95	0.91	736	1.48				
0.99	0.97	872	1.75				
1.00	1.00	1,098	2.21				

[a] The interpolation method cannot be used in this case.
Source. Computed from Tables 2 and 3.

ADELMAN AND SUNDING

TABLE 5

NATIONAL LORENZ CURVES

Cumulative percentage of population	Cumulative income share						
	1952[a]	1958[b]	1961[b]	1966[b]	1968[b]	1978[a]	1983[a]
0.05	0.02	0.02	0.02	0.02	0.02	0.02	0.02
0.10	0.05	0.04	0.04	0.04	0.05	0.04	0.04
0.15	0.07	0.07	0.07	0.07	0.07	0.07	0.06
0.20	0.10	0.09	0.10	0.09	0.10	0.10	0.09
0.25	0.13	0.11	0.12	0.12	0.12	0.12	0.12
0.30	0.17	0.13	0.15	0.15	0.15	0.15	0.15
0.35	0.20	0.16	0.18	0.18	0.18	0.18	0.18
0.40	0.24	0.19	0.21	0.21	0.21	0.21	0.22
0.45	0.27	0.22	0.24	0.24	0.25	0.24	0.26
0.50	0.32	0.25	0.28	0.28	0.29	0.28	0.30
0.55	0.36	0.28	0.32	0.31	0.33	0.32	0.34
0.60	0.40	0.32	0.36	0.36	0.37	0.37	0.39
0.65	0.45	0.36	0.41	0.40	0.42	0.42	0.45
0.70	0.51	0.41	0.46	0.45	0.47	0.47	0.51
0.75	0.57	0.46	0.52	0.51	0.53	0.52	0.56
0.80	0.63	0.52	0.59	0.58	0.59	0.58	0.62
0.85	0.71	0.60	0.67	0.66	0.67	0.66	0.71
0.90	0.79	0.70	0.76	0.75	0.76	0.75	0.79
0.95	0.88	0.82	0.86	0.86	0.86	0.85	0.88
0.99	0.97	0.96	0.97	0.96	0.97	0.97	0.97
1.00	1.00	1.00	1.00	1.00	1.00	1.00	1.00

[a] Computed from Table 4.

[b] Constructed by varying the incomes and populations of the 1978 rural and urban distributions (see text below for further explanation).

Second, rural inequality increased between 1978 and 1983. The increase in rural inequality was due to decreases in the income share of the poorest 40% of peasants and to a large increase in the share of the richest 1%. This is not to say that these poorest peasants were absolutely worse off than they were in 1978. Lardy (1984) indicates that, even after deflating by cost-of-living indices, the incomes of all peasants increased since 1978. The contention of the Chinese leadership that the benefits of decollectivization have been unequally distributed but few peasants, if any, are actually worse off, therefore, appears correct.

Third, total inequality decreased between 1978 and 1983. This decline is due to the unprecedented growth of peasant income and consequent narrowing of the urban/rural income gap, even taking into account the massive subsidies given to urban workers.

TABLE 6

GINI COEFFICIENTS

	1952	1978	1983
Rural	0.230	0.222	0.264
Urban	0.165	0.165	0.146[a]
Total (without urban subsidies)	0.255[a]	0.317[a]	0.284[a]
Total (including urban subsidies)	0.255[a]	0.438[a]	0.412[a]

[a] Computed with the lower bound formula (see text); all others are computed with the Kakwani interpolations method.

HISTORICAL SIMULATIONS

In this section, we simulate the size distribution of income for the years 1958–1977 by using the 1978 rural and urban size distributions constructed by Kakwani's interpolation method. After determining the contribution made by migration versus relative sectoral income changes to the pattern of change in income inequality over time and verifying this time pattern through the use of three alternative base-year distributions, we examine the relationship between the simulated pattern of inequality and changes in policy regimes.

These simulations are based on the 1978 rural and urban distributions of Table 4 which give the percentage of the population and the ratio of mean class income to the overall mean income. This array, which preserves the distributional content, can be adjusted to derive the approximate size distribution for a particular year by multiplying the population share by sectoral population and the mean income ratio by mean income per capita. Aggregating the resulting sectoral distributions empirically yields the national size distribution (see Table 7).

To derive this table, we needed time series on average per capita incomes and populations. Sectoral populations (Table 8) are published in the *SYC* (State Statistical Bureau, 1984, p. 81). Information on average income, however, is not directly available and must, consequently, be derived. For the period 1958–1977, average peasant income per capita (Table 8) is computed as

$$\frac{\text{income distributed from collectives} * w}{\text{rural population}}$$

where $w = 1/(1 - p)$, and p is the percentage of total income from noncollective sources. To derive p, the percentage of income from sideline production is set at 27 for 1958–1977 (Perkins and Yusuf, 1984, p. 113) and that from remittances and other sources at 11% for 1958–1965 and 6.9% thereafter (State Statistical Bureau, 1984, p. 113).

TABLE 7

SIMULATED NATIONAL GINI COEFFICIENTS[a]

Year	Base run	Varying population	Varying income	World Bank distribution	20% inflation of rural income
1958	0.377	0.312	0.383	0.421	0.341
1959	0.368	0.319	0.366	0.410	0.331
1960	0.368	0.322	0.361	0.408	0.331
1961	0.314	0.321	0.311	0.362	0.282
1962	0.321	0.316	0.323	0.370	0.288
1963	0.338	0.314	0.342	0.386	0.305
1964	0.328	0.318	0.327	0.375	0.295
1965	0.318	0.317	0.318	0.366	0.286
1966	0.323	0.317	0.323	0.371	0.290
1967	0.315	0.317	0.315	0.364	0.283
1968	0.310	0.316	0.310	0.360	0.279
1969	0.307	0.316	0.308	0.358	0.276
1970	0.311	0.316	0.313	0.362	0.280
1971	0.308	0.315	0.310	0.359	0.278
1972	0.325	0.315	0.327	0.374	0.292
1973	0.312	0.315	0.314	0.363	0.281
1974	0.317	0.315	0.319	0.366	0.285
1975	0.329	0.315	0.331	0.377	0.296
1976	0.335	0.316	0.337	0.382	0.301
1977	0.333	0.316	0.334	0.381	0.300

[a] Estimated using the lower bound formula.

Per capita income distributed from the collectives is constructed as income distributed from teams∗1.2012, to account for income distributed from collectives beyond the team level (e.g., income earned through employment with collective enterprises such as factories). The adjustment factor of 1.2012 was derived from the ratio of average per capita income distributed from collectives for 1978 (State Statistical Bureau, 1984, p. 471) to average per capita income distributed from teams (State Statistical Bureau, 1984, pp. 81 and 199).

Average urban income per capita is estimated with

$$\frac{\text{average annual worker wage} * \text{number of workers}}{\text{urban population}}.$$

All three series are contained in the *SYC* (State Statistical Bureau, 1984—for average wage, p. 459; number of workers, p. 107; and urban population, p. 81). The resulting income series is given in Table 8. The treatment of income and workers employed in urban collectives is unclear from the published data. The Statistical Bureau indicates that the income data were collected from surveys stratified by area of residence and the sampling was irrespective of

TABLE 8

SECTORAL POPULATION AND AVERAGE PER CAPITA INCOME

Year	Population (10,000)			Average per capita income (Rmb)		
	Urban 1	Rural 2	Urban as a percentage of total 3	Urban 4	Rural 5	Ratio 6
1958	10,721	55,273	0.16	280	75	3.72
1959	12,371	54,836	0.18	235	69	3.42
1960	13,073	53,134	0.20	254	76	3.34
1961	12,707	53,152	0.19	232	90	2.57
1962	11,659	55,636	0.17	237	87	2.73
1963	11,646	57,526	0.17	261	86	3.02
1964	12,950	57,549	0.18	254	91	2.80
1965	13,045	59,493	0.18	264	99	2.66
1966	13,313	61,229	0.18	263	96	2.74
1967	13,548	62,820	0.18	261	99	2.63
1968	13,838	64,696	0.18	260	102	2.56
1969	14,117	66,554	0.18	263	104	2.53
1970	14,424	68,568	0.17	274	106	2.59
1971	14,711	70,518	0.17	287	112	2.56
1972	14,935	72,242	0.17	309	110	2.80
1973	15,345	73,886	0.17	304	116	2.61
1974	15,595	75,264	0.17	316	118	2.68
1975	16,030	76,390	0.17	324	113	2.86
1976	16,341	77,376	0.17	331	113	2.95
1977	16,669	78,305	0.18	339	117	2.91

Sources. Columns 1–3: State Statistical Bureau, 1984, p. 81. Column 4: State Statistical Bureau, 1984, pp. 81, 107, and 459. Column 5: State Statistical Bureau, 1984, pp. 81, 113, and 199: and Perkins and Yusuf, 1984, p. 113. Column 6: State Statistical Bureau, 1984.

nature of employment of the household head. If so, it should include collective workers. If it does not, the urban income figures are too high (Lardy, 1984) and increasingly overstate urban incomes over time. The correction, if appropriate, would thus reinforce the conclusions concerning the decline in overall inequality between 1978 and 1983.

The percentage of the Chinese population living in urban areas reached its peak during the tumultuous 1958–1961 period following the withdrawal of Soviet aid and bottomed in 1963 during the years of recovery and "Agriculture First" development. The urban/rural income ratio was 1.8 in 1952 (Schran, 1976, p. 9; and Lardy, 1978, p. 179), peaked during the 1952–1958 period of capital-intensive industrialization, and dropped to 1.51 in 1983. Thus, this income ratio exhibits the archetypal "inverted U" pattern described by Kuznets (1955), Adelman and Morris (1973), and Ahluwalia et al. (1979).

It is desirable to assess the relative importance of changes in income and population for the simulated Gini coefficients. Table 7 contains the results of two further simulations—the third column is derived by varying population and keeping sectoral incomes constant at 1978 levels and the fourth column is obtained by varying per capita incomes and keeping sectoral populations constant. These data then give, for example, the partial effect of migration on inequality holding incomes constant.

It is obvious from Table 7 that relative changes in sectoral populations have not had much impact on the distribution of income in China. Inequality has tended to increase, however, as the percentage of urban population increased because despite the "enrichment effect" even when urban population rises China's population remains overwhelmingly rural. The data in Table 7 also suggest that changes in national income inequality have been due primarily to changes in the urban/rural income gap.

As a final experiment in this simulation, we assess the sensitivity of the estimated Gini coefficients to changes in the rural income distributions. One alternative is to use the 1979 rural size distribution constructed by the World Bank (World Bank, 1983, p. 313). The World Bank distribution is much more unequal than the distribution estimated in Table 4 (the associated Gini coefficient is 0.315) and thus generates a more unequal national size distribution. Another is to inflate the rural incomes by 20% to account for underestimation of rural output (Travers, 1982). Since the yield-corrected rural distributions effectively lower the urban/rural income gap, they produce a more equal national size distribution. It is evident from Table 7 that the pattern of inequality over time as measured by the Gini coefficients is invariant to the choice of these base-year distributions. The level of inequality, of course, differs between the alternative distributions.

INEQUALITY AND DEVELOPMENT STRATEGY

There are clear relationships between the pattern of inequality revealed by these simulations and Chinese development strategies (Tables 5, 6, and 7). The First Five Year Plan was strongly Stalinist. The Chinese had an overriding commitment to high rates of growth through rapid capital accumulation particularly in heavy industries. Industrialization was explicitly designed to come at the expense of the rural sector since agricultural institutions were transformed (through collectivization) to facilitate a high rate of involuntary saving through taxation and manipulation of the internal terms of trade. This surplus extraction gave monopoly profits to state trading companies, and these profits were then paid into the government budget and used for investment in industry. The Stalinist growth plan did lead to impressive industrial growth (Eckstein, 1977). However, it also generated the highest levels of income inequality in postrevolution China. The wildly divergent growth paths of agriculture and industry led to a peaking of the urban/rural per capita income ratio in 1958 at a level over 3.7:1.

Collectivization was imposed partly to facilitate industrial accumulation. Another reason was the belief that collectivization would increase agricultural output by taking advantage of economies of scale, even without more intensive application of modern inputs. Agricultural output did increase between 1952 and 1958. However, the increases in output due to institutional transformation were largely one-time increases, and thus agricultural output reached a plateau. Food shortages in the cities began to occur in 1956 and 1957. Largely in response to these failures, the Chinese became convinced that, if their experience was to be successful, they would have to place greater emphasis on agriculture.

The Great Leap Forward strategy, which followed the First Five Year Plan, was influenced by these considerations (Eckstein, 1977, p. 56). It was clear that something had to be done with regard to agricultural inputs as well as the structure of production. Because the state was unwilling to commit resources to agriculture in the form of modern, manufactured inputs, the Chinese decided to increase usage of traditional inputs. Surplus labor was mobilized on a massive scale to collect human and animal excrement, institute flood control, and irrigate land. The second major objective of the Great Leap Forward was increasing industrial output via the introduction of small-scale industrial production in the countryside. The Chinese argued that, in those industries which were characterized by fixed capital–labor ratios and significant economies of scale, the scale of production should be expanded by capital-intensive and large-scale methods. On the other hand, in those industries where there is a wider choice of techniques, emphasis should be placed on small-scale, labor-intensive methods. Thus, the simultaneous development of agriculture and industry sought by the architects of the Great Leap would come through technological dualism or "walking on two legs."

Unfortunately, while not conceptually flawed, the Great Leap was plagued by inadequate, disorganized, and technically deficient implementation. Compounding this poor execution were the profoundly disruptive effects of communalization and poor weather conditions between 1959 and 1961, all of which helped produce a succession of bad harvests and stagnant rural incomes. Indeed, this agricultural crisis reached such severe proportions that by 1961 the Chinese faced the prospect of serious famine. The Great Leap Forward also helped precipitate a crisis in urban areas and served to depress urban incomes. The agricultural decline most severely affected consumer goods industries which began to operate well below capacity. Other nonagricultural sectors were, in turn, depressed through decreased demand for their output and through shortages of raw materials. Finally, the withdrawal of Soviet aid in the summer and fall of 1960 reinforced the downward path upon which the Chinese economy found itself.

Our simulation results indicate that the Great Leap Forward and these related events improved the distribution of income, but not in a welfare-increasing manner. That is, the large decline in the Gini coefficient between 1958 and 1961 was due not to increased incomes of the poorest members of Chinese society but, rather, to the misfortunes of urban workers. Average urban income declined from 280 to 232 yuan per capita in these years—a drop of over 17%—while peasant incomes showed no clear trend. Thus, the national Gini coefficient dropped sharply from 0.3781 in 1958 to 0.3149 in 1961.

Chinese development policy in the years 1961–1966 was shaped largely by the lessons learned from the disastrous period which preceded it. The leadership realized that there was no substitute for increased provision of modern inputs into agricultural production. Whereas the Great Leap tried to use institutional reforms coupled with traditional techniques to stimulate production, during the "Agriculture First" years, the Chinese believed that the diminishing returns which had contributed to the failure of communalization to improve output growth could be overcome only through technical modernization in agriculture. Thus, in 1962, Chou En-lai announced a policy which had crystallized in 1961: Agriculture was to be given first priority in state investment, consumer goods industries second, and investment industries third. Along with this reversal of investment priorities, greater reliance was placed on material incentives in all sectors. This major break with the Great Leap Forward had lasting impacts—in fact, its basic structure was not altered by the tumultuous years of the Cultural Revolution.

Urban and rural incomes per capita increased more or less together between 1961 and 1966; consequently, there was no significant change in inequality. Urban income increased sharply in 1963 following the cessation of economic crisis; but beyond this jump and accompanying increase in inequality, the simulated Gini coefficients remained at or near 1961 levels.

The trend in income distribution was somewhat clearer during the Cultural Revolution of 1966–1968. Due primarily to Mao's desire to keep the Cultural Revolution out of agriculture, rural production and incomes increased steadily. The urban areas and industry suffered greater disruptions, particularly with regard to transportation, as a great deal of freight space was devoted to the movement of Red Guards. The result was raw material and input shortages throughout the country and industrial slowdowns (Eckstein, 1977, pp. 204 and 205). Politically induced violence also served to depress industrial activity, especially in 1967 and 1968. Not surprisingly, average urban incomes declined slightly but consistently throughout the worst years of the Cultural Revolution. This trend, combined with the continued agricultural expansion and reduced percentage of population residing in urban areas, reduced income inequality. The estimated national Gini coefficient declined from 0.323 in 1966 to 0.310 in 1968.

Following the Cultural Revolution, which was in many ways short-lived, the Chinese economy entered into a period of sustained moderate growth. From 1968 to 1978, agricultural output and rural incomes expanded at a moderate rate, while urban incomes expanded at a much higher rate. The simulations show that the result of this widening income gap was a clear upward trend in inequality.

The increasing disparity during this period was perhaps a reflection of the urban bias resulting from Mao Zedong's desire to transform China into a fully modern industrial power. Despite increases in agricultural investment and rhetoric about "agriculture as the foundation," the years during which Mao wielded the greatest control over economic policy (1958–1959 and 1966–1976) were also the years of greatest emphasis on machinery and steel (Perkins and Yusuf, 1984, p. 5). During the years after the Cultural Revolution, there was little desire on the part of the Chinese leadership to pursue policies which would benefit an urban, technocratic elite. State investment in urban infrastructure such as housing was kept at a minimum, and limits were imposed on rural/urban migration as a means of preventing the existing infrastructure from being overwhelmed. This policy, designed to limit investment in urban areas, however, produced phenomena commonly associated with urban bias: capital-intensive industry and a widening urban/rural income ratio.

The poor performance of agriculture vis-à-vis the urban sector, played a significant role in the adoption of the 1978 reforms. The liberalization of agriculture resulted in an unprecedented growth of peasant income which, even in the face of massive and increasing subsidies to urban workers, caused national income inequality to decline between 1978 and 1983. This latest policy regime is the only time in postrevolution Chinese history when significant and consistent declines in national income inequality may be attributed to increases in peasant income rather than to declines in urban incomes. The two previous episodes of declining inequality—the Great Leap Forward and the Cultural Revolution—were both periods when urban incomes fell relative to rural incomes.

CONCLUSION

Despite vast differences in institutions, China's experience with inequality generally confirms what we know about development inequality in other less-developed countries. First, even though the inequality index is sensitive to which base and price assumptions are used in the calculation, inequality in China is clearly one of the lowest in the world. The low inequality is due primarily to very equal sectoral distributions. This confirms the importance of institutions, especially property relations in agriculture and industry for inequality. Second, it is interesting to note that, after the initial drop in inequality following land reform, China also experienced an inverted U-shaped relationship between growth and inequality. Even with socialist institutions, capital-intensive industrialization leads to increases in inequality. Third, China's pattern of inequality change confirms that the nature of growth strategy matters. Income inequality changed significantly with different policy regimes. Finally, strategies which improve the relative lot of the peasant reduce national income inequality. The most striking example of this proposition is the decline in national income inequality since 1978.

It is interesting to speculate on the future course of inequality in China. As the responsibility system spreads to the urban industrial sector and raises both growth and income in urban areas, it is likely that inequality in China will again increase. Dengist growth extended to the urban sphere will lead to a new inverted U-shaped relationship, with the eventual turnaround, due mostly to urban–rural migration and labor absorbtion in the urban sector, far into the 21st century.

REFERENCES

Adelman, I., "Redistribution before Growth: A Strategy for Developing Countries." Inaugural Address for the Cleveringa Chair, University of Leiden, 1977.

Adelman, I., and Morris, C. T., *Economic Growth and Social Equity in Developing Countries.* Stanford: Stanford Univ. Press, 1973.

Ahluwalia, M., Carter, N., and Chenery, H., "Growth and Poverty in Developing Countries." *J. Devel. Econ.* **6,** 3:299–341, Sept. 1979.

Chang, S., "China's Agricultural Policy: An Independent Appraisal." *Econ. Planning* **22,** 2:3–8, May–Aug. 1986.

Eckstein, A., *China's Economic Revolution.* Cambridge: Cambridge Univ. Press, 1977.

Kakwani, N., *Income Inequality and Poverty.* New York: World Bank, 1980.

Kakwani, N., "On the Estimation of Inequality Measures from Grouped Observations." *Rev. Econ. Stud.* **43,** 2:483–492, June 1976.

Kuznets, S., "Economic Growth and Income Inequality." *Amer. Econ. Rev.* **45,** 1:1–28, March 1955.

Lardy, N., *Agriculture in China's Modern Economic Development.* Cambridge: Cambridge Univ. Press, 1983.

Lardy, N., "Consumption and Living Standards in China, 1978–83." *China Quart.* **100:**849–865, Dec. 1984.

Lardy, N., *Economic Growth and Distribution in China.* Cambridge: Cambridge Univ. Press, 1978.

Ma Hong, *New Strategy for China's Economy.* Beijing: New World Press, 1983.

Perkins, D., and Yusuf, S., *Rural Development in China.* Baltimore: Johns Hopkins, Univ. Press, 1984.

Roll, R., "The Distribution of Rural Income in China: A Comparison of the 1930's and the 1950's." Unpublished Ph.D. dissertation, Harvard University, 1974.

Schran, P.,"China's Price Stability: Its Meaning and Distributive Consequences." Unpublished manuscript, University of Illinois, 1976.

Shen, R., "A Perspective of Economic Development in PRC." *Rev. Bus.* **7**, 1:14–17, Winter 1985.

State Statistical Bureau, *Statistical Yearbook of China, 1984.* Hong Kong: Economic Information Agency, 1984.

State Statistical Bureau, *Statistical Yearbook of China, 1981.* Hong Kong: Economic Information Agency, 1982.

Travers, S., "Bias in Chinese Economic Statistics: The Case of the Typical Example Investigation." *China Quart.* **91**:478–485, Sept. 1982.

World Bank, *China: Socialist Economic Development,* Vol. 1. Washington, DC: Johns Hopkins Univ. Press, 1983.

JOURNAL OF COMPARATIVE ECONOMICS 11, 462–478 (1987)

Reform: Results and Lessons from the 1985 CESRRI Survey[1]

CHEN YIZI, WANG XIAOQIANG, AND COLLEAGUES

China Economic System Reform Research Institute, Beijing, China

Chen Yizi and Wang Xiaoqiang—Reform: Results and Lessons from the 1985 CESRRI Survey

The report summarizes and interprets a very large quantity of data collected during 1985 by a research team directed by the China Economic System Reform Research Institute in Beijing. Data were generated by questionnaires administered on-site at 429 enterprises, and four public opinion polls. The report concludes that initial reform in industry has been very successful, but has generated dangerous inflationary pressures and has biased investment away from producer goods and toward inefficiently small-scale projects. *J. Comp. Econ.*, September, 1987, **11**(3), pp. 462–478. China Economic System Reform Research Institute, Beijing, China. © 1987 Academic Press, Inc.

Journal of Economic Literature Classification Numbers: 113, 124, 514.

The current report is a summary of the major findings of a number of surveys conducted in 1985 by the China Economic System Reform Research Institute (CESRRI). Covered in the report are the results of economic studies of 429 enterprises in 27 cities, two polls on the public reactions to the May 1985 price reform (2409 and 2060 questionnaires respectively), a survey of young people on job preferences and their basic attitudes toward social and economic life (76,000 questionnaires), and an opinion poll concerning the reform of the social security system. The report attempts to make a general analysis of the present state of economic reform, its problems, and strategic priorities for the reform in the next stage, on the basis of the above surveys as well as an overall assessment of the nationwide situation.

---

[1] This Report was presented to the State Council in October, 1985. The organization, research, and drafting of the report involved Chen Yizi, Wang Xiaoqiang, Zhang Gang, Zhang Shaojie, Diao Xinsheng, Li Jun, Gai Nangfeng, Jiang Sidong, Xia Xiaojing, Jiang Yao, Ji Xiaoming, Xu Siaobo, Xu Gang, Cao Yuanzheng, Zhao Yujiang, Shen Hong, Liu He, and others. The full version of the report was published in Chinese in 1986, and will be published in English in 1987 under the title, *Reform: Challenges and Choices.*

172

CHINESE ECONOMIC REFORM

Reforms have imbued enterprises with greater incentive and accorded them more autonomy. The introduction of market mechanisms has enlivened the market and raised the sovereign status of consumers. But the expansion of consumption spending and of investment demand pose a serious challenge to reform.

The expansion of consumption spending is the result of the upward adjustment of wages intensified by the immobility of labor. The runaway consumption-oriented investment and the softening of the bank constraint both feature prominently in the issue of excessive investment growth, while the miniaturization of the investment scale and the tilt toward light industry in the composition of production-oriented investment will become a serious drag on economic revitalization in the days to come.

The problem lies in the micro mechanisms. The proper choice is, in step with a strengthening of administrative and indirect controls over wages and credits, to launch bold yet prudent microeconomic reforms. To keep wages from rising continuously, it is necessary to reform the systems of social welfare and security, throw open the labor market, take advantage of the abundant supply of labor, and encourage a certain degree of employment competition. To quench the thirst for investment and reverse the trend toward light industry in the industrial composition, such alternatives as a reform in bankruptcy laws, strengthening horizontal ties among enterprises, opening non-bank financial markets, and encouraging the formation of investment consortia by enterprises may be steps in the right direction.

China's economic mechanisms in the "switchover" period are more complicated than either the traditional model of the Soviet Union or the mature market economies of Europe and North America. Therefore, in our attempt at exercising effective macroeconomic control, it would be far from adequate to adopt the methods of the traditional model or to introduce the macroeconomic indicators of the developed countries, before our microeconomic mechanisms have been correctly understood. Gaining an understanding of the current economic mechanism through positive, in-depth studies and investigations is the prerequisite.

1. ACHIEVEMENTS OF REFORM THUS FAR

Since 1979, based on the idea of simplifying administration and decentralization, the reform of the economic structure designed to create a commodity market and deregulate and enliven the enterprises has made substantial progress. The reform of the systems of interenterprise distribution, planned resource transfer, and allocation and price control has gained noticeable results. Market mechanisms have begun to play an important role in the operation of the economic system.

The reform of the distribution system has highly motivated enterprises to generate profit. In 1984, the enterprises studied retained 21.9% of the gross profit realized and 36.7% of the retained profits was disbursed as bonuses. The correlation coefficient between the increased rate of retained profits and the increased rate of gross profits realized was 0.57, while the correlation coefficient between the increased rate of per capita bonus and that of retained profits is 0.29. The interests of the enterprises and their workers are closely related to the profits of the enterprises. Enterprises which for a long time sought mainly to fulfill production quotas have begun to react to a strong profit incentive. According to statistics derived from 359 questionnaires addressed to factory directors, "improvement of efficiency and benefit" topped the list of 14 management objectives, followed by "improvement of quality" and "development of new products," in that order. "Fulfillment of production quotas" came eleventh with "doubling of product value" bringing up the rear. Such an order of priority is born out by the actual performance indicators of the enterprises: the annual growth rates of product value and of profits of the sample enterprises show a significant correlation, as do the rates of investment in fixed assets and profit (for the former, $r = 0.3249$ and for the latter, $r = 0.1373$, while investment and other indicators do not show such correlations).

The reform in the system of planned resource allocation has afforded the enterprises a certain degree of autonomy in their operations. In 1984, the planned production ratio of the sample enterprises (the proportion of the output under mandatory plans in relation to the gross output) was 23.97%, the planned supply ratio of major raw materials (the proportion of planned supply in relation to the gross materials consumption) accounted for 73.16%, and the planned marketing ratio of products (the amount earmarked for planned allocation in relation to gross sales) took up 57.42%, leaving as much as 32.81% to be marketed by the enterprises on their own. In the period from January to June 1985, the planned ratios of raw material supply diminished sharply. In the gross consumption of major raw materials, the proportion acquired by enterprises autonomously through adjustment and cooperative arrangements between enterprises and in the market has abruptly increased from 26.84% in 1984 to 43.8%, an increase of 17% within half a year.

As regards the overall situation in the enterprises, in 1984 51% of enterprises studied had already gained varying degrees of autonomy, 77% of them found it necessary to adapt their production plans to market demand, and 90% relied to a certain extent on marketing at least part of their products by themselves.

The "two-tier" pricing system has obviously played a positive role. An important function of enterprise-coordinated prices and self-marketed prices is to reflect more truthfully the supply and demand situation of the market and, through the accompanying marginal effect, to regulate enterprise activities. Take steel for example: to producer and consumer alike, the possibility of selling additional steel output or the need to buy additional steel products at the high free-market price would imply that with each extra ton of steel produced or saved, a given enterprise would experience increased sales, or reduced cost, calculated according to market prices. The data gathered from 12 medium-sized steel mills suggest that as soon as the self-marketed portion of output exceeds a certain "threshold," a great marginal effect is achieved (Table 1). The "two-tier" pricing system also has a noticeable effect on economizing of materials. In 1984, 300 steel-consuming enterprises reduced steel consumption for each 10,000 yuan of output value by 18%.

The market has begun to exert a strong influence on enterprise production, supply, and marketing. Vested with more decision-making power, enterprises have to cater to market demand in order to realize profits. The correlation coefficient between the growth rates of output value and sales revenue of the sample enterprises is a high 0.74. The fastest-growing lines of trade and enterprises are also the most successful sellers.

The city of Shashi, a model in this reform campaign, is known throughout the country. Its gross industrial output value increased by 7.1% in 1984, only half as much as the previous year and far below the national average increase of 14%. Other indicators of economic performance such as the utilization of circulating funds also failed to maintain the level of the previous year. The simple reason is that the textile industry, the output value of which accounts for 60% of the city's gross industrial output value, faced an unfavorable market. By contrast, the city of Xiamen registered a 57.7% increase in its industrial growth in the first half of 1985. The reason lies in the 890% increase in the industrial output value of the much sought-after electronic products, which account for 58.3% of the total increment in industrial output value.

The Hungarian economist Janos Kornai takes the ratio between the input inventory and the output inventory of an enterprise (referred to as "Kornai index") as the most important comprehensive index capturing the essential difference between the resource-constrained, sellers' market economy and the demand-constrained, buyers' market economy (Table 2). The Kornai index of our sample enterprises was 4.5 in 1983, 4.4 in 1984, and 3.8 in the first half of 1985. The relative reduction of the input inventory and increase of

TABLE 1

THE RELATIONSHIP BETWEEN THE SELF-MARKETING RATE AND THE OUTPUT
GROWTH RATE OF 12 STEEL MILLS

Number of enterprises	Self-marketing rate (%)	Average	Output growth rate (%)	Average
Lowest 6	0–7.8	2.96	−10.98–5.80	−9.32
Highest 6	20.0–34.0	18.78	2.30–69.73	14.38
All 12	—	11.00	—	5.26

TABLE 2

"KORNAI INDEX" FOR SIX COUNTRIES[a]

Buyers' market economies	Years	Kornai index	Sellers' market economies	Years	Kornai index
Australia	1972–1977	1.5	U.S.S.R.	1967–1977	9.2–12.3
Sweden	1968–1972	0.7–0.74	Poland	1975	10.3
U.S.A.	1960–1977	0.94–1.16	Hungary	1971–1980	7.26–8.53

[a] Janos Kornai, "The Dual-Dependency of State Industry." *Econ. Res.* No. 10, 1985.

output inventory of the enterprises imply a greater room for choice to the enterprises as buyers, and a greater constraint of market demand on enterprises as sellers. Different methods of computing all affirm the significant change in the effect the market mechanism has on enterprise operations. Along with the deepening of the reform, the sovereign status of enterprises as independent buyers is rising steadily, whereas the monopoly status of enterprises as sellers is gradually receding.

The introduction of market mechanisms has accustomed the people to life under a commodity economy and has won widespread support (Table 3).

The interval between the two surveys in Table 3 was less than six months but the score for strict state control over prices plummeted. Shortly after the opening of prices for nonstaple foodstuffs, quite a number of people turned from a negative attitude to show support for price management by market forces, thanks to their as yet limited experience with market practices.

In the survey conducted in February 1985 on the social and psychological effect of the price reform, we found that in the list of 11 factors affecting people's views on the reform, "evaluation by changes in the standard of living" (subjective indicator) scored the highest, whereas "evaluation by per capita family income" (objective indicator) scored the lowest. What is more, there

TABLE 3

PUBLIC REACTION TO PRICE CONTROL ALTERNATIVES

Alternatives	February survey (%)	July survey (%)
All prices should be fixed and strictly controlled by the state	61.8	34.7
All prices should be open to market quotation	5.9	6.7
Some prices should be open and some others subject to state control	30.8	58.2

did not seem to be any significant correlation between the two. People did not think that their standard of living was markedly correlated with their actual levels of income. This interesting phenomenon shows that in a seller's market, where money cannot always get what one wants, consumption ceases to be a direct function of income and the level of income cannot be equated with the actual standard of living.

For this reason, it is far from adequate to base macro control over inflation on commodity price indices which include many planned prices that do not reflect market supply and demand. What affected people's opinions most during the switchover period was their realized purchasing power and the actual improvement of their living standard. The second opinion survey last July reaffirmed the above conclusion. The prices of nonstaple foodstuffs have a direct bearing on people's livelihood. At a time when wage adjustments had not yet fully caught up, when the very sensitive and risky reform of the price system had just been launched, people who claimed a "substantial" and a "slight" improvement in their standard of living still accounted for 73.4% (11.1% less than in the February survey). Is that attributable to the income subsidies? Our conclusions point to the contrary. Especially worth mentioning is the encouraging attitude of understanding and support of the broad masses toward the reform, as reflected in another survey entitled "The Social and Psychological Reaction of People to the Reform of the Social Security System" (see Table 4).

It is safe to conclude that the reform over the last few years has been a great success. As far as the functioning of the economy is concerned, the goal

TABLE 4

PEOPLE'S UNDERSTANDING OF THE REFORM

Statement	Total and partial aggreement (%)	Total and partial disagreement or uncertainty (%)
As long as the reform measures are conducive to social and economic development, they are worthwhile even if entailing greater risks to one's own welfare	78.3	21.7
The reform may be somewhat disorderly at present, but it is better than "eating from the same big pot"	77.8	22.2
As long as one has skill and ability, one won't suffer from the reform	80.7	19.3
If the reform succeeds in the end, we don't mind suffering a lower standard of living for the time being	75.3	24.7

of production has begun to shift from the fulfillment of state quotas to the satisfaction of market demands, and supply is actively responding to demand. The development of production has increasingly been motivated by profits and sales returns instead of output volume, output value, and growth rate. More autonomy to enterprises has led to changes in their operational objectives and enhancement of their managerial capability. The constraining effect of market demand on enterprises has to some degree edged the enterprise behavior away from the track set by the old mode of control. The introduction of market mechanisms has helped acclimatize people to life under a market economy, and is steadily fostering ever greater support reform.

The achievements of the reform over the past have provided favorable conditions for pushing reform efforts from product markets into factor markets, and have laid a solid foundation for more effective and active government intervention in economic life while adopting the market mechanism as a guideline. The task we are facing now is not to reintroduce the Procrustean bed and shove our national economy back on to the old track nor is it to brush aside the great breakthroughs already made in the reform and to start wholly anew. Rather, we should come to grips with problems in real life and resolutely carry forward the reform on the basis of what has already been achieved.

2. NEW CHALLENGES

Having established the constraint which market demand now imposes on the orientation of the economic system, this report focuses next on trends and problems in consumption, investment, and microeconomic mechanisms. The expansion of consumption spending, and the "thirst for investment" which seems to be embedded in the system, have become serious challenges to economic development and structural readjustment, just at a time when reform over the past years has begun to bear fruit. This is a syndrome common to economic reform in all socialist countries.

(1) The Expansion of Consumption Demand

Structural wage inflation. "More work, more pay" is a fair demand by workers. Wages should rightfully be determined by market supply and demand. Such a system would draw forth well-motivated labor. But the lack of job mobility in China required that we motivate workers by linking wages to enterprise profit.

Unfortunately, the performance of an enterprise is affected not only by the enthusiasm of its workers, but also by a mix of various other factors. The planned allocation of factors of production, enforced over a long time in the past, has resulted in extremely uneven operational conditions among the enterprises in China. Take fixed assets for example. The ratio between the highest and lowest per worker value of fixed assets in the sample enterprises is roughly 200. Under these circumstances, average labor productivity, a main indicator of the productive enthusiasm of the labor force, does not reflect the quality or quantity of work, and, in fact, shows a negative correlation with profit. The 56 sample enterprises whose profit increase rate is below 14% show an average labor productivity increase rate of over 10%, whereas for the 43 enterprises with profit increase rate in excess of 120%, the average labor productivity increase rate is below zero. Presumably, these enterprises increased profit by increasing fixed assets. In this context, it would obviously be inadvisable to link labor to profits.

But, in practice it is hard for a profitable enterprise to resist pressure for wage hikes, in the absence of a labor market. When wages in one sector shoot up, workers in every other enterprise or industry press for "matching" wage hikes in their "home base," in an inflationary process which has been labeled "upward emulation." After the taxi companies in Beijing achieved wage raises, the bus drivers applied to be transferred to taxi companies. When their applications were turned down, they were usually compensated by a wage increase close to the level achieved by the taxi drivers. Whether we admit it or not, wages are already being determined by supply and demand. If there were enough drivers competing for jobs with taxi companies, wages there could not remain high. If the bus companies could enroll drivers from the community, then they would not need to raise wages without regard to economic efficiency.

This structural wage inflation due to the lack of a labor market has not yet received adequate attention. Wage reform is more inflationary than price reform. Although the removal of price controls leads to a rise in the general price level, the simultaneous reform of the system of planned allocation, and the expansion of enterprise autonomy over supply, production, and marketing, allows factors of production to flow and form new combinations. The resulting increase in supply of products helps to check the general price rise. But reform in the system of planned labor assignment and allocation has not even started. As a result the partial lifting of wage control is not accompanied by a labor reallocation which might mitigate wage inflation.

Since any one sector's wage increase is merely a result of the rigid economic mechanism, a call for "upward emulation" (matching wage hikes) naturally is received with sympathy by factory managers, local governments, banks, tax authorities, and auditing and other management departments. According to data on 429 enterprises, in 1984 alone, enterprises were able through "negotiations" with these higher-ups to raise the percentage of retained profit in gross profit from 19.36 to 21.59% and to increase the percentage of bonus disbursement in retained profit from 25.43 to 36.70%. Despite great differences in profitability, labor productivity, and operating conditions, the sample enterprises sharply reduced the Gini coefficient of per person retained profit from 0.208 in 1983 to 0.182 in 1984. Undoubtedly, "upward emulation" has contributed to this situation. And these are only the facts on record in the accounts. Off-the-accounts "loopholes" are too numerous to stop up. According to our investigations, the enterprises employ more than 40 different methods to dodge wage control and secure more bonuses and benefit. These include, inter alia, transferring funds through labor service companies or auxiliary companies, unmerited disbursement of income, illicitly diverting funds from the set purposes, disbursing administrative appropriations to benefit individuals and adding the amount thus spent to the cost, using the bank accounts of collective enterprises to escape detection, unauthorized marketing of products by enterprises and omitting part of the returns from account books, awarding shares to individuals and paying them dividends, and increasing the disbursement of tax-free bonuses. According to a rough calculation, "off-the-book" losses alone amount to some 20 billion yuan in the whole country.

Hidden expansion of consumption funds. China's planned job assignment system combines employment with welfare and social security. Any redistribution of national income must all take place at the point of employment. Consequently, social welfare and security expenses have become components of gross labor cost. Hence, the "upward emulation" and the resultant expansion of consumption funds in the form of wages are sure to kick off a substantial increase in various welfare funds. In the period from 1978 to 1984, the disbursements of wages and wage-related cost by the banks throughout the country increased by 11% annually; state subsidies for commodity prices increased by 36% annually (from 1978 to 1983); and the disbursement for labor welfare increased by 21% annually. In 1984, the state appropriated to various cities 60 billion yuan for workers' welfare and subsidies, which equalled 66% of wages. From 1978 to 1983, the per capita national income created by city workers increased by 9.28%, and their average cash and noncash income doubled in the same period. If the hidden expansion of consumption funds is also counted, wage cost reaches 13% of total cost, equalling the level of Japan.

Consumption demand is far in advance of level of production. The expansion of consumption funds in the form of wages and the hidden expansion of consumption funds has led to an overall advance of consumption demand far ahead of the level of production. In the consumption of foodstuffs, the caloric intake per person per day in China was 2877 calories in 1983, which amounted to the 1979 level of Japan, and was 1.3 times that of the average level of all developing countries (1977). The intake of animal calories is also close to the world average, reaching Japan's level when its per capita national income was $413 (China's per capita national income in 1983 was only $231). In consumption patterns, the proportion of durable goods consumption climbed from 24% in 1979 to 44% in 1984. In 1985, the average level of possession by urban residents of such durable consumer goods as TV sets, electric fans, tape recorders, and sewing machines matched the level in Japan when its per capita national income was $1600. Consumption in terms of housing, transportation, and medical care has also gone up with the tide. This concentrated and vigorous consumer demand exerts a heavy pressure on the market and a strong pull on industrial production and investment.

In 1984, the accumulated purchasing power of our urban and rural residents approached 200 billion yuan, amounting to 60% of the gross cash income of the residents in the same year and 36% of gross national income. In 1985, consumption demand increased by about 80 billion yuan. The irreversible momentum of the expansion of consumption spending, which has taken up 80% of national income outlays, poses a grave threat to structural reform, economic development, and social stability. It must receive adequate attention and be dealt with seriously.

(2) The Expansion of Consumption-Oriented Investments and the Shift of the Industrial Structure toward Light Industry

In 1984, extrabudgetary investment in fixed assets accounted for 80% of the gross social investment in fixed assets. The continued expansion of the retained segment of enterprise profits, the continued decentralization with respect to the authority to invest, the reduction of state budgetary investment, and the conscientious implementation of the policy of "substituting loans for budgetary appropriation" are reform objectives decided on for the Seventh Five-Year Plan period. These extrabudgetary investments, which have been increasingly determined by the interplay of supply and demand in the market, will become a major factor in the sectoral distribution of investment. The resource allocation pattern established thereby will, to a great extent, determine the fate of the overall economic revitalization drive after 1990.

Expansion of consumption-oriented investment. A main characteristic of the current investment expansion is the rapid growth of consumption-oriented investment, and insufficient producer goods growth. As of August 1985, non-productive investment was 42.43% of the national capital construction during the Sixth Five-Year plan period. It is now a common practice to divert funds for technological renovation and reform to housing construction. Even if funds for technological renovation and reserve funds were both lumped under productive accumulation, the investment rate in China has fallen from 29.14% (1976–1979) to 24.41% (1981–1984). By the end of 1985, it is estimated, the productive capital construction projects completed in the Sixth Five-Year Plan will have increased by only 6.4% over that of the Fifth Five-Year Plan, whereas the nonproductive capital construction projects completed will have increased by 128.76%. The increase in the nonproductive investment amounts to 87.75% of the gross increase in capital construction in the Sixth Five-Year

Plan. According to statistics provided by 19 cities surveyed, in the period between 1983 and the first half of 1985, the proportion of nonproductive investment in gross investment was roughly 60%.

Investment in housing accounted for 70% of gross nonproductive investment in the whole country. From 1982 to 1984, investment in housing occupied 28% of gross social investment. More alarming still, the rapid growth in housing and similar nonproductive investment seems to be particularly insensitive to overall contraction of investment, perhaps due to the rigid employment system under which housing is a major fringe benefit. In the period of investment contraction from 1981 to 1982, the share of nonproductive investment in gross investment rose from 43.0 to 45.5%. In 1983 and 1984, as investment expanded, the share fell to 41.7 and 40.3%. The share rose again to 42.5% in the first half of 1985, during the renewed contraction in gross investment. Over the recent past, investment in housing has hardly been affected at all by state macroeconomic policies but has maintained a steady and rapid growth. And the share of such investment in the total tends to become greater when overall investment shrinks. Housing investment seems to be as "downward-inflexible" as wages. If such a trend is allowed to continue, the long-term development of the national economy will surely be hampered by insufficient productive investment.

The danger of a softening bank constraint: "Investment thirst." Given expanding and inflexible consumption investment, to guarantee the necessary productive accumulation would presuppose an undesirable expansion of overall investment. The traditional thirst for investment in socialist systems poses another threat to economic development and to the relaxation of control over investment.

Conventional wisdom attributes the thirst for investment to the "everyone eating from one big pot" system that ignores economic accounting. However, it should be pointed out that the investment expansion today differs substantially from previous fiscal investment expansions, for it occurs at a time when the budget constraint on enterprises has become harder. At present, enterprises are still not really wholly responsible for their profits and losses and the cadre system in enterprises had not been thoroughly reformed. The investment decision-makers are in the enviable position of engaging in profit-seeking adventures and being credited with success in operations without having any qualms about investment losses rebounding on themselves. The factory directors are not afraid of bankruptcy and workers do not fear unemployment— this is what fuels investment expansion. And yet, with the progress of the reform, the constraints on enterprises have, after all, become more stringent. Except for a few priority projects, the era of wrangling for free fund appropriations and resource transfers is no more. The investment decision-makers have at least to bear the burden of paying bonuses to workers and staff as long as their enterprises still remain in operation. Such developments should at least have eased to a certain extent the thirst for investment. Then how can we explain the reemergence of an investment upsurge that shows no visible signs of abating?

We believe that the rampant investment expansion in 1984 and thereafter was to a large extent brought about by excessively liberal bank lending. National investment in fixed assets financed by domestic loans in 1984 increased by 47.3% over 1983. In the period between January and August 1985 an increase of 129.8% was registered (despite the high increase in 1984), while investment through enterprise self-financing rose by only 49.6%. The proportion of extrabudgetary capital construction and technological renovation financed by loans was, respectively, 18.7 and 29.3% in 1982, and these figures abruptly jumped to 20.5 and 35% in 1984; and again to 26.5 and 44.3% in the first half of 1985. As a result of the general tightening of credits and loans, the banks have readjusted their loan structures. According to itemized reports from the banks in 18 cities, the proportion of loans for fixed assets in the sum total of loans was 6.3% in 1983, 6.8% by the end of June in 1984, 7.7% by the end of 1984, and reached 8.9% by the end of June 1985. Our sample enterprises financed 31.84% of their gross investment in fixed assets by bank loans. The loans for investment by rural enterprises have increased by a similar margin.

When we asked factory directors to rank operational constraints, "inadequate financing" won second place in a list of 16 alternatives. Asked to rank their preferred sources of funds, "to borrow from a bank" scored first out of 8 options. And each of 14 enterprise subgroups without exception named it as their first choice. This shows that the reform has hardened the fiscal constraint, while bank loans have become an important source of capital funds. Of the loans provided by the construction banks in seven cities, the overdue arrears in repayment of loans by the end of 1984 increased by 6.6% over the previous year, and shot up by 44.7% by the end of June 1985, as compared with the same period of 1984. The data in Table 5 show the same pattern. All these statistics testify to the softening of the bank constraint, once the most rigid area of the Chinese economy.

The softening of the bank constraint poses an even greater threat than fiscal investment expansion. Within government finance, an increase in the fiscal

TABLE 5

INSOLVENCY LOSSES OF CONSTRUCTION BANKS IN 18 CITIES

	June 1983	Dec. 1983	June 1984	Dec. 1984	June 1985
Ratio of insolvency to arrears (%):	24.29	36.93	41.90	47.66	51.80

reserve must necessarily be accompanied by a decrease in consumption. However, the banks possess unlimited power to create money and can achieve high accumulation at the same time as consumption expands. Nowadays, it has become common practice for enterprises to pay bonuses and welfare expenses from their own funds and carry on construction projects on borrowed money. The profit retained by the enterprise is mainly earmarked for consumption, which generates additional investment demand through the accelerator mechanism. The resulting effects—a shortfall in productive investments and accelerated investment prospects—in turn exert a two-pronged pressure on bank financing, compelling the banks to grant loans and finally compelling the central bank to issue currency. In this pattern, there seems to emerge a new economic mechanism, which satisfies through bank loans both the enterprise's welfare needs and its production needs. For the local banks, a handsome investment turnover might be expected. But what seems rational and feasible at a micro level is not necessarily healthy for the macroeconomy. While the microeconomic entities are rejoicing over their respective gains, the softening of bank control may have kicked off a general inflation characterized by excessive money supply.

The lesson of Yugoslavia is that when enterprises assume responsibility for their own financial gains and losses, the consumption spending from enterprises' retained funds lurches forward, a piling up of bank loans for investment follows closely behind, and the issuance of money brings up the rear. Compared with 1970, in 1976 in Yugoslavia, individual consumption increased by 273%, collective consumption increased by 330%, investment in fixed assets increased by 290%, and accumulation by 40%. The cost of this dual satisfaction of welfare and production needs was a high foreign debt and inflation, which could hardly be due to fiscal expansion.

"Stunted trees": The miniaturization of unit investment scale. The expansion of overall investment is only one aspect of the problem. Along with the increase in the share of enterprise retained profit, decentralization in investment authority, and the expansion of the overall level of investment, the neglected question of miniaturization of the scale of investment projects looms increasingly large.

In 1984, of the extrabudgetary funds of 23 cities, the enterprises and their upper management bodies accounted for 76% of the income and 89% of the outlay. The objective of the reform is to strengthen and not weaken the trend of enterprises controlling their own resources. However, because 90% of China's enterprises are small in size, the growth of enterprise-controlled funds implies a scattering of these funds over hundreds of thousands of enterprises, and thus a reduction in the amount of money available to any one unit. Of the enterprises we investigated, 57% are large and medium sized, which is a much higher proportion than the national average. The profits they retained averaged 1.53 million yuan, only 0.5 million of which was earmarked for the development of production. The retained profits of the small enterprises averaged 0.26 yuan, and funds for the development of production only 0.1 million yuan. These are tiny amounts.

In China today, the financial market has not yet developed. There is no way to concentrate financial funds. The division of labor among enterprises is not well-developed, and mechanisms for enterprise integration and merger are rudimentary. Thus, the scattered distribution of funds inevitably leads to their scattered utilization. Enterprises can't lend or borrow funds, so they use what they happen to have. Our survey found that for 10 cities, of 3212 capital construction projects in 1984, only 5.5% exceed 10 million yuan, and 52.0% were lower than 0.5 million yuan, averaging 0.237 million yuan. The projects which fell between 10 million and 0.5 million yuan averaged only 1.18 million yuan. If we look farther away from the central cities, we find the situation even less encouraging. Investment by urban and rural collectives and individuals amounts to 35% of gross social investment in fixed assets. Here, the miniaturization problem is even more conspicuous. By the end of 1984, the fixed assets owned by rural enterprises averaged 35,000 yuan each in terms of their original value, less than 0.5% of the average for state-owned enterprises.

The miniaturization of the scale of investment has seriously hampered economic performance. During the period of high economic growth in Japan, nongovernmental investment created the then world's-biggest iron and steel works, chemical complexes, shipyards, automobile works, and so on. Generally speaking, large-scale investment stimulated by a promising economic environment on the one hand, and large-scale production and expansion of the scale of investment on the other, are two sides of the same coin. The reality we are facing today, however, is the expansion of gross investment coupled with a decline in the scale of investment. Take for example, those projects that have caught the fancy of many investors. The minimal optimal production scale of a washing machine factory should be 200,000 units per annum. In 1984, of 130 washing machine factories in the whole country, only 9 reached such a capacity. Of 110 refrigerator factories nationwide, average output was 4600 units per annum, which is far below the rational scale. There are over 110 motor factories in China, distributed all across the country except in Tibet and Ningxia. Their average scale is 2000 cars per annum. Only a few state-financed automobile works established in former years operate up to the requirements of scale economy.

The minuscule unit investment scale is a challenge to current strategic thinking on reform. The emergence of more than 1000 "bucket-size blast furnaces" has sounded the warning. In one sense, the problem reflects the success of the price reform. As the two-tier price system for steel generated an accurate price signal, market demand stimulated supply. It is impossible to revitalize the national economy by relying on a nationwide blooming of "stunted trees" like these.

"Short-term investment and quick turnover": The light-industrialization of the industrial structure. Within productive investment, extrabudgetary financing is biased toward short-term payoffs. Since 1978, our country has decided on a policy giving priority to the development of consumer goods, which has helped improve the economic situation and contributed to social stability. But in the long run, the proposition that the economy of a big country can depend on light industrial growth is not borne out by any historical precedent. As matters now stand, the increased demand of consumers for durable consumer goods is exerting a strong pull on production and investment, and on the other hand, the miniature scale of unit investment resulting from the decentralized investment operations has led to inadequate investment in the heavy and chemical industries, with their low elasticity in scale of financing and technology. The tight-money policy and difficulties in fundraising have converged to make the unit investment scale even smaller and the investors even more desirous of short-term gains. "Short-term and quick turnover" has become a principle governing the choice of investment targets. This is yet another problem that endangers long-term development.

The increase in general-purpose investment has far surpassed investment in energy, transportation, and other priority construction activities. From January to June 1985, the proportion of delivered investments in the energy sector in relation to gross investment fell from 23.8% for the same period in 1984 to 19.7%. In the sectors of transportation and telecommunications the ratio concerned fell from 15.1 to 13.9% for the same period. A bias toward light industry has led to light industrialization of the industrial structure. The net increments of productive capacity in the railroad, highway, steel making, electricity generation, and other sectors in the Sixth Five-Year Plan period have all declined. The development of the raw materials industry is falling even farther behind the needs of economic development. In the first half of 1985, based on the share of the metallurgical industry in gross industrial output value (the annual average of which was 0.084 from 1980 to 1984) and the investment output ratio of the metallurgical industry (0.66), investment in the metallurgical industry should have been 10.4 billion yuan. However, the actual investment in the metallurgical industry in the period mentioned was only 3.384 billion yuan, representing a shortfall of 207%. The insufficiency of investment in the metallurgical industry will undoubtedly hinder the effort to reverse the increasing dependency on imports.

As to the age of the productive equipment of China's metallurgical industry, the equipment of the seventies only comprises 15%, that of the fifties and sixties comprises 70%, and that of the forties still occupies 15%. The need for investments in energy and transportation sectors is even more pressing. With the further advance of the reform and the increase in the retained profit of enterprises (which implies a reduction of the portion for state fiscal use), investment will more and more be undertaken using scattered extrabudgetary funds. In the light of the trend toward short-term gains in extrabudgetary financing, it is safe to predict that the light industrialization of the industrial structure will in time become a most serious drag on the takeoff of the national economy.

3. CONCLUSION: OPEN THE FACTOR MARKETS

Reform—that is, simplification of administration and continued decentralization—presents three touchy problems. (1) "Relaxation of control always breeds expansion." Reform conflicts with economic stability. Reform requires the delegation of power to enterprises, for without authority over such matters as wages and investment, the enterprises will have no genuine room to maneuver. But with any renewed reform, the expansion of consumption is bound to provoke an inflationary upsurge of investment and an overheated growth rate. (2) Reform conflicts with the need to emphasize heavy industry. Reform means using indirect economic levers to stimulate particular industries, regions, or enterprises. But the mechanism of upward emulation quickly turns any local incentive policy into a widespread consumption expansion, threatening a loss of macro control. (3) Reform conflicts with effective long-term economic development. Reform seeks to lodge the investment decision in those enterprises which are responsible for their own losses and gains. But miniaturization of the scale of investment caused by this decentralization, the expansion of nonproductive investment, and the shift toward light industry, all deviate in varying degrees from long-term development goals.

Thus the expansion of consumption funds and investment set obstacles in the way of the reform. How can they be overcome? The rising expectations for income, the entrenched upward emulation mentality, and the experience with markets in recent years, have combined to imbue the broad masses with a desire and an expectation to change jobs or choose professions, which was out of the question under the "big pot" system. The attitude of people toward employment has switched from seeking security and avoiding risks to seeking opportunities in spite of risks. This has laid the foundation for the opening up of a labor market. The thirst for investment and the miniaturization of the scale of investment will induce enterprises to pool resources and to open wider channels for the concentration of capital, making them more inclined to integration. This in turn prepares the groundwork for the opening up of a capital market, the reform of the financial system, and active intervention by government.

The macro imbalance which confronts us is severe indeed. Until we are able to curb the "two expansions" (consumption and investment), some remedial measures are unavoidable. For the sake of preserving reform, this recentralization must be carried out resolutely. With so many problems arising from our microeconomic mechanisms, to rashly change mandatory administrative control into indirect economic regulation at the macro level would run the risk of "one move amiss, the whole game a mess." Besides, the capacities of macro control, even in western countries with full-fledged market mechanisms, are limited. So, the correct direction is to strengthen administrative control over aggregate wages, credit, and loans, while resolutely deepening the reform of the micro mechanisms.

An essential prerequisite to containing the expansion of consumption funds is the unemployment of some workers. Similarly, the essential prerequisite to quenching the thirst for investment is the bankruptcy of some enterprises. During the Seventh Five-Year Plan period, then, we should face these challenges squarely. On the basis of a product market and a reformed price system, we must push forward to the next stage: Establishing a labor market and a capital market, along with adjustments in consumption policies and industrial organization policies.

Practical experience tells us that the state of the microeconomic base determines the effectiveness of macro control. As we seek substantial and risk-free advances for reform, we must promote indirect control at the macro level through reform at the micro level. By combining three aspects—opening up the factor markets, creating the micro preconditions for a change in the mode of macro control, and carefully developing the new organizational functions of government while maintaining certain necessary administrative control measures—we can map out a dynamic reform strategy that has structure, continuity, and gradually evolving priorities. This strategy, different from yet linked to the previous one of simplifying administration and decentralizing, will mark a new stage of reform and provide a logical point of departure for our future study.

JOURNAL OF COMPARATIVE ECONOMICS **11**, 479–489 (1987)

Trade, Employment, and Inequality in Postreform China[1]

BRUCE L. REYNOLDS

Union College, Schenectady, New York 12308

Reynolds, Bruce L.—Trade, Employment, and Inequality in Postreform China

The paper uses provincial-level Chinese foreign trade statistics, and a 1981 World Bank input–output table for China, to explore the impact of economic reform on employment, trade, and income inequality. The author concludes that trade increases regional inequality, and that 1981 trade decreased total employment in China, but that by 1985, due largely to the agricultural response to reform, net trade had become job-creating. *J. Comp. Econ.,* September 1987, **11**(3), pp. 479–489. Union College, Schenectady, New York 12308. © 1987 Academic Press, Inc.

Journal of Economic Literature Classification Numbers: 421, 824, 941.

INTRODUCTION

Foreign trade has been condemned as immiserizing, and glorified as an engine of growth. This study explores the role which foreign trade is playing, and may play in the future, in furthering two major Chinese policy objectives: urban full employment and equality of income distribution.

The paper proceeds as follows. Section 1 reviews the urban unemployment which arose in China in 1978, and the measures used to bring it under control. The central argument is that open unemployment has been traded for underemployment, and that this unhappy compromise, which cannot survive true industrial reform, stands as a barrier to it.

Section 2 reviews success stories of the "newly industrialized countries," associated with trade liberalization and export-led growth. In these countries, industrial employment has grown virtually as fast as industrial output, eliminating urban unemployment as a major problem. Implicit is the suggestion that such a policy shift might soften the dilemma presented in Section 1. I then consider China's own policy changes in foreign trade since 1978, and

[1] This paper benefited considerably from criticisms at the Arden House Conference and the Union College Economics Workshop, and in particular from the comments of Dwight Perkins, Dwight Phaup, and Tom Wiens. Remaining errors are my own.

189

conclude that despite false starts and pullbacks, China's trade sector is dramatically liberalized when compared with the traditional Soviet model. However, the concentration of trade and foreign investment in rich provinces probably increases interregional inequality.

Section 3 asks: would continued liberalization of foreign trade, and continued trade expansion, increase employment opportunities in China? The estimates of the sectoral labor requirements of China's imports and exports, and of the aggregate employment-creating effects of China's foreign trade, suggest that in 1981, China's imports displaced more employment than exports created; China was a net importer of labor. But by 1985, this paradoxical pattern had shifted, due largely to the impact of reform on production and trade of agricultural products.

1. Unemployment

In the years immediately following 1976, urban unemployment became a major policy problem. In the decade 1966–1976, as many as 17 million young people had been rusticated to the countryside. But by 1981 (Feng, 1981, p. 189), "except for a small number, all of the 17 million have returned to the cities. All of them demand employment." In addition, up to 8 million people fired during the Cultural Revolution had to be reinstated in their jobs; this was done by the end of 1979.[2] Meanwhile, middle schools were graduating new job-seekers at a rate of roughly 3 million a year. To make matters worse, urban enterprises had become accustomed to recruiting low-wage, unskilled labor in the countryside. Up to 14 million workers entered the urban labor force in this fashion between 1970 and 1976 (Taylor, 1986, p. 235). The resulting urban unemployment is shown in Table 1. These figures reflect only job-seekers registered with the municipal labor bureaus. True unemployment may easily have been twice as high at the 1979 peak.

In the 6 years 1978–1983, more than 44 million urban job-seekers found employment (Taylor, 1986, p. 255). This was accomplished in three ways. First, State Council decrees made it more difficult to recruit peasants into urban jobs. Second, a new practice, termed the "substitution system," permitted parents to retire in favor of a child. In the first few months of 1979, 100,000 such jobs changed hands in Shanghai alone.[3] Last, urban enterprises were prodded into accepting many more workers than they truly needed (Zhao and Yao, 1983, p. 21). By 1983, these policies had greatly reduced unemployment (but aggravated underemployment) in cities.

---

[2] Li Xiannian, quoted in *Ming Bao* (Hongkong), 14 June 1979.

[3] Taylor (1986). This may partially explain Shanghai's extraordinarily high proportion of retirees—10% of the population. It may also contribute to Taylor's estimate of Shanghai's unemployment rate, the lowest of any province.

TABLE 1

URBAN UNEMPLOYMENT, 1978–1983

Year	Million	Percent
1978	5.31	5.3
1979	6.36	5.5
1980	4.09	3.6
1981	3.05	2.6
1982	3.04	2.6
1983	2.71	2.3

Sources. Beijing Review, 3/28/83, p. 21 and Zhonqquo Laodong, 18 (9/28/84), p. 13.

Underemployment is a very severe problem in China. A number of Chinese studies place rural underemployment at 30–40% of the labor force. Zhao and Yao (1983) place underemployment in 1983 at one-third of industrial employment. The extremely low rate of productivity growth in both industry and agriculture since 1957 is indirect evidence of a consistent social policy of storing surplus labor inside production units rather than outside.

If economic reform in Chinese industry is to proceed, it is crucial that underemployment be brought under control. The industrial reforms propose to transform Chinese enterprises into autonomous entities, responsible for their own profit and loss. Clearly, the first action which would occur to an enterprise which faced losses, and was being held responsible for them, would be to fire any surplus workers on its staff. If the government withholds from enterprises (as it did in the period under review here) the freedom to fire workers (and in fact forces them to hire unneeded workers), enterprises are unlikely to accept responsibility for losses as well.

2. Trade, Reform, and Interregional Inequality

A. Import-substitution versus export-promotion. During the 1950s, trade policy in developing countries was dominated by the "elasticity-pessimism, import-substitution" approach.[4] Assuming low price- and income-elasticities of demand for primary products (relative to manufactures), theorists predicted that as trade expanded, the terms of trade faced by developing countries (exporters of primary products) would worsen. In the long run, LDCs could produce (and even export) manufactures as well, but only after reaping the cost-reducing benefits of scale expansion and learning-by-doing. Thus in the short run, tariffs and import quotas would be needed to facilitate the process of substituting domestic manufactures for imports.

[4] This section is heavily indebted to Kreuger (1986).

By the 1960s, the costs of this policy were apparent. Trade contracted sharply, especially exports, and the static losses in foregone gains from trade were large. The tariff barriers, which in effect subsidized use of capital, discouraged employment. In Brazil, India, and Taiwan during the 1950s, the annual growth rate was 7–10% for manufacturing output, but only 1–2% for manufacturing employment (Baer and Horve, 1966, p. 91). Import quotas, which produced de facto rationing of critical imported inputs, protected inefficient producers (in much the same way that Chinese rationing of key materials dictates and preserves domestic Chinese market shares). Under these government-sponsored cartels, producers naturally concentrated on lobbying the government. Cost reduction was ignored, and efficiency fell.

In reaction to this, several countries—Brazil, Taiwan, South Korea—sharply changed the nature of government intervention in trade. Administrative quotas gave way to tariff and subsidy levers. Foreign exchange was no longer worth more than its official (rationed) price. The incentive structure shifted away from *saving* foreign exchange and toward *earning* it. The explosive growth which resulted is well known. In the years after the policy shift, real GDP growth shifted from around 5 to around 10% for these three countries. Even more startling, annual growth in industrial employment rose to between 6

TABLE 2

GROWTH OF FOREIGN TRADE[a]

Year	Exports	Imports
1971	22.8	1.3
1972	21.6	25.5
1973	10.0	39.5
1974	−9.4	5.0
1975	9.0	−8.4
1976	0.5	3.9
1977	−6.1	9.0
1978	19.0	36.9
1979	25.6	15.7
1980	20.3	6.5
1981	10.6	−6.7
1982	12.5	0.5
1983	16.3	19.8
1984	7.9	33.8
1985	4.0	52.0
1986	4.2	−4.6

[a] Real terms; annual % change.

Source. 1971–1985: Ministry of Foreign Economic Relations and Trade, *Foreign Trade Almanac, 1985,* p. 797; 1985; State Statistical Bureau, *Monthly Statistical Bulletin,* March 1986; 1986: *China Daily* (17 January 1987) p. 1. 1986 figures are in nominal terms.

and 10%. Export growth was also double-digit in Korea, 28% per year for 1960–1978 (Kreuger, 1985, p. 21).

B. *Trade reform in China.* China's foreign trade stagnated through most of the 1960s. In real terms, it was lower in 1969 than in 1958. As the Chinese policy agenda shifted toward economic growth in the 1970s, trade grew rapidly, in two 3-year surges: 1971–1973 and 1978–1980 (70% real growth each time). In part to relieve the growing burden on central government trade organs, and in part to stimulate further export growth, the government began to transfer important trade powers to provinces, municipalities, and enterprises.

The experience of Shanxi Province is representative. Beginning in 1977, the Ministry of Foreign Trade permitted some measure of local control over exports, under a system called *xian hui.* During 1978, the locally managed portion of exports grew somewhat. This new set of arrangements was formalized at the 3rd Plenum (December 1978) as *ziying chukou* (self-managed exports). By 1982, more than 40% of Shanxi export procurement was under self-management.

Beginning in January 1981, local control of some imports (purchased with locally retained foreign exchange) was also allowed, through six provincial foreign trade importing corporations; a significant portion of 1981 provincial imports, including one-third of machinery imports, were "self-managed" (*ziying jinkou*). But the large 1978–1980 deficits soon led to a clamp-down on provincial imports, which accounted for only 4% of the total for Shanxi in 1982. Central control remained tight for the next 2 years.[5]

Then in September 1984, the State Council issued a new set of reform documents for the foreign trade sector. The trade system was expected to change in two ways. First, foreign trade enterprises were to become more independent of their administrative superiors, and to be judged on the basis of efficiency and profitability. Second, the FTCs were gradually to become merely agents for the exporting and importing enterprises or units. They would receive commissions for managing foreign transactions, but the producer, or the end-user, would bear the profit or loss from the transaction. The agency system would extend to all imported items, and to all nonagricultural exports. To facilitate this loosening of the system, the government reduced to 100 the number of export items which would be balanced through the traditional planning process by the State Planning Commission or the Ministry. Imports would henceforth be regulated through an import quota system (Chan and Sung, 1986).

One objective of this reform was probably to eliminate a large drain on the state's financial resources: export subsidies to foreign trade corporations. (Given China's overvalued exchange rate, most exports sold at a renminbi

---

[5] Information on Shanxi is drawn from Ministry of Foreign Economic Relations and Trade, *Foreign Trade Almanac, 1985,* pp. 359–362.

price lower than the price at which they were procured domestically. These losses had been routinely covered by budgetary transfers of billions of yuan annually.) But when the subsidy was withdrawn, exporting units reacted just as one would predict. Exports rose in 1984 by only 7%. Meanwhile, imports soared: a 37% increase in 1984, and 55% in 1985, including huge increases in imports of steel and other producer goods, as well as television sets, cars, and other consumer durables. Despite government countermeasures beginning in March 1985, it was 8 months before the situation had stabilized. The trade deficit for the year was nearly $8 billion.

Clearly, China has not found the path to export-led growth a smooth one. Administrative decentralization, in the presence of "incorrect" prices, has generated unacceptable trade deficits. The response has been to recentralize. But China has also reacted through price changes, such as the exchange rate devaluation in 1985. Although the foreign trade system is still constrained by numerous administrative controls, in comparison with the 1970s the number of agents empowered to engage in foreign trade has vastly increased. And their motivation has changed as well: the trade sector, like much else in the economy, has become monetized.

C. *Regional inequality.* China's rapid trade growth has probably increased regional inequality. Table 3 shows the breakdown of exports and foreign investment by province. A province gains from exports through both job-creation and retained foreign exchange. When one ranks these provinces in order of per capita income (World Bank, 1981, p. 54), one finds that the richest 15 provinces, accounting for 43% of the population, generated 75% of exports, while the poorest 9 provinces, with 37% of the population, account for only 9% of exports. Provincial per capita foreign investment is also highly correlated with per capita income. Thus to some extent, trade exacerbates interregional inequality. The World Bank (1985) notes this side effect of trade growth, and lists a number of possible remedies. One is to extend trade decentralization and liberalization to the poorer provinces such as Gansu, rather than restricting authority over trade to the richer provinces like Jiangsu and Guangdong.

3. Trade and Employment

In this section, I ask: to what extent does trade expansion increase employment in China? I explore this question in two ways. First, what is the employment effect of a one billion yuan increase in exports? The answer depends critically on the sector from which the exports come. Second, what about the employment effect of a balanced trade expansion? When exports and imports grow together, does the employment expansion from increased exports more than offset the employment contraction as imports displace domestic production and jobs? Rather unexpectedly, I find that on the contrary, balanced trade expansion which followed the trade pattern of 1981

TABLE 3

PROVINCIAL TRADE AND FOREIGN INVESTMENT, 1983

Province	1983 Exports ($100 M)	Direct foreign investment ($U.S. M)
Shanghai	33.90	43.10
Jiangsu	13.73	5.65
Zhejiang	6.52	3.15
Anhui	7.30	.36
Fujian	3.95	23.62
Jiangxi	2.43	.69
Shandong	18.10	11.69
Beijing	5.94	11.80
Tianjin	11.20	10.57
Hebei	6.8	1.12
Shanxi	.27	.11
Neimenggu	.70	.30
Liaoning	11.07	4.57
Jilin	1.67	.14
Heilongjiang	3.0	.52
Shaanxi	.57	.16
Gansu	.45	.03
Qinghai	.62	2.35
Ningxia	.60	.30
Xinjiang	.82	.33
Henan	2.80	.60
Hubei	4.12	4.99
Hunan	3.98	3.46
Guangdong	24.00	141.11
Guangxi	2.90	2.67
Sichuan	1.23	2.89
Guizhou	1.46	.29
Yunan	1.10	.15
All China	167.85	275.80

Source. Ministry of Foreign Economic Relations and Trade, *Foreign Trade Almanac, 1985, passim.* Export figures include provincial self-managed (*ziying chukou*) only.

would reduce employment in China. In other words, China in 1981 was a net importer of labor. The input–output methodology employed in this analysis parallels Levy (1982). The data employed are from the 1981 input–output table constructed by the World Bank (1985, Annex 5).

A. *Sectoral employment effects of trade.* Table 4 shows, for each of 15 sectors which enter into China's foreign trade, the total labor required, and the direct labor required, to produce one yuan of gross output. That is, column one shows total wage payments per yuan of gross output, taking into account the wage payments embodied in that sector's other inputs, whereas column

TABLE 4

LABOR COEFFICIENTS[a]

| | | | | | 1982 Trade (by) | |
Sector	Total labor requirements	Rank	Direct labor requirements	Rank	Exports	Imports
Agriculture	0.864	1	0.689	1	2.99	5.50
Food processing	0.625	2	0.050	14	2.65	1.28
Coal mining	0.552	3	0.337	2	0.33	0.09
Misc. manufactures	0.468	4	0.132	6	2.80	1.57
Paper	0.467	5	0.102	9	0.33	0.58
Commerce	0.453	6	0.210	4	3.44	1.46
Textiles and clothing	0.407	7	0.065	12	10.99	6.50
Transport	0.392	8	0.247	3	2.46	1.16
Machinery (narrow)	0.348	9	0.121	7	2.83	7.88
Chemical manufactures	0.340	10	0.071	10	2.96	4.56
Metallurgy (mining)	0.319	11	0.173	5	0.55	0.24
Metal products	0.315	12	0.116	8	1.51	2.08
Metallurgy manufactures	0.313	13	0.066	11	1.20	2.95
Petroleum mining	0.168	14	0.055	13	1.58	—
Petroleum manufactures	0.113	15	0.007	15	1.21	0.02

[a] Wages per unit of gross output, in yuan.

Source. Calculated from data in World Bank (1985), Annex 5: Economic Structure in International Perspective, Table C4.

two reflects only wage payments in the sector itself. Thus in food processing, wage payments to workers employed in that sector account for only 5% of gross output value. But once one takes into account the large role of agricultural products as inputs to the sector, and the labor embodied in those products, the figure rises to 62.5%.

One obvious implication of the results in Table 4 is that in considering the job-creating effects of export expansion in particular sectors, it is crucial to take indirect labor requirements into effect. Not only food processing, but paper, textiles, and clothing as well, shift their ranking dramatically in column one as compared with column two.

A second implication is that the job-creating effects of export expansion depend critically on the sector which expands. To take the extreme case, consider agriculture versus petroleum manufacturing. If, through a wave of some planner's magic wand, China had exported one billion yuan more in the former sector, balancing that with a one billion yuan reduction in petro-leum exports, total exports would have required an additional 751 million yuan of labor (0.864–0.113). If we assume a figure of 1500 yuan for annual wage payments per worker in each sector, this reallocation of exports would have created roughly 500,000 jobs.

To draw a third implication of Table 4 requires the assumption that the Chinese economy is labor-rich relative to the economies with which she trades, to such an extent that labor-intensity swamps other considerations in evalu-ating the rationality of China's sectoral pattern of trade. Under this assumption, and using the traditional Heckscher–Ohlin–Samuelson comparative advantage framework, one could say: to maximize gains from trade, China should be a net exporter in sectors toward the top of Table 4's ranking, and a net importer in the lowest-ranked sectors. By and large, the trade pattern in Table 4 con-forms to this prescription (and one suspects that this would be even more true at a higher level of disaggregation). The glaring exceptions, agriculture and petroleum, are discussed below.

B. *Aggregate employment effects of trade.* Let A = matrix of input–output coefficients; X = vector of net exports; Q = vector of gross output required to generate X; N = vector of direct labor requirements per unit of output; L = direct and indirect labor required to produce X. Then we can write

$$Q = (I - A)^{-1} X$$

and

$$L = QN.$$

Applying this methodology to the 1981 input–output matrix yields a value for L of -0.394. The interpretation of this result is as follows: the net impact of the job-creation due to exports, less the job-displacement due to imports, was to reduce employment by 394 million yuan. Exports by themselves re-quired 16.606 billion yuan of labor inputs. The amount of labor which would have been required to produce the goods which were imported was greater, 17.000 billion yuan. China, although clearly a labor-rich economy, was a net importer of labor in 1981. Using, again, a figure of 1500 yuan earnings per worker, we can say that 1981 trade cost roughly 265 thousand jobs.

If labor and capital were the only productive factors, one might conclude from this result that China's trade pattern in 1981 was allocatively inefficient—perhaps due to a lack of scarcity prices, or of profit-maximizing behavior, in foreign trade decision-making. But a more logical explanation for this "Leon-tief paradox" result is the exclusion of other productive factors—in particular, land and other natural resources—from the analysis. Two trade categories—petroleum, a capital-intensive export, and agricultural products, a labor-in-tensive import—largely account for the paradoxical result. But clearly, China exports petroleum because she is endowed with petroleum deposits, and im-ports agricultural products at least in part because she is land-scarce.

C. Trade, employment, and the impact of reform since 1981. Has China's pattern of trade shifted since 1981, to either increase or decrease job-creation? If so, can the shift be attributed to reform? Aside from a mild shift from manufactures toward primary products, the composition of exports in 1985 was virtually identical to that in 1981.[6] In imports, however, change was considerable. In reaction to very rapid growth in domestic agriculture, agricultural imports' share in the total fell from 36 to 12%. The gap was filled principally by imports of machinery and transport equipment, and textiles and other light industrial products, whose share of imports rose 50% each.

This 1985 trade composition was imposed on the 1981 aggregate trade figures, and the analysis in Section 2, part B was performed again. This hypothetical trade pattern would have required direct and indirect labor totalling 1.47 billion yuan (compared with the earlier result: −0.39 billion yuan). The interpretation of this result is that had trade in 1981 followed the 1985 pattern, employment in China would have been higher by 1.86 billion yuan (or some 1.2 million jobs). Clearly, China's foreign trade by 1985 was playing a much more positive role in employment-creation.

Is this result related to economic reform? Yes, the rapid agricultural growth which underlies it is clearly linked to the introduction of the production responsibility system in agriculture. On the other hand, this study found no evidence to suggest that reform in industry or in the foreign trade system was affecting the job-creation potential of foreign trade.

CONCLUSIONS

(1) Although the open urban unemployment which arose after 1978 was largely eliminated by 1983, China has not really solved her urban employment problem. Job-seekers were provided with "ricebowls," but not always with productive employment. Reform, insofar as it creates profit-seeking (and bankruptcy-fearing) producing units, will transform underemployment into unemployment. Even assuming that some unemployment compensation system emerges, urban unemployment will mean increased urban income inequality.

(2) Foreign trade, in countries which have dismantled protectionist trade regimes, has mitigated this source of inequality by generating rapid employment growth. In China, export procurement is concentrated in rich provinces, which presumably reinforces regional inequality.

(3) In addition, the composition of trade in 1981 was such that China appears to have been a net labor importer. This pattern shifted, by 1985, such that net trade had become job-creating. However, the source of the shift was growth in (rural) agriculture, rather than in (urban) light industry. Thus it is unlikely that trade is sharply reducing urban underemployment.

---

[6] State Statistical Bureau, *Monthly Bulletin of Statistics,* section 9, various issues.

REFERENCES

Baer, Werner, and Horve, Michel, "Employment and Industrialization in Developing Countries." *Quart. J. Econ.* **80,** 1:88–107, Feb. 1966.

Chan, Thomas M. H., "Reform in China's Foreign Trade System." Paper presented to Conference on China's System Reforms, University of Hong Kong, March 1986.

Feng, Lanrui, "Current Problems of Employment." *Zhongguo Shehui Kexue,* p. 189, November, 1981.

Kreuger, Anne O., "Import Substitution versus Export Promotion." *Finance Develop.* **22,** 2:20–23, June 1985.

Kreuger, Anne O., "The Relationship between Trade, Employment and Development." Paper presented to the Conference in Celebration of the Twentieth Anniversary of the Yale University Economic Growth Center, New Haven, April 1986.

Levy, S., "Foreign Trade and Its Impact on Employment: The Mexican Case." *J. Devel. Econ.* **10,** 1:47–67, Feb. 1982.

Ministry of Foreign Economic Relations and Trade, *Foreign Trade Almanac, 1985,* Beijing, 1986.

Sung, Yun Wing, "Decentralization of China's Foreign Trade: Problems and Prospects." Paper presented to the Conference on China's System Reforms, University of Hong Kong, March 1986.

Taylor, Jeffrey R., "Labor Force Developments in the People's Republic of China, 1952–1983." In *China's Economy Looks Toward the Year 2000,* Vol. 1, p. 222. Comp. of Papers, Joint Econ. Comm., U.S. Congress. Washington, D.C.: U.S. Govt. Printing Office, 1986.

World Bank, *China: Long-Term Development Issues and Options.* Washington, 1985.

World Bank, *China: Socialist Economic Development.* Washington, 1981.

Zhao, Lukuan, and Yao, Yuyuan. *Jingji Wenti Tansuo* **12:**21, Dec. 1983.

JOURNAL OF COMPARATIVE ECONOMICS 11, 490–502 (1987)

A Tentative Plan for the Rational Sequencing of Overall Reform in China's Economic System[1]

JOHN FEI

Yale University, New Haven, Connecticut 06520

AND

BRUCE REYNOLDS

Union College, Schenectady, New York 12308

Fei, John, and Reynolds, Bruce—A Tentative Plan for the Rational Sequencing of Overall Reform in China's Economic System

The authors review Chinese economic reform to date, and sketch a linked sequence of reforms stretching over the coming 20 years. They argue that the logical interrelations of a market system require that markets in China be developed in a particular order: first commodity markets, then loanable funds, then capital goods, and finally labor. In addition, they argue that legal reforms, and a revival of traditional Chinese cultural values, are essential for the success of market institutions in China. *J. Comp. Econ.,* September, 1987, **11**(3), pp. 490–502. Yale University, New Haven, Connecticut 06520; Union College, Schenectady, New York 12308. © 1987 Academic Press, Inc.

Journal of Economic Literature Classification Numbers: 027, 052, 124.

INTRODUCTION

1978 witnessed the beginning of a reform of China's economic system. The process entered a new stage in 1984, with the Central Committee's Decision on overall economic reform. This resolution is a comprehensive blueprint, a vision of a future economic system.

But like any blueprint, the Decision can only suggest the eventual structure of the building. It offers no guidance concerning how to proceed with construction. That is our objective here. We seek to provide, not so much an alternative blueprint of a reformed economy, as a plan for reform: a "flow chart" showing the smoothest step by step transition path to the "Chinese" socialism envisioned by the decision.

[1] The authors are indebted to the conference participants, and in particular to Wu Jinglian, Ma Bing, and Xu Jingan, for their thoughtful comments on an earlier draft of this paper.

ISBN 0-12-587045-0

200

Chart I sketches that transition process. Our periodization is based on the successive, sequential opening of a series of markets: first for commodities, next for loanable funds, and last for capital goods and labor. We break the reform process into three periods. In the initial period, from 1978 to the present, the critical breakthrough was the monetization of the system, or the rebirth of a money economy in China. The middle period, from 1986 to 1998, will feature the full establishment of markets for commodities. Only during the late period, from 1998 to 2006, will capital goods and labor markets be opened.

Whether any particular stage might in practice take a longer or shorter time, or whether one stage might overlap somewhat with another, is a matter best left to further debate and experience. What we wish to stress above all is that reform should logically follow the particular sequence which we present.

As suggested by the rows in Chart I, we believe that reform must proceed at several different levels simultaneously. Rows B, C, and D contain the changes customarily associated with the notion of economic reform. Here economic power, formerly centralized in government hands, is increasingly dispersed and exercised by individual decision-makers, who interact in markets and thereby generate the prices which inform and regulate their decision. But simultaneous with these changes, we argue, China must foster a change in the "management culture" of state enterprises (row E). That is, the members of China's state enterprises—managers, workers, and cadres—must gradually change their notions of their appropriate roles and behaviors in a market-oriented system. This evolution can be stimulated by and in turn will stimulate the legal system reforms suggested in row F. Laws can be effective only to the extent that they accurately reflect the values (the social definition of a "necessity") of the society as a whole. As row G suggests, and as we will argue in what follows, traditional Chinese cultural values do in fact reinforce the legal system and management culture which will be necessary in China in the future. Thus a revival of traditional Chinese cultural values is, in our view, an integral part of reform.

A. The Impact of Monetization after 1978

In the command economy, from 1958 to 1978, money was merely an accounting unit, an appendage to the real sector. (One is reminded of the Six Dynasties period, during which the disappearance of the money system precipitated a brief period of "natural economy.") Without money as a medium for horizontal information exchange, and without the initiative and drive which the profit motive brings, producers, especially in industry, could only "look upward," puppets whose strings were manipulated by central bureaucrats.

The October 1984 Central Committee Decision resolved to cut those strings, and to activate money as a medium of exchange and a carrier of value in-

CHART I

PROGRAM FOR TOTAL REFORM OF THE ECONOMIC SYSTEM (1986–2006)

	1949	1958	1978	1986	1990	1994	1998	2002	2006
	Socialist transformation	Totally politicized system		Transition period to a depoliticized economic system					Chinese Socialism (exclusively indirect control)
				Initial period	Middle period			Late period	
B. Sequential order for establishing various markets				Advent of a money economy (government monetary guarantees persist)	Establishment of a commodity market			Capital goods market	Labor market
				(0)	(I)	(II)	(III)	(IV)	(V)
C. A five-stage reform program				Dispersion of economic and political decision-making process	Price system reform (government acts as guarantor for i. Smooth urban–rural exchange ii. Successful outcomes for state enterprises)	Reform of interest system	Reform of profit system	Reform of financial property	Reform of human relations
D. Content of each reform				i. Agriculture: collapse of communes; marketization, privatization ii. Collectives pursue profit iii. Tax replaces profit in state enterprises	i. Prices float ii. Government deficit controlled iii. Free purchase and sale iv. Inflation controlled	Establishment of a loanable funds market	Production efficiency profit (Marshallian profit)	Capitalized future profit, risk, and embodied technical change are basis for value of capital goods	Labor mobility

E. Sequential establishment of a management culture in state enterprises	Individual initiative begins to replace command system	Business/politics separation (concerning current operations)	Business/politics separation (concerning long-term growth)	Business/politics separation (halfway to profit/loss responsibility)	i. True profit/loss responsibility ii. Enterprise a legal entity iii. Property rights depolitized	i. Firm now pure production unit ii. Labor contract system iii. Labor/management relations depoliticized
Attitudinal basis for legal system	State enterprises develop sense of independence	Commercial cost culture established	Commercial interest/debt culture	Profit culture (profit apolitical)	Entrepreneurs: group identity, social status	Workers: sense of integrity and independence
F. Reform of the legal system	Rule still primarily by party or political force sprouts of legalism	Antitrust spirit, private legal system	Banking laws	Corporate income tax law	Bankruptcy and contract law	Labor relations law
	Gradual separation of party and government			Independent judicial system		
G. Rebirth of traditional chinese cultural values	Family values	Spirit of independence; self-reliance	Trust and honesty	Apolitical entrepreneurs	Respect for intellectuals	Independence of labor class
						Cultural revival (basis for reunification)

formation. Just like Western conservative political philosophers, who place the highest value on self-reliance, freedom, and every human's responsibility for his own fate, the framers of the Decision seek state enterprises weaned from government subsidies, taking initiative on their own, and responsible for their own profits and losses.

The Decision does not address the ideological underpinnings of monetization. We believe that, rather than glossing over the moral aspects of this issue, reformers strengthen their case by openly acknowledging its moral content. Economic freedom is conducive to human economic creativity. In addition, monetization provides a productive outlet for human impulses which might otherwise lead to much less desirable behavior. As Keynes puts it in the General Theory:

> Dangerous human proclivities can be canalized into comparatively harmless channels by the existence of opportunities for money-making and private wealth, which, if they cannot be satisfied in this way, may find their outlet in cruelty, the reckless pursuit of personal power and authority, and other forms of self aggrandizement. It is better that a man should tyrannize over his bank balance than over his fellow-citizens.

Although Keynes was referring to the brutality of Nazi Germany, his remarks seem equally applicable to the catastrophe of the Cultural Revolution. While some fear that monetization of the economy threatens to generate a chaotic lawlessness, we believe, with Keynes, that monetization is the best hope for rule by law, because it erodes the law's competitor: rule by the "personal forces" of the prevailing political party.

When most people in China are principally interested in earning money, interest in getting ahead by joining the Party will be reduced. The critical difference between these two ways of "getting ahead" is that under the first, success hinges on what you do (i.e., be creative economically) rather than on who you are (i.e., be a Party member). As business and politics are increasingly separated—that is, as the Party's role as an adjuster of "marketplace outcomes" is increasingly circumscribed—conflicts arising from money-making will necessarily be handled in the courts. The need for such a system of conflict resolution will automatically call forth economic law; indeed, in the years since monetization began, this transition has already begun.

If monetization is such a panacea, what explains the two most pressing policy problems today in China: price inflation and chaotic price structure? In our view, these result from the persistence, into the monetized period, of the dependent attitude and dependency relationship between enterprises and the center. The government has withheld a crucial freedom: the freedom to fail. But now, in a monetized environment, protecting enterprises from "bad" economic results takes the form of money creation (excessive bank loans) and price manipulation.

The pursuit of "monetary guarantees" of this kind is widespread among less developed countries. Rather than setting China apart, price inflation shows that China has "joined the club." China should study carefully the negative example of those LDCs in which money creation is used to promote growth in name, and inflation in reality. Nor can she follow the example of the industrial nations, where aggregate demand management aims to stabilize the level of employment. She would do best to limit the growth of money to a rate not much higher than the GNP growth rate, and to solve her economic problems by nonmonetary methods.

B. The Middle Period of Reform: Prices, Interest, Profit

The central requirement of price reform (1986–1990) is what one might call anonymity of buyers and sellers (or an antitrust spirit) such that a particular product (of a particular quality) must not be sold to some consumers at a higher price than to others (or denied to them entirely). This requirement is, of course, equivalent to the more usual definition of price reform: allowing markets to generate market-clearing prices competitively. Resistance to price reform at present stems mainly from concern over the government budget deficit and price inflation, as well as from certain problems at the enterprise level.

At the present time two types of commodities are subsidized by the government. On the one hand, the official prices for agricultural goods paid by urban consumers are less than the procurement price paid to the farmers. The loss in state trading due to the difference must be subsidized out of the government budget. On the other hand certain basic raw material prices (e.g., petroleum) are set lower than the cost of production, meaning that the producers must be subsidized. If these government subsidies are eliminated, other adjustments—principally a rise in the urban wage—will be politically inevitable. The net effect of all these changes on the budget deficit—whether they occur through readjusting fixed prices or by allowing those prices to float—is difficult to predict. It depends on the elasticity of supply and demand responses. Price reform must proceed cautiously when the government is confronted with such a knowledge vacuum.

Effective functioning of the price mechanism will require a sharp increase in those mercantile service sector activities which link buyers and sellers and centralize the forces of demand and supply in a competitive market. It will take some time to weaken the ideological rejection of all such mercantile activities as "evil" and "speculative." A similar attitudinal shift is required in the dependent mentality of state enterprises, accustomed to being rescued via monetary interventionism. In the last analysis, price reform cannot succeed until state enterprises relinquish these politically based privileges; until a moral conviction leads them to feel ashamed of depending on the government for survival.

In our sequence, the next logical step (1990–1994) is reform in the system
for determining the interest rate, through the opening of a loanable funds
market. This step can logically come only after the opening of commodity
markets, for several reasons. First, the nature of the transaction is more complex. The commodity market transaction involves exchange of goods and
services for money at one point in time—a "spot" transaction. Transactions
on the loanable funds market involve the exchange of monetary purchasing
power at different points in time. Second, the loanable funds market requires
the creation of more functionally specialized financial institutions than does
the commodity market, to be the intermediaries between savers and investors.
Marketing institutions for commodity transactions already exist in China,
whereas the specialized agents and experts needed for financial intermediaries
(such as commercial or saving banks) can only be created in a slow learning-
by-doing process. Third, the cultural change involved here is much greater.
To make effective decisions concerning this new market, production management must now take on responsibility not just for current output decisions,
but for future growth. They must lengthen their time horizon, and begin to
learn the art of debt management. While price and cost are concepts which
they were familiar with before 1978, interest rates and debt management are
notions quite foreign to them. Cultural values play a key role at this point.

Several policy issues must be addressed at this stage. In a mixed economy
with public and private enterprises, the savers and borrowers can be private
or public. At the present time of transition, the public component is still
overwhelming. Financing public investment out of tax revenue is a major
issue of the reform of the financial institutions in the years ahead. Furthermore,
to implement interest reform, the Ministry of Finance will have to divert a
significant portion of its tax income from direct allocation by decree to chan-
nelization as loans through the banking system. Needless to say, the banks
must themselves be profit-oriented enterprises, to enhance their competitive
efficiency as financial intermediaries. There must also be a sufficient number
of such banks to promote active competition among them, because China is
so huge that otherwise the allocation of loanable funds will continue to be
influenced by political power. Last, the vigorous growth of private enterprises
in the rural sector and in the coastal cities has posed a new issue: shall China
permit financing private investment by private saving, through the informal
financial market of friends and relatives? The informal market always plays
an important role for medium and small scale industries at the early stage of
development of an LDC. In the process of interest reform, passive government
nonintervention with the informal market is at least as important as active
government intervention to construct the formal financial market.

All this boils down to the time-consuming process of building an interest
culture in China. In the United States, where this culture is in full flower, a
corporation's financial vice president, responsible for debt management, is

invariably the second in command. In Taiwan, by contrast, there are no powerful financial vice presidents in state enterprises, because these enterprises have always relied on the Ministry of Finance for investment funds.

A crucial cultural component of this interest rate system is that a high value be placed on trustworthiness and creditworthiness. Moral behavior in business has deep roots in traditional Chinese culture, beginning with the rise of a business culture, between the Ming and Qing Dynasties. Combined with neo-Confucianism, it has become an integral part of Chinese economic culture. "One cannot go far without creditworthiness," we are told in the Five Constant Virtues of the ancient Chinese ethical code.

The latter part (1994–1998) of the Middle Period should witness profit reform. Profit is the excess of revenue over costs. Prices, including the interest rate, are the basis for making a profit calculation. Thus profit cannot fully take its place within a reformed system until after reform of prices and interest rates. Of course, something called "profit" is already calculated by Chinese enterprises. But this profit is "monopolistic profit" (i.e., sustained by inflexible, state-set prices). The following discussion presupposes that reform at this point will have created an environment within which most profit serves a social function.

Functional profit can be further subdivided into managerial efficiency profit and risk premium. The former, Marshallian profit, has always been recognized in China, even before 1978. The desirability of entrepreneurial behavior and modern management were merely translated into a socialist framework. The barrier to a profit culture in the Marshallian sense is technical, not ideological. But risk premium, or Frank Knight profit, meaning a reward for undertaking an uninsurable risk, runs into much stiffer resistance in China, because of the long tradition under which the uninsurable risk ordinarily borne by enterprises was, in fact, "insured" (i.e., absorbed) by "the whole people." The well-known defect of such "whole people insurance" is the accumulation of investment errors. In the modern age, where technological change is very rapid, the social function performed by this type of profit is just as important as that of Marshallian profit.

These ideological barriers to the acceptance of a role for Knight-profit in the economy might soften if were recognized that what the country needs to create here is not capitalists, but entrepreneurs. In the United States entrepreneurs are the helmsmen of the economic system. In Taiwan, private entrepreneurs are often called the lifeblood of the economy. Their contribution far outweighs that of the mediocre bureaucratic managers of state enterprises. Now, must entrepreneurs necessarily be capitalists, sharing in ownership of their corporation? On the contrary, a U.S. corporate executive is no more owner of the corporation than is a Chinese manager in a state enterprise. The separation of ownership and management transcends doctrine and ideology. Chinese entrepreneurs in a reformed system must have a healthy interest in the profitability of their corporation, as those in the U.S. do, but they will make their contribution as entrepreneurs, not as capitalists.

We anticipate that toward the end of the middle period of reform, a group of professional, apolitical managers will begin to emerge in China—individuals who will take the success of the enterprise as their sole goal in life. Of course, as long as profit comes primarily from political string-pulling, rather than from managerial expertise, a professional class of apolitical managers can never appear, because there is no standard of success by which to measure them, and no raison d'etre for the group. Indeed, such individuals could hardly prosper or even survive within the present system, where politics and business are not yet separated.

Is traditional Chinese culture receptive to such a group? From the Spring and Autumn Period to the early Han Dynasty, merchants regularly participated in politics. After that time, a contempt for merchants began to develop; they were barred from politics, although money-making was never restrained. In the 20th century, prior to the establishment of the People's Republic, national entrepreneurs who took no interest in becoming officials were present in China's major cities. It was this apolitical Chinese entrepreneurial class that brought about the economic miracles of Hong Kong and Taiwan during the postwar years. That China has such a tradition can be seen clearly from the dominant role of Chinese entrepreneurs in Southeast Asian countries. It needs only to be revived in China itself. Of course, the emergence of a helmsman-class in the economic arena can only proceed in step with the evolution of the Party from a totalitarian organization to one of several power centers in a modern pluralistic society.

C. Development of the Capital and Labor Markets (1998–2006)

1. Capital markets (1998–2002). In their eagerness to explore all aspects of the market economy, Chinese reformers have proposed the establishment of a stock market. This seems premature. Given a durable capital asset A (e.g., a steel mill), the ability to attach a monetary value P_a to A, so that the title to A can be traded, is usually found only in a highly developed commercial culture. For P_a reflects the consensus of all potential traders as to the value (discounted by the interest rate) of the anticipated stream of future profits. A capitalized value P_a can be meaningful only after interest and profit are rationalized by reform, over the course of one or two decades.

Other issues must also be addressed. Who will be the owners and traders of stock shares? What legal framework would be required? And what function would such a market serve? In China, the traders (i.e., those who have saved in the past) cannot be private families, which save relatively little at the present time. One group of participants in a stock market would probably be those public enterprises which are interested in holding the stock of other public enterprises. In addition, if government continues to be the major saver in the economy, inevitably various levels of government will be major stockholders, perhaps through "public investment corporations" which would manage government assets. As for the legal framework, presumably any durable capital goods would become the assets of a corporation, with a secure, continuous legal (rather than political) existence over time. The stock of the corporation could then be bought and sold. Under these conditions, an increase in the stock price reflects a strengthened confidence in the entrepreneurial ability of the corporation's managers to generate growth, while a decrease reflects a vote of "no confidence" which, if strong enough, can lead to bankruptcy. Such a market would serve important incentive and distributional functions. Bureaucratic supervision of state enterprises in China could be replaced by monitoring by profit-seeking stockholders. Ownership of state enterprises by "the whole people," which was only an empty phrase before 1978, would become operationally relevant. Of course, we can only have a vague impression of what the landscape of Chinese socialism in the 21st century will be like. This is only natural, since the restoration of the un-Marxian idea of property rights in a socialist economy is unprecedented.

The central issue in designing a financial and capital assets market is: in China's future, who will be the entrepreneurs, making investment decisions and bearing risk? The traditional answer before 1978 was: the State owns the capital and bears the uninsurable risk on behalf of the whole people; therefore, the bureaucrats were the entrepreneurs. The enterprise itself bore no risk, because the state guaranteed to each enterprise that bad investments would not be reflected in lower pay, demotion, firings, or plant closings. Effective operation of the market-oriented system envisaged for China by the end of this century depends on the appearance of a class of apolitical, professional managers. This is not wishful thinking. Chinese culture has fostered just such a group in Taiwan, Hong Kong, and the Southeast Asian countries. In this regard, a useful bridging role in a postreform economic system can be played by Chinese intellectuals, who have traditionally interacted with both businessmen and bureaucrats.

II. Reforming the labor system (2002–2006). A full reform of the labor system must be postponed to the 21st century. It hinges on full separation of the party from the economy, and this, in turn, cannot come until Chinese workers accept that the legitimacy of party rule is not based on the narrow endorsement of the proletarian class. Since it is difficult to eradicate this sense of power and privilege from the minds of older workers, the real hope for labor reform lies with a new generation of young workers, inspired by a revival of traditional Chinese cultural values.

Prior to 1978, the labor system was strongly centralized. The government fixed the money wage rate throughout Chinese industry. New high school graduates were given compulsory job assignments, and job shifts were seldom permitted. State enterprises became multiple-function communities, providing housing, food, welfare benefits, and even employment for workers' offspring.

Clearly, the system places a very high value on job security. It also achieved (apparent) full employment. But the single most startling statistic from this 20-year period (1958–1978) is stagnant or even declining labor productivity.

What were the shortcomings of the pre-1978 system? At the macroeconomic level, the principal shortcoming was the mistaken belief that the real industrial wage and the level of employment could be fixed and maintained through an act of political will. As the past 35 years have taught the industrialized countries, political force (using Keynesian macro policy) cannot guarantee full employment. China's attempts to do so only served to generate even more disguised unemployment than in the typical LDC, along with considerable labor misallocation.

At the microeconomic level, centralized job assignment has created a motivational structure within which workers are discouraged from being productive, thrifty, or loyal to their enterprise. Consider the reaction of a worker assigned to a state enterprise. He may say (if he remembers the "old society"), "What good fortune that we have a system where I don't have to fear unemployment." But when a state enterprise is poorly run and near bankruptcy, rather than joining together to raise productivity, each worker is likely to think, "What concern is that of mine? The government put me here; I'm not free to leave. The government must ensure that the enterprise can continue to pay my wages."

Reform in this system since 1978 has been negligible. The job assignment system continues to foster dependency. The fact that enterprises cannot refuse assigned workers clearly means that "responsibility for own profit and loss" is unenforceable. The one significant change since 1978—the decentralization of the wage-setting power—is major, but harmful rather than helpful. In the absence of labor mobility, wage flexibility (and an accommodating monetary policy) is generating severe wage-push inflation. The problem is aggravated by the government's lack of experience in administering the money supply and the tax system, and also by the weak incentives to save.

We propose five guiding principles for reform in the labor system in the years ahead.

(1) Replace centralized job assignment with free contractual choice. This change, which will convert a Chinese state enterprise from a "political adhesive community" to a "voluntary contract association," will eliminate the range of serious problems outlined above, particularly a dependent attitude by both workers and enterprises. However, the change should be gradual. One possible transition mechanism: give workers over the age of 40 job tenure, while converting younger workers to a contract basis. Recent social surveys suggest that younger people would be particularly willing to trade job security for free job choice.

Such a change would also strip away the government's principal lever for controlling rural–urban migration: immigrants to cities could no longer be denied a job there. The implication is that development policy will have to strive even harder to minimize rural–urban and interregional gaps, while the individual state enterprises learn to hire (and are empowered to fire) their workers.

(2) Enterprises should be profit-seeking production units. A pre-1978 Chinese firm was a "revolutionary unit." Although the state enterprise has been somewhat depoliticized, much progress needs to be made to convert them into profit-seeking units. Many of the present fringe benefits should be "commercialized" or eliminated. Otherwise, a worker who leaves an enterprise gives up too much (job mobility will be constrained)—and an enterprise which closes down costs the community too much (bankruptcy will be politically unpalatable). In particular, enterprise pensions should gradually be replaced by a modest national social security system (subordinate to that of the Chinese family system). The "iron ricebowl" should be replaced by a modest level of unemployment compensation. The Chinese government should consider that Taiwan and Hong Kong, relying on the traditional Chinese family, did quite well for labor welfare without a government-sponsored social security or unemployment compensation system. Furthermore, China introduced these welfare systems prematurely, and could afford them only as long as the systems covered only a small aristocratic minority of the urban dwellers.

(3) Let the basic wage float. This will be particularly important in the 21st century, as China begins the transition from a labor-surplus to a labor-scarce economy. Until that point, a stable basic wage will be practicable, and will even make economic sense. As the Lewis labor-surplus model makes clear, marginal product of urban labor, determined by marginal product in agriculture, is low and stable up to this point. In other words, despite the Chinese fears of wage inflation if the labor market were opened, a market wage would not have been, and will not be, much different from the state-set wage.

But in the 21st century, as productivity begins to rise, the wage must follow it. In Taiwan, although the government sets the wage rate for a sizeable number of workers (civil servants and soldiers), it can look to the large private labor market as a guide to what the wage should be. China will have to find some such mechanism to link wages to productivity.

(4) Basing the system on enterprise loyalty (as in Japan) is impracticable; replace it with family loyalty. Worker motivation, and labor–management relations, are fundamentally determined by the culture of the country in question. When we compare the American industrial enterprise with the Japanese, this fact stands out clearly. American individualism is reflected in the purely economic nature of the motivation, the short time-horizon of the worker–firm relation, the strong protection for workers' rights, and the formal, legalistic contractual and grievance arrangements. In Japan, dominated by a community-oriented culture, it is just the opposite.

In China, the government has attempted, over the past 30 years, to inculcate a collectivist, enterprise-oriented culture in workers. We believe that this attempt has backfired. As we approach the 21st century, China should search out the displaced Chinese cultural values and, based on them, reconstruct workers' social personalities and the interpersonal relationships within the state enterprises.

What are the relevant cultural values? Loyalty to the family group; independence, thriftiness, and a sense of social obligation; and a stress on social harmony (rather than class conflict). A state enterprise compatible with this culture would be one in which firm and worker enter into a contract, and where efficiency is maintained by appealing to the worker's sense of social and family obligation.

(5) Stimulate saving by dispersing property rights. If workers in the future are encouraged to make money, but not allowed to invest, they will go out and consume! To encourage saving, we should get rid of the idea that property rights inevitably are the beginning of exploitation. Private ownership of housing stock would be a beginning. But it seems likely that to soak up personal savings, China's industrial workers must eventually be allowed to become (minority) shareholders of state enterprises.

SUMMARY AND CONCLUSION

Reform is a complex process. It is also unprecedented: no economy in the centrally planned group has ever reformed so fully that market forces became the principal source of initiative for whole sectors of the economy. Clearly, then, no one can look 20 years into China's future and purport to see precisely what lies ahead.

Our objectives here have been more limited. First, we wish at least to place the long time horizon for reform, and its sequential nature, we also seek to the easel—so that others may paint there their own view of the future. Second, we seek to remind the reader that some parts of the reform logically must follow others. In particular, an effectively functioning capital market must build on successful reform of prices and interest rates. Third, while stressing the long time horizon for reform, and its sequential nature, we also seek to underscore the dramatic change which has already occurred: the monetarization of the economy. Last, we hope to enlarge the framework of "reform" to include, not just institutional rearrangements of a narrow sort (reduction of planned allocation, improved incentive structures, and so forth), but legal and cultural change as well. And in that context, we suggest that traditional Chinese culture provides many of the prerequisites for a successful commercial culture.

This paper is ambitious—indeed, presumptuous. But so is reform itself. If we are to fully comprehend its dimensions, we must at some point try to mark them out, as we have done here, in a comprehensive conception (however faulty) of China's future.

JOURNAL OF COMPARATIVE ECONOMICS 11, 503–508 (1987)

Enlivening Large State Enterprises: Where Is the Motive Force?

MA BIN

Economic, Technical, and Social Development Research Center, Beijing, China

AND

HONG ZHUNYAN

Beijing University, Beijing, China

Ma Bin and Hong Zhunyan—Enlivening Large State Enterprises: Where Is the Motive Force

The paper considers the proposal to convert state ownership in Chinese industry to a stock-share ownership system. While accepting that in the present period of exploration, the stock-share system can be experimented with, the authors argue that such a change would block the road to Communism in China. *J. Comp. Econ.,* September, 1987, **11**(3), pp. 503–508. Economic, Technical, and Social Development Research Center, Beijing, China; Beijing University, Beijing, China. © 1987 Academic Press, Inc.

Journal of Economic Literature Classification Numbers: 313, 513, 614.

The Third Plenary session of the 12th Party Central Committee unveiled urban economic reform in order to pump new life into large state enterprises and mobilize the enthusiasm of the workers and staff. Put simply, the reform is designed to provide the motive force from within the state enterprise while bringing pressure to bear on it from without. To convert large numbers of state enterprises into collective economic entities, the following five measures were taken: (1) linking workers' income with the result of enterprise's performance; (2) replacing profit delivery with levies of income tax; (3) shifting state responsibility for the enterprises' gains and losses to the enterprises themselves; (4) separating management from ownership, which means converting ownership by the whole people to collective ownership; (5) changing direct state control of enterprises into indirect control, and changing mandatory planning to guidance planning.

These measures, however, have failed to work satisfactorily because they failed to draw a clear distinction between state enterprises and collective enterprises. They have failed to work effectively in the 6000 leading enterprises

213

which cannot do without direct state control; neither are they any good for those enterprises which are publicly owned in name but have long been changed to collective enterprises in fact. Many people, therefore, suggested classifying the different economic undertakings into five ownership categories. (1) Publicly owned state enterprises, referring to the more than 6000 leading state enterprises which account for 60% of China's total value of fixed assets and total value of production. They will remain under state management. (2) Medium sized and small publicly owned enterprises, which will operate under collective ownership, with fixed funds granted in the form of state loans. (3) Labor cooperatives in which members own their own means of production and participate in labor as shareholders. These cooperatives should be developed in large numbers. (4) Private economy. (5) Joint ventures with Chinese and foreign capital and wholly owned foreign companies.

It seems that these measures have succeeded in mobilizing the enthusiasm of nonpublicly owned enterprises. Collective ownership, once readjusted, also enjoys a bright future. But so far no effective measure has been devised to provide an interior motivating force for large state enterprises. In its 1984 report a World Bank economic study delegation pointed out that to fire workers and staff in large state enterprises with enthusiasm, non-socialist countries often use the method of establishing boards of trustees which have decision-making power free from government intervention. The report suggested that the capital owned by state enterprises be scattered, funds be raised from various forms of ownership, and a socialist joint-stock ownership system be instituted. This suggestion soon drew pros and cons from at home and abroad. Those who are for the joint-stock system listed the following five reasons.

First, when a large enterprise is divided into shares and absorbs new shares to form joint-stock management, the state will retain its ownership of the enterprise because it holds the majority of the shares, while the presence of non-state shares enables the enterprise to separate its management from the state administration. The chairman of the board of such an enterprise is appointed by the state, and it is up to the chairman to choose the manager for the enterprise. In this way management is separated from ownership, and government administration from enterprise. The participation of government, local departments, collectives, and individuals as shareholders enables the enterprise to absorb idle funds while the state retains public ownership of the enterprise. Second, once individual workers and staff members become shareholders, their fate becomes integrated with that of the enterprise, and they will enjoy their say in management. This "socialist joint-stock system" will become a new form of public ownership of the means of production different from ownership by the whole people and collective ownership. Third, the experience of advanced capitalist countries shows that an ill-managed state enterprise often starts to improve its performance once it has been sold to private joint-stock companies. Fourth, the institution of the share-holding system will help channel consumers' saving deposits of more than 100 billion yuan in the Bank of China into enterprises as investment in fixed assets. Fifth, under the joint-stock system, stocks and the market situation will serve to guide investment in capital construction. Once such a capital market appears, it will combine with the commodity and labor markets to form a comprehensive market. Some people even quoted Marx as saying that without the shareholding system it would be impossible to construct railways even today. As Marx once said that the system was private property's self-negation within the framework of the capitalist mode of production, many believe shareholding conforms with Marxism.

The new system is now being widely discussed in China, and some enterprises are trying it out. We believe that it is necessary to make a concrete and historical analysis of it and to work out clear stipulations concerning the content and form of the stock system. We deem the institution of such a system in large enterprises as inconsistent with China's actual conditions. It is our view that shares are tantamount to ownership—the power to occupy, use, and deploy the means of production.

Joint stocks of private capital are, needless to say, of a private nature. Everyone knows that in history this system played a large role in organizing production forces. Marx once spoke highly of cooperatives, and today, we also advocate such labor cooperatives, which, however, are different from enterprises under public and collective ownership in that members own their shares although they share the public accumulation funds. So such cooperatives are privately owned, in which members take part in labor and get paid according to work done. Cooperatives are also different from publicly owned enterprises in that shareholders are entitled to dividends and once a member withdraws or dies, his shares may also be withdrawn.

The joint-stock system does have a role to play in a country's economy: it raises the funds needed to meet the demand for socialized production, technological progress, and economic planning. It is also undeniably a major way of collecting idle funds in rural and urban areas. But we do not think the shareholding system can serve as the internal motive force for enlivening large state enterprises, for the following reasons.

First, there is simply no way to divide a publicly owned enterprise into shares, so that one worker owns a blast furnace and another owns a steel rolling machine. This means that the enterprise's public ownership remains unchanged while its property is divided into shares and put under a board of trustees. But can this facilitate democratic decision-making by letting shareholders dispute with each other, or, when they fail to reach a concensus, can the manager make the final decision? If the shareholders are industrial departments or local governments, this will only lead to contradictions between these departments and local governments. Only countries not yet unified or countries under the federal system can consider this form of shareholding.

Depending on state investment to ensure the public ownership of the enterprise takes one nowhere. To avoid state intervention by setting up a board of trustees and giving the manager the final say is not realistic either. On the contrary, precisely what a state enterprise needs is state control and sensible state intervention. Actually any large enterprise, no matter what its ownership, is invariably managed by a special group of people, be it capitalist joint-stock companies or capitalist state enterprises. An enterprise under social ownership by all the people should also have its own group of managers. Even a collectively owned enterprise should be managed by a panel of directors and managers elected by all the members.

The World Bank report says that factories in national defense, power supply, and railway transport should be directly managed by the state. Even such "direct management" should be done by a group of managers. But does this mean separating ownership from management? The two should, generally speaking, not be separated because ownership entails the power to occupy, use, and deploy the means of production.

When the state controls shares, it certainly has an impact on non-state shares. This serves only to put private shareholders at loggerheads with state control, and as a result, individual shareholders will impinge on state shares. Such a chaotic situation is inevitable because no distinction can be made in the ownership of such an enterprise, and no definite policy can be worked out to handle this. As to dividing dividends according to shares, this should be decided by shareholders, which is different from the contract system in joint ventures. The result will be that while the enterprise cannot remain publicly owned, private investors will hold it at arm's length.

Second, if the workers become shareholders but are not allowed to handle the share certificates on their own, the enterprise will not be truly owned by shareholders. If the workers are allowed to handle share certificates, their interests are not linked with those of the enterprise but with the stock market, where stock exchange holds sway. When a worker shows an interest in his dividends, this does not mean he is concerned with the property of the enterprise, because, motivated by his own interests, he will only compete with the enterprise for his own interests. Dividends and bonuses represent the surplus labor of all the workers of an enterprise and the share certificates allow individuals to seize the surplus labor of others. So won't this give rise to class polarization and contradiction in a country where public ownership of the means of production is introduced?

Because in a joint-stock company some people hold shares and others don't and some have more shares than others, this will inevitably lead to class polarization when the enterprise has greatly increased its profits. So the joint-stock system is not as simple as putting everybody's money together. There will be no public ownership to speak of once some means of production are privately owned. In a nutshell, shareholding can only drive an enterprise apart.

Third, the fact that in capitalist countries state enterprise can be sold to individual joint-stock companies does not mean that private ownership is superior to other forms of ownership, nor does it justify selling socialist state enterprises to joint-stock companies. In a capitalist country, barons can afford to buy an enterprise and, by putting it under a joint-stock company, to keep its production going. But in China who can afford to purchase a state enterprise? Even if it is sold to individual workers and staff members, it still needs a group of managers to keep it alive.

Fourth, those who suggest using the shareholding system to pool money and channel residents' savings deposits into capital construction are often ignorant of the fact that the savings deposits are a result of an irrational consumption system. Under this system, people, not knowing where to send their money, have to put it into the bank. Both the people's incomes and living standards are very low, but some people are still trying to make use of their savings at a time when investment in fixed assets is already overheated. Actually these savings have already been used to develop the economy. If a state enterprise worker or staff member wants to save money, he may put the money into the bank, so that he can increase his income by earning the interest and the state bank can use his savings to boost production.

Fifth, those who want to introduce the joint-stock system mainly intend to establish a stock exchange market and use the market situation to guide investment. But if the state holds the majority of the stocks, it is still the state calling the shots; if one wants to do without state planning, this is possible only when private shares make up the majority in an enterprise. There simply is not a third choice.

From the foregoing analysis, the system of joint-stock companies and the cooperatives are nothing new. If such a system is introduced to collective enterprises, it will turn collective ownership—in which stockholding and withdrawal is unheard of—into ownership by individual cooperative members who take part in labor as shareholders. To change state enterprises owned by the whole people into the joint-stock system is tantamount to allowing private ownership to make inroads into public ownership with the motivation to gain the largest possible profits. Although the World Bank report did not specify this point, some economists are already arguing that only private ownership is in accord with Vilfredo Pareto's theory for producers to gain maximum profits and for consumers to gain maximum consumption. They also say that the joint-stock system is the only way to mobilize people's enthusiasm and develop a sizeable economy.

This is perhaps what is behind the idea of introducing the joint-stock system: on the one hand, because they dare not negate public ownership they want to pass off the joint-stock system as public ownership of the means of production, i.e., ownership by the whole people; on the other, they believe that only by putting the means of production under private ownership will people really care about production and management. Why is there the practice of "everyone eating from the same public pot"? Why do people not concern themselves with the management of their enterprise? Why do people waste enterprise property? In their eyes, the answer is because people do not own the enterprise property and the enterprise itself. Some even go so far as to say that private ownership in a slave society is much better than public ownership in primitive communism.

But if these ideas are put into practice, the road to communism will be blocked. The *Manifesto of the Communist Party* says that the purpose of communism is to eliminate capitalist private ownership of the means of production and eliminate the system of man exploiting man. Private ownership runs counter to communism; it certainly does not apply to the actual conditions of China.

How, then, can the enthusiasm of workers and staff members in large state enterprise be brought into full play? The state enterprise can successfully improve its efficiency and labor productivity only if it has a fixed payroll and production quota, closely examines the workers' performance, and if skilled labor is paid a premium over unskilled labor and everyone, from blue collar to white collar and from the enterprise director to janitors, is paid according to the quality and quantity of his labor, knowledge, skill, responsibility, and actual performance.

Turning enterprises into joint-stock companies and putting them under private ownership, mobilizing workers' enthusiasm as shareholders and on this basis developing a capital market on which shareholders depend for their income on labor market changes—these are obviously things of the Western capitalist countries; they do not accord with the actual conditions of China. The development of a joint-stock market and labor market is inevitable, and permissible as one of the experiments of reform, if it serves as a supplement to a socialist economy in which a private economy still exists. These markets, however, should not be developed in big enterprises where the means of production are publicly owned. To mobilize the enthusiasm of workers and staff in a publicly owned enterprise, the only thing to do is to administer communist education and carry out the principle of "to each according to his work."

JOURNAL OF COMPARATIVE ECONOMICS 11, 509–514 (1987)

The Stock-Share System: A New Avenue for China's Economic Reform

Xu Jing'an

China Economic System Reform Research Institute, Beijing, China

Xu, Jing'an—The Stock-Share System: A New Avenue for China's Economic Reform

The paper reviews the development of the stock-share ownership system in Chinese collectively owned industry. It considers the feasibility and desirability of extending the system to include state-owned industry. While noting the absence of necessary preconditions (in particular, tax, price, and legal reforms), and the presence of ideological barriers, the paper concludes that such a system should be developed. *J. Comp. Econ.,* September 1987, **11**(3), pp. 509–514. China Economic System Reform Research Institute, Beijing, China. © 1987 Academic Press, Inc.

Journal of Economic Literature Classification Numbers: 313, 513, 614.

This paper considers the feasibility and desirability of instituting a stock-share system in China. Such a system is already in use for collectively owned industry. After reviewing that situation, the paper considers the question of stock-share ownership of state-owned industry, and in particular, the possible use of holding companies for managing state assets. A concluding section considers ideological difficulties in the way of implementing such a system.

1. STOCK SHARES IN COLLECTIVE INDUSTRY

In 1984 and 1985, faced with a shortage of funds coupled with the tightening of bank credit, Chinese enterprises started to use stock issue to raise funds both from their own staff and workers and from society at large. This fund-raising method was widely used in Guangdong, Jiangsu, Shanghai, Beijing, Henan, Hebei, Anhui, Hubei, Liaoning, and Inner Mongolia. By the end of 1985, approximately 10 billion yuan had been raised nationally by means of stocks and bonds. 850 enterprises issued stocks in Guangdong Province alone.

This form of raising funds was at first limited for the greater part to the staff and workers within each enterprise. For the year 1985, funds raised in this way in Shanghai accounted for 95% of the total stockholders there, and

70% of the total funds. In those cases where only the newly invested funds were used as the asset base, with the original assets of enterprises being excluded, interest and dividend payments were large. In some enterprises, stock interest and dividend accounted for over 30% of the stock capital (and even 100% in a few enterprises), far exceeding the normal profit ratio of capital. This, in effect, became a means of issuing bonuses in a disguised form.

In response to this problem, it was then stipulated everywhere that in general the income ratio of stock capital could not exceed 15%. Two problems arose. One was that the rate of return on stock capital was divorced from the economic performance of the enterprise, leading to indifference of stockholders to the operation of the enterprise. Another was that the ceiling made it unattractive for stockholders to bear the risk of the operation. In order to encourage buying of stocks, enterprises had to permit full withdrawal, adopting the practice of "ensuring stable yields despite drought or flood": guaranteeing capital and interest. At this point, stocks exist in name only; there is no difference between them and bonds.

Most of this early use of stock shares has been in collectively owned industries. One such case of the experimental use of stock shares is the Shenyang Compressor Plant, part of the 1985 CESRRI survey. Here, the assets of the enterprise are divided into three parts: publicly owned stock (120 thousand yuan), collectively owned stock (1.38 million yuan), and private stock (42 thousand yuan). Collectively owned stock is broken down and allocated to every staff and worker, taking into account their length of service. This part of stock capital cannot be withdrawn by them when they are transferred elsewhere or retire, but only serves as a basis for distributing dividends.

The profit made by the enterprise is distributed, after deduction of income tax, in accordance with the proportion of publicly owned, collectively owned, and private stock. The dividends on the publicly owned stock are not paid out to the company this enterprise is affiliated with, but instead are used to increase the publicly owned stock. The dividend on the collectively owned stock is divided into accumulation fund, public welfare fund, and stock dividend. The last part is distributed to staff and workers in proportion to their share of stock. The dividend on private stock is distributed to stockholders.

This reform has brought about profound change in the enterprise. The property relations of the enterprise have been put in order. Formerly, nobody cared about the enterprise assets or was responsible for them. Now, with the growth of the enterprise accumulation fund and the appreciation of collectively owned stock, the amount of stock and dividend payments of each worker increases accordingly. They truly feel that the collective assets belong to every worker.

Two issues remain. First, how should the assets be divided up? It is difficult to separate state investment from accumulation by the enterprises themselves. In practice, this question must be settled by working out a rough proportion.

Second, how much income should be paid to stockholders? The amount to be distributed depends on the amount of profit. Let enterprises make their own decisions, subject to the risk of bankruptcy. If a few enterprises are closed down after the entire assets are used up, or go bankrupt due to mismanagement, that is not a bad thing. It can sound the alarm for other enterprises.

2. STOCK SHARES IN STATE-OWNED INDUSTRY

Can the stock system be carried out in enterprises owned by the whole people? There is a heated dispute on this issue. No definite opinion has been expressed either at home or abroad. By studying the experience of reform in Yugoslavia, Hungary, and China, one finds that three types of mechanism exist.

The first type is nonparametric restraint. Here, the responsibilities and benefits of the enterprise are determined according to its particular conditions. This method has some defects. First, the state has to determine the responsibilities and interests of enterprises through separate negotiations with each of them. This causes great arbitrariness and unfairness. In most cases, a low profit target with a large margin left is used as the basis for a high assessment. Second, the constraint over enterprises cannot be stiffened. Since it is initially based on negotiations, an enterprise will ask to conduct new negotiations in the event that some change in the environment takes place which is unfavorable to it.

The second type is parametric restraint. This includes the change of profit into tax in China and the autonomy of enterprise in Yugoslavia. Distribution of income between the state and the enterprise is based on uniform tax laws. This exercises some restraint on the enterprise. However, there is a major shortcoming: lack of adequate motive force. If an enterprise is well run, there is not much left for staff and workers after deduction of tax, development fund, and welfare fund. Conversely, if the enterprise is not well run, the profit is lower and the award fund is first guaranteed, so the workers' income does not decrease. In comparison with contracted enterprises, enterprises practicing the "change profit to tax" system often lack enthusiasm.

The third type is self-restraint by the enterprise. The stock system belongs to this category. When staff and workers buy stocks, their relation with the enterprise is no longer that of earning a wage for doing their job. They have an additional tie with the enterprise assets. The stock brought by the staff and workers may seem negligible compared to the total assets of state-owned enterprises, but can prove decisive to the staff and workers. As the proverb goes, "when you have cargo in a ship, the ebb and flow of the tide arouses your concern." Compared with the two other types of restraint, the stock system creates stronger incentive pressures on the enterprise and workers. Furthermore, this restraint does not originate from negotiations with the state and a specific assessment target, but from the enterprise's own interest in its survival and development. There is a short-term tendency among stockholders to seek high stock dividends. However, this is constrained by the interests of the various parties within the enterprise, and the income paid out can become enterprise accumulation again through self-circulation. Therefore, the stock system is so far the best of the various mechanisms, and possibly the medicine for curing China's enterprises of their current illness.

Of course, a number of preliminary issues must be resolved before the stock-share system can be implemented. Major changes are needed in the tax system. There are fundamental problems associated with appraisal of assets, given the lack of a well-functioning stock market. In the initial stages, conversion of assets to stock will be complicated; it is not clear, for example, whether assets formed by an enterprise at an earlier time through retained profits should be treated as enterprise stock in a corporation with various stockholders. Last, it must be clearly stipulated what the leadership system will be in a stock-share enterprise. A board of directors, selecting an entrepreneurial factory director but bearing ultimate responsibility itself, seems the appropriate form for modern, complex industrial enterprises.

In addition to these issues, internal to the stock-share system itself, there are important external preconditions. First, the irrational price system must be reformed. The great disparity of profit rates across industries and enterprises causes enormous difficulties in asset appraisal. Moreover, the existence of a developed and sound commodity market where materials can easily be bought with money is also vital to a stock system. Second, bond and stock markets must be opened systematically. As a first step, banks could be agents responsible for the circulation of stocks. Third, laws and regulations must be amplified, and cadres trained. The successful implementation of a stock system requires, in particular, a group of talented people who are familiar with its operation and management.

3. HOLDING COMPANIES AS MANAGERS OF STATE ASSETS

How should the state manage its assets? Some people feel concerned that in the stock system, participation in enterprise management by the state in its capacity as stockholder may undercut the separation of government administration from enterprise management. It would be little different from the current direct management. Such concerns are justified. This situation may arise if the existing machinery is not reformed and the behavior of administrative organizations is not changed. The principle for correct reform should be that the organizations in charge of managing state assets must be accountable for their effective use. We propose that state asset operating companies, or holding companies, be responsible for the direct management of state assets.

Their responsibilities would be twofold. First, they would designate representatives of the state as directors or chairmen of the enterprise board of directors. Second, the state holding companies would reinvest their assets, in compliance with state industrial policy and regional arrangements. By using this form of investment, state planned management is combined with the principle of economic effectiveness and project construction is integrated with enterprise management, thereby avoiding blind investment and loss of accountability.

The reform described here will fundamentally improve investment in China. At present, government at each level fails to assume its appropriate economic responsibility. A group of ill-run enterprises is set up, as a result of blind investment. It then needs to rely on administrative power for protection. Such a system survives only through the intermingling of government administration and enterprise management. This system depends on the monopoly of raw materials, the blockade of markets and strangulation of competitors. From this system flow the subsidies and tax exemptions, the practice of taking from the fat to pad the lean, and propping up money-losing enterprises. The mistakes of investors are covered up by the fact that ill-run enterprises *can* be protected.

Under these conditions, it is naturally very difficult to do away with Kornai's "investment hunger." But the stock system makes investors assume the responsibility for unprofitability of their investment from the very beginning. Only through such an investment mechanism can macroregulation and macrocontrol work.

4. IDEOLOGICAL RESISTANCE TO THE STOCK-SHARE SYSTEM

The biggest obstacle to the implementation of a stock-share system is the resistance of traditional ideas. Our tendency to belittle or ignore the role of capital among the factors of production has led to strange phenomena in our practice of socialism. On the one hand, public property is regarded as sacred and inviolable, while on the other, it is often ruined, damaged, wasted, or lost, with no one shedding a tear. On the one hand, building socialism requires large-scale investment while on the other, the people are not offered the opportunity of directly making such investment and indeed are prohibited from doing so. On the one hand, the state runs short of investible funds, and cannot generate sufficient employment, while on the other, it does not recognize the price of funds, the appreciation of funds, and the role of funds in organizing production and supply. On the one hand, the state urgently needs to curtail consumption and withdraw currency from circulation to increase accumulation, while on the other, it regards as forbidden territory a method of raising funds which can shift consumption directly to accumulation and which is readily accepted by the people.

We are presented with the argument: one can take his reward for labor, and deposit the unused portion in the bank at interest, but he cannot buy the stock of enterprises or own their assets. The asset is publicly owned, and may not be owned by individuals. Otherwise the title "proletariat" will be changed into "capitalist" and "socialism" will be transformed into "capitalism."

When the system of fixing farm output quotas at the household level was implemented in rural areas, some people described it as a retrogression, pandering to the private ownership mentality of peasants. They complained, "after thirty years of hard work, things overnight go back to where they were before the land reform." When small industry and commerce moved back from state ownership to collective ownership, and even contracted out or leased to individuals, some people claimed that this showed a lack of confidence in public ownership—we were pinning our hopes on capitalism. But in this stage of a socialist commodity economy, the relation between the individual and the society is still that of commodity exchange. One of the tasks of economic reform is to combine the material interests of individuals with the need to increase social wealth and improve economic efficiency. The stock system mixes together private and public assets and merges the interests of staff and workers with the interests of enterprises. Both sides share weal and woe. This system promotes the development of enterprises and pushes forward productive forces. How can this be described as bestowing high praise on capitalism?

Under the stock system, interest is received on the basis of stock ownership or "capital." Doesn't this run counter to the socialist principle of distribution according to work? Under the stock system, the main bodies which receive enterprise profit are still the state and the enterprises. Individuals invest a part of their reward from labor in the enterprise and help to organize production, create supply, and cause an appreciation of capital, so they should receive the income. It is justified that the income is higher than the interest on bank deposits, because of the risk taken in buying stocks. The question of usurers who profit by other people's toil has to be settled through regulation of distribution. Banning the stock system is no cure.

Some people worry about the growth of a "speculative mentality." But "speculation" should not be a derogatory term if we accept a commodity economy. Broadly speaking, to carry out production and exchange of commodities is an act of speculation. Whether a commodity can find a market depends on the correctness of the producer's prediction of the market. The same question of making a correct prediction exists in investing in enterprise stocks for income.

The socialist stock system needs to be developed. The socialist cause needs to forge ahead. There is no trodden path before us. It is up to us to break new paths.

JOURNAL OF COMPARATIVE ECONOMICS 11, 515–516 (1987)

Arden House Conference on Chinese Economic Reform Participants

United States

IRMA ADELMAN, Department of Agricultural and Resource Economics, University of California, Berkeley

BELA BALASSA, Department of Economics, Johns Hopkins University

JOSEF BRADA, Department of Economics, Arizona State University

WILLIAM BYRD, Senior Economist, China Division, World Bank

GREGORY CHOW, Department of Economics, Princeton University

JOHN FEI, Department of Economics, Yale University

NICHOLAS LARDY, School of International Studies, University of Washington

BARRY NAUGHTON, Department of Economics, University of Oregon

DWIGHT PERKINS, Department of Economics, Harvard University

QIAN YINGYI, Department of Economics, Harvard University (President, Chinese Young Economists Forum)

BRUCE REYNOLDS, Department of Economics, Union College

T. N. SRINIVASAN, Department of Economics, Yale University

THOMAS WIENS, Senior Agricultural Economist, World Bank

CHRISTINE WONG, Department of Economics, University of California, Santa Cruz

Europe

JANOS KORNAI, Institute of Economics, Hungarian Academy of Sciences

RICHARD PORTES, Department of Economics, Birkbeck College, University of London

People's Republic of China

CAO YUANZHENG, Chief, Division of Scientific Research, China Economic System Reform Research Institute (CESRRI)

HONG JUNYAN, Department of Economics, Beijing University

HUANG FANZHANG, Standing Director, International Monetary Fund

CHINESE ECONOMIC REFORM
225
ISBN 0-12-587045-0

MA BIN, Deputy Director, Economic, Technical, and Social Development Research Center, State Council

WU JINGLIAN, Economic, Technical, and Social Development Research Center, State Council

XU JINGAN, Deputy Director and Senior Researcher, CESRRI

ZHAO RENWEI, Deputy Director, Economic Research Institute, Chinese Academy of Social Sciences

ZHOU XIAOCHUAN, Deputy Director and Senior Researcher, CESRRI

Observers at the Conference

CHEN YANNAN, Department of Economics, State University of New York at Albany

ZSUZSA DANIEL, Institute of Planning, Hungarian Academy of Sciences

SONG GUOQING, Director, First Research Office and Senior Researcher, CESRRI

WU XIAOLING, Director, Finance Research Office and Researcher, Bank of China

DIAO XINSHEN, Researcher, Rural Development Research Center, State Council

TIAN YUAN, Researcher, State Council

ZHANG XUEJUN, Deputy Director and Researcher, Institute of Economics, Chinese Academy of Social Sciences

MAO YUSHI, Department of Economics, Harvard University

PETER GEITHNER, Ford Foundation

KAZIMIERCZ POZNANSKI, Northwestern University

LLOYD REYNOLDS, Yale University

WU RUOSI, *China Daily*

Conference Secretary:

JAMES HAVARD, Union College

Critical Bibliography

The explosion since 1978 of information about the Chinese economy has produced a similar expansion in the secondary literature on the subject. The World Bank's China Division has published voluminously. The Joint Economic Committee of the U.S. Congress has produced biennial compendiums of articles, the most recent of which is listed here. Work also appears in the form of scholarly monographs, conference volumes and journal articles.

The best single bibliographic tool to explore this material is the *Journal of Economic Literature.* The following review covers only books.

I. Textbooks on the Chinese Economy. Most of the following provide an introduction to the basic institutions of the economy, as they evolved between 1949 and 1978, and a periodization of those three decades (usually based on shifts in development strategy or broad political line).

Cheng, C.Y. *China's Economic Development: Growth and Structural Change.* Boulder, CO: Westview, 1982.

Chow, Gregory. *The Chinese Economy.* New York: Harper and Row, 1985.

Donnithorne, Audrey. *China's Economic System.* New York: Praeger, 1967.

Eckstein, Alexander. *China's Economic Revolution.* Cambridge: Cambridge University Press, 1977.

Howe, Christopher. China's Economy: A Basic Guide. New York: Basic Books, 1978.

Kraus, Willy. *Economic Development and Social Change in the People's Republic of China.* New York: Springer-Verlag, 1982.

Prybyla, Jan S. *The Political Economy of Communist China.* Scranton, PA: International Textbook Co., 1980.

II. Background Reading. In understanding post-1949 China, and in particular the reforms since 1978, it is very useful to have some sense of the history of the Chinese economy, of the Stalinist central planning model, and of the attempts in Russia and Eastern Europe to move away from that model. The following works address these issues.

Bornstein, Morris, ed. *Comparative Economic Systems: Models and Cases.* Homewood, IL: Richard D. Irwin, 1979.

Kornai, Janos. *The Economics of Shortage.* Amsterdam: North-Holland, 1980.

Kornai, Janos. "The Hungarian Reform Process: Visions, Hopes, and Reality," *Journal of Economic Literature* **XXIV** (December 1986) p. 1694.

Myers, Ramon H. *The Chinese Economy Past and Present.* Belmont: Wadsworth Press, Inc., 1980.

Nee, Victor, and David Stark, eds. *Remaking the Economic Institutions of Socialism: China and Eastern Europe.* Stanford, CA: Stanford University Press, forthcoming.

Perkins, Dwight H. *Agricultural Development in China: 1368–1968.* Chicago: Aldine, 1969.

Perkins, Dwight H. *China's Modern Economy in Historical Perspective.* Stanford: Stanford University Press, 1975.

III. General Works on the Economy. This section lists three major reviews of the economy as a whole, including the most recent Joint Economic Committee volume, and then four more specialized monographs (Byrd, Jamison, Kueh and Lardy).

Barnett, A. Doak. *China's Economy in Global Perspective.* Washington, D.C.: Brookings Institution, 1981.

United States Congress. Joint Economic Committee. *China's Economy Looks Toward the Year 2000.* Washington, D.C.: U.S. Government Printing Office, 1986.

World Bank. *China: Socialist Economic Development.* Washington, D.C.: World Bank, 1981.

Byrd, William. *China's Financial System.* Boulder, CO: Westview Press, 1983.

Jamison et al. *China's Health Sector.* Washington, D.C.: World Bank, 1984.

Kueh, Y.Y. *Economic Planning and Local Mobilization in Post-Mao China.* London: Contemporary China Institute, 1985.

Lardy, N. *Agriculture in China's Modern Economic Development.* Cambridge: Cambridge University Press, 1983.

IV. Economic Reform in China. The following works deal with 'institutional change since 1978.

Barnett, A. Doak, and Ralph Clough, eds. *Modernizing China*. Boulder, CO: Westview Press, 1986.

Byrd, William, and Gene Tidrick. *Recent Chinese Economic Reforms: Studies of Two Industrial Enterprises*. Washington, D.C.: World Bank Staff Working Papers, No. 652, 1984.

Byrd, William, and Lin Qingsong, eds. *China's Rural Industry: Structure, Development and Reform*. Washington D.C.: World Bank, forthcoming.

Chai, J.C.H., ed. *China's Economic Reforms*. Hong Kong: Centre of Asian Studies, University of Hong Kong, 1987.

Perry, Elizabeth J., and Christine Wong, eds. *The Political Economy of Reform in Post-Mao China*. Cambridge, MA: Harvard University Press, 1985.

Tidrick, Gene, and Chen Jiyuan, eds. *China's Industrial Reforms*. London: Oxford University Press, 1987.

World Bank (Lim, Edwin, et al). *China: Long-Term Development Issues and Options*. Baltimore: Johns Hopkins University Press, 1985.

V. Translations from Chinese Authors. The following works, by major Chinese economists, date from 1978 to the present. The intellectual paradigms employed, and the methodology used to support assertions, are different from the Western academic tradition (although this is less and less true, in both cases, as academic exchange with China strengthens). The volume edited by Reynolds is particularly rich in micro data.

Lin, Wei, and Arnold Chao, eds. *China's Economic Reforms*. Philadelphia: University of Pennsylvania Press, 1982.

Ma, Hong. *New Strategy for China's Economy*. Beijing: New World Press, 1983.

Reynolds, Bruce, ed. *Economic Reform in China: Challenges and Choices*. Armonk, NY: M.E. Sharpe, Inc., 1988.

Wang, George C., ed. *Economic Reform in the People's Republic of China*. Boulder, CO: Westview Press, 1982.

Xue, Muqiao. *China's Socialist Economy*. Beijing: Foreign Language Press, 1981.

VI. Politics and Economics. Economic reform has a major political component. The following is a partial list of major recent monographs dealing with this area.

Harding, Harry. *China's Second Revolution*. Washington, D.C.: Brookings Institution, 1987.
Lampton, David M., ed. *Policy Implementation in Post-Mao China*. Berkeley: University of California Press, 1987.
Oi, Jean. *State and Peasant in Contemporary China: The Political Economy of Village Government*. Berkeley: University of California Press, forthcoming (1989).
Riskin, Carl. *China's Political Economy*. New York: Oxford University Press, 1987.
Shue, Vivienne. *The Reach of the State: Sketches of the Chinese Body Politic*. Stanford, CA: Stanford University Press, 1988.
Zweig, David. *Rural Small Towns and the Politics of Planned Development*. Forthcoming.

VII. Journal Articles. To identify relevant journal articles, an alternative to a full-scale literature search is to scan the indexes to the following journals.

China Quarterly
Chinese Economic Studies
Economic Development and Cultural Change
Journal of Comparative Economics
Modern China
Problems of Communism

Index